"As I settled in for a flight, I asked my seatmate about his work. 'I am a church planter,' he said enthusiastically. 'That's interesting to hear,' I responded, and then asked with apparent naiveté, 'So what does it take to plant a church?' 'Two simple things: a good sound system and a dynamic speaker!' This rich volume offers multifaceted wisdom about how much more church planting actually requires than just those two things. I hope my seatmate, and all who read this very helpful book, will see that church planting is about deep sowing and nurturing, about how much God has a passionate purpose in all of it, and about what a faithful adventure and daunting challenge church planting really is!"

Mark Labberton, president, Fuller Theological Seminary

"If you want to view church planting through a missiological lens, this is the book for you. Written by scholar-practitioners, this volume will be a great primer as you explore the world of church planting and multiplying."

Daniel Im, pastor, podcaster, and author of *You Are What You Do, No Silver Bullets,* and *Planting Missional Churches*

"Drawing from Scripture and the experience of many church starters and reproducing churches, this book has the capacity both to inspire and to guide planting initiatives into healthy, practical activation. Along the way, the authors remain ever attentive to helping startup teams cultivate the supportive environments and practices conducive to their flourishing and the multiplying of new churches. What a helpful resource for anyone or any church considering a role in planting!"

Daniel Steigerwald, missional catalyst and coach at Artesia ReSourcing

"Again I am proud to count Fuller's church planting program among our partners in this work. Cotherman's quick and deep picture of mission history, Woodward's clear and honest take on the work and his journey in it, and Tang's pastoral take on leadership are all gifts to the conversation. Whenever I encounter an honest response to the colonial and mission history of the church and the prevailing culture that surrounds planting in evangelical traditions, I am glad for the courage that gives it voice. This book's four-part structure offers fresh insight, and the third section, reminding us that the God who sends us is also out in front of us, already among those to whom we go, is an insight worth delving into and pushing deeper. Read this book for fresh takes, bubbling up from the canonical work of evangelical and missional theologians and embodied by the familiar voices of practitioners as well as scholars."

Karen Rohrer, director of the Church Planting Initiative, Pittsburgh Theological Seminary

"What I wanted most as a young church planter was the advice of those who had gone ahead of me. *Sent to Flourish* is just that—a compilation of experienced voices answering questions that are on the hearts and minds of church planters. When many voices on several topics all begin with fostering personal growth in relationship with God and responding to the Holy Spirit, you know the wisdom that follows can be trusted. Well done!"

Robert E. Logan, author of *The Church Planting Journey* and *The Missional Journey*

"The honest, experienced, and insightful collection of *Sent to Flourish* authors clearly demonstrates the value of collaboration in church planting. Together they have blessed the church with this beneficial resource. Clearly and compellingly written not only from but for the trenches of church planting, this book reflects and will serve the work of many. Rooted deeply in biblical, historical, and narrative soil, *Sent to Flourish* is refreshingly descriptive versus prescriptive, cultivating contextualized church planting with spiritual nourishment displayed by diverse examples of fruitful ministry. Church planting is frequently biased toward action, and this book provides a healthy contrast, beginning with a foundational understanding of the missio Dei, followed by reflection on critical formation of church planters. The authors continue by providing examples of healthy embodiment of the gospel in and as community. They then recognize the critical importance of communities of faith moving beyond sustainment to propagation. Both scholarly and accessible, *Sent to Flourish* encourages us to prioritize the kingdom of God over our respective castles with both inspiration and evidence."

Nathan "Chivo" Hawkins, regional director, StadiaChurchPlanting.org

SENT
TO
FLOURISH

A GUIDE TO PLANTING
AND MULTIPLYING
CHURCHES

EDITED BY **LEN TANG** AND
CHARLES E. COTHERMAN

An imprint of InterVarsity Press
Downers Grove, Illinois

InterVarsity Press
P.O. Box 1400, Downers Grove, IL 60515-1426
ivpress.com
email@ivpress.com

InterVarsity Press® is the book-publishing division of InterVarsity Christian Fellowship/USA®, a movement of students and faculty active on campus at hundreds of universities, colleges, and schools of nursing in the United States of America, and a member movement of the International Fellowship of Evangelical Students. For information about local and regional activities, visit intervarsity.org.

All Scripture quotations, unless otherwise indicated, are taken from The Holy Bible, New International Version®, NIV®. Copyright © 1973, 1978, 1984, 2011 by Biblica, Inc.™ Used by permission of Zondervan. All rights reserved worldwide. www.zondervan.com. The "NIV" and "New International Version" are trademarks registered in the United States Patent and Trademark Office by Biblica, Inc.™

While any stories in this book are true, some names and identifying information may have been changed to protect the privacy of individuals.

Cover design: David Fassett
Interior design: Daniel van Loon
Images: paper texture: © Dmytro Synelnychenko / iStock / Getty Images Plus
   spiral line illustration: David Fassett
   green spiral: © Westend61/ Getty Images
   blue watercolor square: © kentarcajuan / E+ / Getty Images
   green plants: © Sofya Moskalenko / EyeEm / Getty Images
   graphic green plant: © CSA Images / Getty Images
   Fuller Church Planting logo design: Helen Kim

ISBN 978-0-8308-5268-0 (print)
ISBN 978 0 8308 5546 9 (digital)

Printed in the United States of America ∞

Library of Congress Cataloging-in-Publication Data
A catalog record for this book is available from the Library of Congress.

P	22	21	20	19	18	17	16	15	14	13	12	11	10	9	8	7	6	5	4	3	2	1
Y	39	38	37	36	35	34	33	32	31	30	29	28	27	26	25	24	23	22	21	20	19	

To the next generation of church planters who will come out of Fuller Theological Seminary to plant flourishing churches

CONTENTS

PREFACE

SCOTT W. SUNQUIST

THE HISTORY OF CHRISTIANITY IN NORTH AMERICA is the story of church planting movements. Although most of us were not taught American history this way, the Christian faith spread not only through the preaching of missionaries but predominantly by Christians migrating throughout North America and beginning new churches along the way. This migration, resulting in church planting movements, was part of the earliest period of modern globalization. Thus migration, globalization, and church planting are the heart of the contemporary North American experience. It is helpful for us today, thinking about church planting in the twenty-first century, to see how our work is connected to ongoing migration and church planting in previous centuries. We would suggest that the modern church planting movement is not an anomaly, but simply a newer and important expression of our heritage. The question facing us today is: Will, or can, North America now be renewed by church planting movements?

In the following pages we want to lift up some of the themes and issues of this unique heritage of the American experience in the hope that they will inform (and at times chasten) today's church planting movements:

- The language that we use of planting a community that would honor God is language that is central to the American heritage.

- The earliest church planters in colonial America were among the best educated people in North America—all migrants too!

- All these early church planters (or pastors!) shared a common concern to extend the Christian faith by planting churches in new territories.

- Most of these early church planters wanted also to start schools (as well as monasteries and seminaries).

- Some of the earliest church planters tried to reach diverse populations (including indigenous), but most only wanted to reach their own people.

- Although Baptists and Methodists were smaller groups and they started later, they planted churches faster across the frontier because they did not require three years of graduate education.

These themes will emerge from the historical narrative that follows. Let's listen to the history of the United States, a narrative of national church planting.

SPANISH AND BRITISH CHURCH PLANTING

The earliest Europeans who came to explore, settle, evangelize, and trade in North America sailed from Spain via the Caribbean. These Spanish explorers and monks sometimes died trying to establish churches in present day Florida, South Carolina, and Virginia. This is an important part of our history—that the earliest Christians coming to what would become the southeastern United States were martyred trying to plant churches. They were missionaries, mostly Dominican. Almost all the earlier exploration along the coast was driven by complicated desires both to settle (and trade) and to evangelize. This is true of the early southern Europeans (Roman Catholics) as well as the northern Europeans (Separatist Puritans, Anglicans, Lutherans, and Quakers).

Most of the early European names given to places, towns, and bodies of water expressed Christian identity and hopes. As early as 1513, Florida was named after the term for Easter (*Pascua Florida*, "Paschal Flowers") and within a decade priests arrived with settlers to establish churches and reach out to the Calusa people.[1] St. Augustine, Florida, the oldest city in North America that has been continuously occupied (1565), was named after Augustine because the Spanish sighted land on the feast day of St. Augustine. Other new settlements also were given Christian names, indicating the desire to establish the faith in each place: St. Croix Island ("Holy Cross," Maine, 1605), Santa Fe ("Holy Faith," New Mexico, 1607), Salem ("Shalom," Massachusetts, 1626). On a personal note, I come from Philadelphia, the "City of Brotherly Love," a Quaker experiment in cultural diversity. In each of these places some of the first buildings were churches.

A century after the Spaniards began their migration to the Americas, a church planting movement began farther north along the coast. The first northern European church planters came to Virginia, and they were business folks who were searching for a passage to China. They were also looking for gold. Like the Spanish a century earlier, these Englishmen (for they were all men at the beginning) entered into conflict with the indigenous people, in their case the local Powhatan people, in

---

[1]Dale T. Irvin and Scott W. Sunquist, *History of the World Christian Movement*, Volume II (Maryknoll, NY: Orbis Books, 2012), 247.

1606. These business people settled for growing tobacco rather than searching for gold. Although they did not start out as a church planting network, they did plant the first Anglican congregation in North America. Others would follow, mostly in Virginia and the Carolinas. These churches were initiated by businessmen, not clerics or monks as with the Catholics a century earlier.

Farther north in New England, Puritans from old England came to escape the pressure and persecution from Christian brothers and sisters: the Anglicans! They came not only to plant churches, but they had a much grander and more complete vision. They sought to establish a church that would become a city set on the hill for all to see, a signpost of God's kingdom. Their cities were named after their former homes (Boston, Cambridge, Ipswich) and their future homes (New Haven, Providence). Although many came to seek their fortunes, a major reason for risking all to come to North America was Christian motivation. The pilgrims who landed in Plymouth made a compact—before God and with one another—that read in part, "Having undertaken for the glory of God and advancement of the Christian faith and honor of our King and Country, a voyage to plant the first colony."[2] The language of planting a community that would honor God is also part of the American heritage.

As with many church planting initiatives, these early churches in Massachusetts were (sadly) often inspired by church divisions. The early pilgrims were called "separatists," because they separated from other Congregationalists, who separated from the Anglican Church in 1620. Eight years later another group of Puritans landed in Salem, Massachusetts. This group was a little more organized, for they had formed a company to plant their churches in North America: the Massachusetts Bay Company. Of all the church planting movements from 1513 to the present, this was the best educated group of church planters. Most of the clergy and lay people had been educated at Oxford and Cambridge. They even named one of their towns after their alma mater, Cambridge, and there established a school for training other church planters and pastors, Harvard. Later they started another school for training pastors: Yale. These first pastors, church planters all, were the best educated people in North America.

Thus in these early migrations there were different motivations (commerce, persecution), different visions of the church, different educational and economic levels, but all shared a concern to extend the Christian faith by planting churches in new territories. From the beginning they also wanted to bolster the local churches with other institutions: schools, seminaries, monasteries, and later hospitals. Some had concern to reach out to indigenous people, but most sought to establish churches

---

[2]For the full text of the Mayflower Compact, see www.pilgrimhallmuseum.org/mayflower_compact_text.htm.

among their own people first. Christian mission was mostly understood as extending Christendom.

DIVERSITY OF CULTURES

For our purposes here we need to stop and look at the diversity of cultures that were involved in church planting from the beginning. One theme woven through every chapter of this volume is culture: diverse, changing, and multiple cultures. Church planting requires an attentiveness to our own culture and to the cultures we are called to. The earliest explorers in Florida and the Carolinas spoke Spanish, were Roman Catholic (before the Reformation), and were part of a European culture that accepted the proclamation of the papal bull of Alexander VI: "Among other works well pleasing to the Divine Majesty and cherished of our heart, this assuredly ranks highest, that in our times especially the Catholic faith and the Christian religion be exalted and be everywhere increased and spread, that the health of souls be cared for and that barbarous nations be overthrown and brought to the faith itself."[3] This meant that it was the responsibility of Christian kingdoms to bring other peoples to faith in Christ, even if by force. It was a strange way to think about Christian mission (or church planting), but in practice it meant that Roman Catholic nations (mostly Portugal and Spain) sent out explorers both to increase the nation's income and to spread the faith, mostly by depending on religious orders. Augustinians, Dominicans, Franciscans, and later Jesuits planted churches among indigenous people. This was the Christendom culture of Spanish- and Portuguese-speaking settlers.

The next group of early church planters in North America were the Anglicans in Virginia; they spoke English and were not commissioned by their king or queen to evangelize their new colonies. Most had little to no interest in church planting or any other type of mission work. They did, however, bring their Anglican liturgy, prayers, and style of church building.

British settlers who planted churches in New England differed in that most were Puritan and brought a more simplified worship pattern—for instance, they sang only the Psalms—and plain white church buildings. They built towns around a green with a meetinghouse that was used both for worship and civil meetings. This culture assumed that everyone in town would attend this one church. It was a vision of a homogenous Christian culture: little diversity and no pluralism of beliefs. Of course, this experiment failed in the first generation, but it is important to remember their cultural and theological assumptions. They assumed that everyone in their

---

[3]Pope Alexander VI, "Inter Caetera: Division of the Undiscovered World Between Spain and Portugal," May 4, 1493, www.papalencyclicals.net/Alex06/alex06inter.htm.

town should be Christian, that all would worship together, and that they would create a "city on a hill" for all the world to see. This was a Protestant and Puritan expression of European Christendom.

Other British and Dutch who arrived had other, but similar, cultural assumptions. Soon German and French settlers came bringing other languages and assumptions about the role of their newly planted churches in this new world. Some, like the German Pietists who were shaped by a renewal movement centered in Halle, Germany, had much greater interest in reaching indigenous peoples in the Caribbean, as well as in Pennsylvania. Their theological and cultural assumptions were different than those of the Puritans, Anglicans, and most of the Dutch Reformed.

In the nineteenth century, the Irish came building their Catholic churches and colleges as they sought to protect their identity in this anti-Catholic new world. Their churches worshiped in Latin and did all other work in the Irish tongue. Culturally (especially linguistically) this cut them off from the Protestant churches. They were also involved in outreach to indigenous populations but mostly through men's and women's religious orders. It would be a long time before Irish Catholics and Congregationalists or Presbyterians would respect one another. The major breakthrough was the election of our first Catholic president in 1961.

Those immigrants who planted churches who reached out to indigenous people are important models for church planting today. People like John Eliot should be remembered at least for their theological commitment to reaching out to one's neighborhood. With no textbook on church planting among the locals, Eliot established Puritan-looking "praying towns." One of these towns he named Nonantum, which means "Place of Rejoicing." On Martha's Vineyard and in Nantucket, the Mayhew family, inspired by Thomas Mayhew the younger, established equitable economic arrangements with the community of about three thousand local people (the Pokanaukets, a branch of the Narragansett). Mayhew learned their language and established churches and schools for children. Thus there is a tradition of moving to a new area, attending to just economic relationships with those already in the area, learning the local language and culture, and using Scripture to lead people to faith.[4] Church planting and Christian mission are of the same fabric.

1800 TO THE BABY BOOMERS

In the nineteenth century, church planting took a different turn. This was the century of westward expansion and most of the movement west was purely for economic

---

[4]There were many others who reached out to indigenous populations, the Moravians being the most obvious example, but immigrants are usually struggling to survive and to preserve their own family, language, and traditions. Rarely do they also have a missional understanding of the local church.

and political reasons. As the United States acquired new territory (from France in 1803 and Mexico in ca. 1845) it was important to settle people in these formerly foreign territories. Few pastors or missionaries were migrating to the heartland or farther west, but some denominations set up home mission societies to reach out to people beyond the Allegheny Mountains. These home missions were establishing churches both among indigenous people and the new settlers.[5]

Not all churches cared or saw it as a priority to plant churches among the frontier settlers, and as a result there was a sudden shift in denominational strength in North America. During the first decades of the nineteenth century the larger denominations (Episcopal, Congregational, Presbyterian) were surpassed in numbers by the Baptists and Methodists. The great growth of Methodist and Baptist churches had to do with their commitment to church planting as mission and their willingness to forgo a three-year graduate degree for their church planters. While Presbyterians and Congregationalists required competence in Latin, Hebrew, and Greek language, the Baptists and Methodists did not. Thus, Methodist circuit riders and Baptist evangelists, responding to a call from God and confirmed by their local church, rode to the frontier and planted churches in most new towns across the trails and inland waterways to the west.

Along with the movement west came the forced relocation of indigenous peoples. The Indian Removal Act of 1830 mandated the removal of indigenous people from the southeastern states to regions beyond the Mississippi. This forced migration included members of the Cherokee, Choctaw, Muscogee (or Creek), Seminole, and Chickasaw nations. Because of death from exposure and starvation among the Cherokee, their migration has been called the "Trail of Tears." Some churches worked among native Americans as they were being resettled on reservations. Both Protestant and Catholic missionary work began in these new oppressive social environments where people were in a foreign land living in hard-to-cultivate regions in artificial towns. However, church planting did occur and, as is often the case, schools were started by missionary church planters on the reservations.

Church planting, at its best, was attentive to moving populations, planting congregations and schools that would serve the newer populations as well as the traditional ones. A similar pattern developed in the early twentieth century following two different movements of people. In the early twentieth century there began a

---

[5]One interesting example is First Presbyterian Church in Pittsburgh which, in the early decades of the nineteenth century, would send their pastor to work for one month a year among indigenous peoples. He was, in effect, doing short term missions as a church planter. For a further explanation of this missional spirit in the early nineteenth century see Michael Parker, "175 Years of Presbyterian World Mission," accessed February 13, 2019, history.pcusa.org/history-online/topics-note/history-world-mission.

movement from the rural South to the urban North (the Great Migration of African Americans) and from the urban core to the suburban areas. As people moved north, they brought with them their faith and planted churches in northern cities. These were newer churches with newer forms of worship: African American Episcopal, African American Episcopal Zion, National Baptist, and Church of God in Christ, among others.[6]

Those moving to newer communities outside of cities (often in planned communities) relied on urban churches to help them plant churches in their new neighborhoods. Many churches in urban areas of the East and South have a history of the number of churches they planted over the years. It is a great heritage that began in the early twentieth century and continued through the 1960s. The 1960s were a great era of church building, even as the decline of mainline churches was beginning. The post-war babies were coming of age, so churches were adding on larger sanctuaries and education buildings. But by 1965 almost all the mainline churches were in decline. The decline continues even today.

THE RADICAL 1960s TO TODAY

The 1965 Immigration and Naturalization Act changed both the complexion of US society and the nature of American Christianity and church planting. Prior to the 1960s over two thirds of the immigrants were from Europe. The biggest change over the previous century was that more southern and eastern Europeans immigrated and that meant more Catholic and Orthodox churches were planted in the United States. After this important piece of legislation, there were no restrictions on religion, country of origin, or race. Suddenly Latin Americans, Africans, Middle Easterners, and Asians began to migrate to the States. Many more Roman Catholics from Latin America, Presbyterians from Korea, and Muslims, Buddhists, and Hindus were becoming Americans. For those paying attention to their new neighbors, church planting would begin to look a little more like overseas mission work.

The same time this new diversity in US culture was taking off, US churches were finishing a decade or more of building and rebuilding their churches, and it was a time of major upheaval in US society. The secular 60s was the decade of sexual liberation, new experimentation with drugs, and black power and civil rights. It was a prosperous decade, but the two main institutional threads of traditional American culture—the family and the church—were coming unraveled. The civil rights movement made it clear that neither the government nor the churches had

---

[6]See Deidre Hellen Crumbley, *Saved and Sanctified: The Rise of a Storefront Church in Great Migration Philadelphia* (Gainesville: University of Florida Press, 2012) for an excellent discussion of the development of church planting in stores along urban streets.

completed the reform that the Civil War and reconstruction had started. Church planting was in decline, and the planting that was done tended to ignore the reality of cultural plurality in US cities.

However, there were a few exceptions to this church planting decline of the late 1960s. First, Pentecostal and charismatic churches accelerated their church planting both in traditional denominations like the Assemblies of God and in newer groups like Vineyard USA. These churches had great zeal for church planting. They carried a message of spiritual power for transformation and their church planting in the United States quickly (almost simultaneously) spilled out across the nations of the world. Pentecostalism created a new church planting paradigm centered on the Holy Spirit when mainline churches moved to more of a business model.[7]

Second, newer immigrant churches, especially at the end of the twentieth century and early in the twenty-first century, began planting many churches and even began to experiment with reaching out to other ethnic groups in major cities. Most of these groups began their congregations by meeting in a traditional mainline church building and then they would begin to grow. Presbyterians (or Reformed) from Korea, Egypt, Kenya, or West Africa would meet in Presbyterian churches; Methodists would find Methodist churches; and Anglicans would find Episcopal churches.

The third exception to the church planting decline occurred because of the migration out of the Rust Belt to the Sun Belt that began in the late 1950s. American industrial production was at a peak during and immediately after World War 2, but soon cheaper steel and products were coming from Japan, India, Latin America, and later China, Vietnam, and Sri Lanka. When, for example, much cheaper steel was available from Japan, huge factories closed in the industrial heartland from Connecticut to Chicago, down to northern West Virginia and across to Philadelphia. People searched for jobs, and with greater mobility those jobs were moving south and southwest. Cities like Charlotte, Atlanta, Dallas, Houston, Phoenix, and some in Southern California began welcoming millions of immigrants. Churches were planted in part to reach some of the displaced northerners. This church planting movement involved all the mainline and Catholic churches, as well as Pentecostal and newer churches. Again, church planting followed migrants.

An important final word about this volatile period in US church planting history needs to be mentioned: division. Pentecostalism, as with most renewal movements, started within churches and other existing institutions, but soon it broke out of these

---

[7]Guided by the Holy Spirit, Pentecostals pray about the church plant and move forward through prayer and evangelism and then gather people together in Bible study and worship. In a business model, planting involves a five-year budget plan with financial support worked out on a year-by-year basis with clear goals established (attendance, conversions, income, etc.).

traditional centers. It also started out as an ethnically and racially blind movement, but soon it began to divide according to race. Other groups in mainline churches, both fundamentalist and charismatic, also separated themselves out and began to plant their own churches, even as the ecumenical movement was at its height. From the Presbyterian Church (USA) emerged the Orthodox Presbyterian Church, the Bible Presbyterian Church, and later (from the Southern Presbyterians) the Presbyterian Church in America. Baptists, Lutherans, Episcopalians, and Methodists also had similar experiences. Newer churches developed networks and at times denomination-like structures and focused on planting new churches in the last decades of the twentieth century. Today there are numerous church planting networks and associations, but few are connected with the traditional churches that came to North America from Europe or that developed in North America in the nineteenth or twentieth centuries. This history of renewal, division, and church growth is not unique to the United States, but we do need to be aware of it as we think about our own church planting in the twenty-first century. We should learn from these past experiences that have hurt the church's witness and turned so many away from church. Of course, we also want to be attentive to ways that church planting has been done well in the past. Now we are ready to move forward.

CHURCH PLANTING, CHURCH GROWTH, AND THIS BOOK

Before continuing this book, we would like to look at two final issues. First, we'll explore some key themes that have developed over the past decades for church planters in North America. Then we will address the question: How does this church planting book connect to the traditions of evangelicalism that have come out of Fuller Theological Seminary?

Three key themes in Christian development in recent decades must be part of our thinking about church planting today. First of all, less than 50 percent of Christians in North America today are white or European in background. This means that church planters must be conscious of reaching out crossculturally as well as multiculturally. We take this very seriously. Our church planting program at Fuller Theological Seminary is housed in the School of Intercultural Studies because the study of culture and the view of church planting as missionary work is so important today. While historically there were some church planting movements that intentionally reached out to other cultures and ethnic groups, they were very few. We believe they should be more common in the future.

Second, most of the church planting done today is not connected with a church tradition, so the worship, theology, and understanding of the church (ecclesiology) may not relate to existing churches or even to other churches being planted. We are committed to the church and believe that every local church is part of the great Christian tradition (connected) and relevant to local communities (context). Thus, we have, as part of our quartet of books on church planting, a book that is just about basic concepts of what a church is and what it does; how all churches are both connected and contextual.[8] We recommend that you and your church planting team study this book together to help discern the trajectory of your church. We want to plant churches that are vitally connected to their local communities and to other Christian traditions. We hope church planting will connect and unite Christians in common witness.

Third, beginning in the 1990s, a movement in North America and Western Europe started which has had a great impact on church planting: the missional church movement (see chapter one for more detail). This movement finds its origins in the writings of Lesslie Newbigin after he returned to England from India and from his work with the World Council of Churches. His return to the West was an eye opener for him. Recognizing the anemic state of the churches in the United Kingdom, he wrote extensively about the missionary nature of the church, the West as a mission field, and what it means for the church to be missional: a *foretaste* and *signpost* of God's kingdom and an *instrument* in bringing the kingdom. The adjective *missional* was created to communicate Newbigin's concept of the church in mission for Western culture.[9] His other important concept, which has guided many in recent church planting movements, is that the church is also to be a *hermeneutic* of the gospel. Those wanting to know what the good news is today should be able to see it in the life and ministry of the local church.[10]

Newbigin's concern for the church to see itself as a missionary presence in the West connects this book and the four books in this series together. The School of Intercultural Studies at Fuller was originally called the School of World Mission and Institute for Church Growth. Started in 1955, it was concerned to help churches grow, which meant planting new churches in various countries in the world. Most of the early students were doing studies on how to help the church grow in places like the Punjab, Northern Thailand, and Taiwan. In each case church growth meant studying the cultures and societies to make sure that effective bridges of God evident in all cultures would be utilized to help the church grow. New churches would

---

[8]Scott W. Sunquist, *Why Church? A Basic Introduction* (Downers Grove, IL: IVP Academic, 2019). In the near future there will be a book on the spirituality of the church planter and another on the missional pastor.

[9]See Scott W. Sunquist, *Understanding Christian Mission: Participation in Suffering and Glory* (Grand Rapids: Baker Academic, 2013), 11.

[10]Several contributors will refer to Newbigin in this volume. For a more detailed discussion of Newbigin for church planting, see Sunquist, *Why Church?*, chap. 1. See also www.newbiginresources.org/.

be planted as the church planters understood what bridges God had already placed in each culture.[11]

This is not exactly our approach here, but we do see church planting as essentially a primary element of Christian mission. Thus we think as missionaries about our task. We study the local cultures in our parish or neighborhood. We look for key places, people, and organizations to connect with. And in the School of Intercultural Studies, we have been studying these movements and preparing people from around the world with this focus for fifty-four years.

So we are continuing to live into the *missio Dei* (mission of God) as people sent into contexts where the great American twin themes of migration and church planting are still alive and well. We hope that in these pages you will find encouragement for the journey and an approach that is faithful to the gospel message, sensitive to cultures, and deeply spiritual, for church planting, like all mission, is more about spirituality than strategy. We have seen in the past that church planting movements more often than not spring out of revivals or renewals of the church in various contexts. May what follows, from people who have planted churches in different countries and languages, and from different church traditions, be an inspiration and a guide. This is our prayer.

---

[11]For a study on Donald McGavran and church growth, see Gary L. McIntosh, *Donald McGavran: A Biography of the Twentieth Century's Premier Missiologist* (Pasadena, CA: William Carey Library, 2015); David Hesselgrave and Donald McGavran, *Planting Churches Cross-Culturally: North America and Beyond,* 2nd ed. (Grand Rapids: Baker Academic, 2000).

ACKNOWLEDGMENTS

LIKE THE NARRATIVES THAT FILL THESE PAGES, the story of this book is one of partnership and collaboration, first with the missional God who invites us into the redemptive story he is crafting in creation and second with an amazing team of people intent on following on the heels of this sending God. It has been an honor to be on this team, and it's a privilege to be able to thank a handful of folks who made this project not only possible but enjoyable.

The concept for this book and the larger Fuller Seminary Church Planting Program itself came from the missional heart of Scott W. Sunquist, then dean of Fuller's School of Intercultural Studies, and the vision and generosity of the original donors whose passion for the gospel through church planting helped make a vision for a church planting program at Fuller a reality. It was Scott who also ensured that our team could gather for a two-day brainstorming and relationship-building session in Pasadena in April of 2017. This book has benefitted immensely from the friendships and collaboration that were first forged over these two days.

We are also grateful for the contributors to this volume, who spent hours working to craft each chapter even as they shepherded congregations, church planting organizations, and seminaries.

A heartfelt thanks to the new churches we lead—Missio Community Church in Pasadena, California, and Oil City Vineyard in Oil City, Pennsylvania—which have joined God's mission and have embraced us even as we struggle to embody the lessons contained in this book.

In any project like this, there are unsung heroes who do more behind the scenes than most will ever know. This project is especially indebted to Kathryn Engelmann at Fuller Seminary for her faithful and creative partnership in the church planting program and her diligent and insightful proofreading. We are also deeply grateful to Jon Boyd, Rebecca Carhart, and the IVP Academic team for consistently modeling editorial expertise, Christian commitment, and personal approachability.

Perhaps no one better understands the work and the joys of this project better than our families. Throughout this process Amy, Benjamin, Sam, and Josh Tang and Aimee, Elliana, Anneliese, and Benton Cotherman have been faithful encouragers while simultaneously reminding us daily that some things are even more important than book projects. Thank you for your love, support, and prayers.

Finally, thanks be to God for his indescribable gift. May this book be an offering to you and a catalyst to others whom you are calling to join in your redemptive mission.

INTRODUCTION

LEN TANG

CHURCH PLANTING IS HARD. There are a myriad of pressures that squeeze us. There is leadership stress—since I am the visible leader and the literal face of the church, when something goes wrong there is no one else to blame. There is identity stress—if the church plant fails, then by extension *I* am a failure. And, of course, there is financial stress—if the church plant doesn't flourish, the seed money will dry up and my family may go hungry. The list goes on and on.

In response, our spirits shrivel under the weight of all there is to do and the exposure of our own inadequacies. Our theology shrinks from majestic to merely pragmatic and utilitarian. People are reduced to organizational building blocks rather than beings of infinite worth in God's sight. Families are objectified as giving units. The glorious work of church planting shrinks into a myopic view of a small god who brings a reductionistic gospel and an exploitative view of human beings.

Oftentimes well-meaning denominational leaders or church planting networks respond to these pressures by becoming more technical and practical in their advice for the planter: try this, do that, pray more, tweet more, share the gospel more often, cast a bigger vision. But in responding with quick fixes rather than attentive soul work, they unknowingly short circuit the planter's own formation and the learning moment gets buried under an avalanche of action items. This is not to pretend that church planting takes place in some imaginary, stress-free, ideal world. On the contrary, these very stressors and pressures become the raw material for confession, formation, theological reflection, community building, and even evangelism. The humanity of the planter means that as she embraces her own limitations, she finds herself humbled by Christ and freed by the expansiveness of the gospel and invites others to do the same.

So how can we as church planters be sent to flourish?

Welcome to *Sent to Flourish: A Guide to Planting and Multiplying Churches*. As I write this, it's been less than a month since the public launch of the second church

I have planted, and the joy of gathering people from across the spiritual spectrum, each bringing deep questions to their pursuit of faith, is still fresh. Despite the perception that seminaries are ivory towers, this book is written from the trenches of church planting for the sake of the next generation of church planters, who are our heroes. The eight authors are a diverse group of church planters, seminary faculty, and church planting network leaders (some are all three). Together this team of scholar-practitioners possesses the battle scars of church planting as well as the capacity to reflect theologically on what we believe God is doing in the world through planting new mission outposts. This nexus is what Tim Keller calls a "theological vision," which he defines as "a vision for what you are going to do with your doctrine in a particular time and place."[1] Notice that a theological vision is simultaneously actionable ("what you are going to do"), theological ("with your doctrine"), and contextual ("in a particular time and place").

The particular time and place we find ourselves in is a world that is changing more rapidly than we realize. It's self-evident that the West is becoming post-Christian, increasingly diverse, and spiritually fragmented. The so-called spiritual nones are on the rise, and many churches and seminaries are training pastors and planters for a world that no longer exists. Our country is increasingly fractured around issues of race, economic justice, and politics. And yet I share Christopher James's conviction that "these first decades of the twenty-first century ought to be seen not only as a period of church decline but also, and more importantly, as a vibrant season of ecclesial renewal and rebirth."[2] There is an urgent need to holistically form a new generation of women and men from a multitude of cultural backgrounds who are joining God's mission in the world. In this book we want to give church planters and their teams the tools to be theologically reflective, spiritually grounded, and missionally agile.

Just as a tree needs deep roots in order to grow tall, we believe that the church planter needs a robust root system made up of (1) a biblical theology of church planting, (2) the spiritual formation of the planter, and (3) intercultural competencies to navigate the church planting context. These three roots correspond to the three core values of Fuller's church planting program (see figure 1). As we'll see, these roots are intertwined and interdependent, in continuous interaction within the heart, mind, and relationships of the planter. We hope that the Spirit of God will make it second nature to look on ourselves and our mission contexts through this threefold lens. The first three parts of this book address each of these roots in turn.

---

[1]Timothy Keller, *Center Church* (Grand Rapids: Redeemer City to City, 2012), 18.
[2]Christopher James, *Church Planting in Post-Christian Soil* (New York: Oxford University Press, 2018), 2.

Part one will offer thoughtful reflection on the biblical foundations of church planting. This foundation is rooted in the very nature and character of God, not merely a few evangelistic or social justice prooftexts. Part two's priority is the holistic formation of the planter and their team, since we can only minister out of who we are. Church planting is demanding work and it's crucial to help planters stay grounded in their identity in Christ and develop a missional spirituality that flows out to the world, rather than ride the rollercoaster of numbers or success. Part three will explore missional competencies that equip planters to embody the good news of Jesus Christ in an increasingly post-Christian and multicultural world. Finally, part four will help develop a practical church planting plan while keeping planters' eyes on the broader goal of creating a church-planting ecosystem.

Figure 1. Fuller Church Planting logo

In God's providence, Fuller is uniquely positioned to equip church planters for kingdom impact in a changing world. The wisdom and expertise of Fuller's three graduate schools (theology, intercultural studies, and psychology) map perfectly onto our church planting program's three core values of theology, missional skills, and formation. Frederick Buechner famously writes that "the place God calls you to is the place where your deep gladness and the world's deep hunger meet."[3] The deep gladness and depth of competency of Fuller Theological Seminary lies in the very places that we feel the church planting world hungers for.

Throughout our history, Fuller has sought to integrate scholarship with evangelism, theory with practice. It's no wonder, considering that the seminary was founded by Charles Fuller, a radio evangelist, and Harold John Ockenga, a pastor and theologian. In 1947 they founded Fuller Seminary to train evangelists and missionaries. Then in 1964 Charles Fuller wrote of his desire to start the School of World Mission (now known as the School of Intercultural Studies):

> I feel that the time has come to found a school of worldwide evangelism. . . . Such a
> school would provide dedicated people with a chance to study under scholarly and
> godly [people] who have had rich experience in establishing the church of Jesus Christ
> in the various nations of earth. Here they could learn how to use the means available
> today for communicating with the masses, such as radio, television, and the printed

---

[3]Frederick Buechner, *Wishful Thinking: A Theological ABC* (New York: Harper & Row, 1973).

page. Here they could receive training in how best to meet linguistical and cultural differences so as to be increasingly effective in proclaiming the Gospel.[4]

We take a great deal of inspiration from the fact that over a half-century ago, Fuller envisioned a setting in which professors who had themselves been involved in God's mission would train students to innovatively share the gospel using the latest technologies (which at the time were radio and television). At the same time, a deep intercultural awareness meant that students needed training to understand and respect the "linguistical and cultural differences" in such a way as to point various people groups to saving faith in Jesus Christ. In like manner, our team of scholar-practitioners seeks to harness our own church planting experiences, using an intercultural approach, so that the gospel might be respectfully and boldly proclaimed and demonstrated.

We at Fuller Seminary are honored to walk with you as you respond to the unique and daunting call of catalyzing and forming a new community of faith for the sake of the gospel. This book is called a guide because it offers a broad roadmap of church planting. It's neither a how-to manual nor a theology textbook. It's meant to point out some theological potholes and spiritual points of interest, but not in an exhaustive fashion—merely enough to whet your appetite and give you encouragement along the way. We encourage you to read this book with other church planters or members of your church planting team, using the discussion questions at the end of each chapter.

Let's explore the relationship among the three roots of formation, theology, and mission, understanding what each one means and delving into their continuous interplay. As you read, consider how these roots function in your own life, ministry, and church planting context.

4Gary L. McIntosh, "The Life and Ministry of Donald A. McGavran," McIntosh Church Growth Network, March 16, 2015, www.churchgrowthnetwork.com/freebies2/2015/3/13/the-life-and-ministry-of-donald-a-mcgavran.

PART 1

WHAT ROOTS DOES A CHURCH NEED TO FLOURISH?

A BIBLICAL THEOLOGY OF CHURCH PLANTING

BEGINNINGS MATTER. In life, ministry, academics, art, sports, books(!), you name it, the early stages of development are important. Sure, as Christians we follow a God of redemption, so there's no beginning that can't be altered nor early wound that can't be healed, but as good as healing is, we all know there's also a deep goodness and grace to avoiding wounds in the first place. That's why we care for our children and introduce them to Jesus at an early age. We don't want them to be wounded. We know beginnings matter.

Beginnings matter for churches too. From the birth of the church in Acts 2 to the beginning of church plants today in cities, suburbs, rural villages, and at the end of dirt roads all around the world, the roots we put down in the early stages of a faith community's life set a largely unnoticed but hugely important trajectory for the visible life that will follow above the surface. In church life, as in the natural world, roots precede fruit.

That's why the first part of this book focuses on establishing deep, life-giving roots anchored in Scripture and the goodness of the triune God who is working through his Holy Spirit in the church and in all of creation. The first chapter sets the course by rooting us in the ongoing mission of God—the *missio Dei*. It is only by discerning God's ongoing redemptive work in our context and then humbly joining him in it that our efforts as church planters, pastors, and Christ-followers can begin well. Chapter two builds on this understanding of the church as a sent people participating in the mission of a sending God by framing the general contours of this mission. What framework orients our understanding of our efforts on a micro and macro scale? The general framework in which all our church planting and ministry efforts are rooted is the biblical concept of the kingdom of God as seen throughout Jesus' teaching, in the Lord's Prayer, and finally in the consummation of God's kingdom in the book of Revelation. No one (if they are wise!) starts a journey without knowing the means of transportation and the destination. As followers of Jesus our means of travel is joining in on the ongoing work of a missional God and our destination is the kingdom of God, something that we along with the church universal pray will "come, on earth as it is in heaven."

From these roots chapter three will begin to shift our focus to the next stages of the life cycle—growth and reproduction—by asking how God's story spreads. As we start new faith communities, how do we make sure that the good news isn't just good news for us but good news for our neighbors on our street, across town, and around the world? How do we move from roots to fruit, from birth to multiplication? Is there a biblical framework for this kind of church life cycle? As we will see, the answer is yes.

Now let's get started! May the Holy Spirit guide you as you read and as you lead the small part of God's big church that God has called you to. It's his mission and his kingdom, not ours. May we begin rooted in these realities, and may his good news spread.

HOW DO WE DISCERN GOD'S ACTIVITY IN SCRIPTURE AND OUR COMMUNITY?

THE *MISSIO DEI* AND THE MISSIONAL HERMENEUTIC

CHARLES E. COTHERMAN

ABOUT SEVEN MONTHS INTO PLANTING A CHURCH in western Pennsylvania, I found myself seated across from Dan in the dimly lit back room of Karma Coffee. For the better part of an hour Dan had invited me into his story, a story filled with betrayal, loss, and a numbing sense of hopelessness. Now he looked at me, his new pastor, for a response.

Dan's pain followed a trajectory I had grown somewhat accustomed to in my small, poverty-stricken town, so one might think that I would have learned enough even in a few months to respond with an answer that was both compassionate and theologically rich. I wish I could say I did. Instead, I shot from the hip, and blurted out, "You need to run to Jesus."

Fortunately, Dan was honest (or desperate) enough to call my pastoral bluff. "What does that even mean?" he shot back just as fast. For someone who had prayed for years, seemingly to no avail, for God to save his marriage and free him from addiction and chronic underemployment, another clichéd action step was precisely *not* what he needed.

Thankfully, God was gracious to both of us. In the midst of my blundering pastoral care, God helped me see that Dan needed to develop a sense of God's active and redemptive presence, a presence that was there in the midst of his past pain and continued into his current struggles. I asked Dan where he saw the presence of Jesus in the events of his life. As Dan took a moment to reflect, I noticed his expression change. Unlike my first question, which focused on his action, Dan found my second

Mission has its origin in the heart of God. God is a fountain of sending love. This is the deepest source of mission. It is impossible to penetrate deeper still; there is mission because God loves people.

DAVID J. BOSCH

question, which focused on God's action, liberating. For Dan, considering anew the reality of a God who draws near in compassionate and redemptive presence helped shift his perspective from his own problems and failures to the goodness of a God who has always been actively working for the good of creation.

"BAD THEOLOGY KILLS"

Why begin a book on church planting with a story like this? Obviously not to wow you with my pastoral skills! My initial, emotionally charged response was hardly what Dan needed. Yet as simple as it was, my conversation with Dan illustrates one of the most fundamental aspects of church planting and every other activity of the church: God's action always precedes ours. Ministry begins with God, not us. It is his mission, not ours. Put another way, "it is not individual Christians or even the Church who has a mission in the world; rather, it is the God of mission who has a Church in the world."[1] For church planters this means that our calling is one of recognition and response. Instead of beginning with our own "failproof" strategies, custom logos, exquisite websites, and five-step action plans and then inviting God to bless them, we begin with eyes, ears, and hearts open to sensing how the living God has moved in the past through Scripture and the history of the church and is currently moving in our midst. As church planters and congregations our question becomes not What can I do? or What can we do? but How is the missional God inviting us into a mission much larger than anything we could dream up on our own?

This may seem like a small distinction, but as the rest of this book will argue, the theological lens through which we see Scripture and our calling as church planters and church communities matters. This is not always a popular stance to take in a church planting culture where the tendency to value action over reflection is pronounced and sometimes explicitly celebrated. We give our churches names like Action Church and stress activity—sometimes any activity. I have even seen a church plant boast on its website that its *modus operandi* was "ready, fire, aim." For the most part, the heart behind these sentiments is probably good. These churches want to actively spread the good news of Jesus to their community in innovative ways. What a great impulse! (Plus, truth be told, I would rather attend a church called Action Church than one called Theology Church. At least action implies some excitement and passion.) Yet what would happen if soldiers and hunters followed these ready-fire-aim guidelines? Not only would they usually miss the real target, there would likely be plenty of casualties to go around. Unfortunately, this same dynamic can be true in the church. Whether we recognize it or not, all church

---

[1]David J. Bosch, *Transforming Mission: Paradigm Shifts in Theology of Mission* (Maryknoll, NY: Orbis, 1991), 390.

planters have a theology—a way of thinking about God. The question is, does our theology help us hit our intended target by helping us better live as outposts of and signs pointing toward the inbreaking of God's kingdom, or does it lead to unintended consequences?

Whether we think of ourselves as theologians or not, what we think about God and how those thoughts translate into our actions and teaching matters. I know a professional theologian who sums up this reality in an oft-repeated three-word sentence: "Bad theology kills." At first I thought her mantra was an overstatement. Over time, however, I have come to believe that she is right. Faulty understandings of God and God's mission in this world really do stifle life and growth in both individuals and the church. Church planting is no different. So much of what we do as church *planters* is encouraging the life cycle that comes naturally to all living things (birth, growth, flourishing, reproduction). As living bodies, churches are naturally prone to follow this life cycle. The various stages of this progression—including reproduction—should not be exceptions to the norm but the natural outflow of the life of Christ's body.

However, as we see in the natural world, not all living things follow this process. Sometimes a plant can put all its energy into growing larger and larger and neglect the production of fruit that will ensure reproduction and long-term sustainability through future generations. In other cases, an outside force like disease, environmental factors, or genetic engineering curtails the regular life cycle. The same can be true for churches. A host of internal and external forces can stunt a local church's growth. Sometimes the problem is unconfessed sin or unhealthy leadership. Other times a lack of growth stems from a failure to accurately discern the local climate or wisely cultivate a healthy environment for growth and reproduction. The following chapters in this book will address these and other concerns, but more basic than them all is the theological soil into which a new church is planted. Just as plants cannot thrive in poor soil, our efforts as church planters will be stunted or wither altogether if we fail to begin with a theology that places the task of planting in right relationship to the ultimate Source of life.

MISSIONAL GOD

Over the past half century or so, theologians, missiologists, pastors, and church planters have increasingly recognized that the theological basis for church planting and all other Christian endeavors is the *missio Dei,* the "mission of God." Drawing on the meaning of the Latin word *missio* (sending), the *missio Dei* points to the sending nature of the triune God: The Father sends the Son, and the Father and Son (or for Eastern Christians, the Father) send the Spirit to complete God's redemptive mission in creation. Only recently has the church rediscovered an appreciation for the divine origin of mission. Its earliest Protestant manifestations trace back to the work of European theologians like Karl Barth (1886–1968) in the 1930s and only began to crystallize following the 1952 Willingen Conference of the International Missionary Council. From that point on, the concept of the *missio Dei* found a ready reception. By the mid-1970s the idea that all Christian mission found its origin in the missionary (i.e., sending) God was making its way from theological classrooms and ecumenical conferences to the books of popular authors like John Stott. Writing in 1975, Stott conveyed the idea of the *missio Dei* in clear terms that readers then and today could hardly miss. "The primal mission is God's," Stott asserted, "for it is God who sent his prophets, his Son, and his Spirit."[2] Stott even anticipated later developments by taking God's sending task one step further—to the church. Stott pointed to passages like John 17:18 and John 20:21 as evidence that "Jesus did more than draw a vague parallel between his mission and the *model* of ours, saying '*as* the Father sent me, *so* I send you.' Therefore, our understanding of the church's mission must be deduced from our understanding of the Son's."[3] Through his international ministry and regular speaking engagements at places like InterVarsity Christian Fellowship's triannual Urbana Conference, Stott no doubt helped many begin to think through the implications of God's missionary nature.

It was not Stott, however, who played the leading role in helping the church better understand the practical implications of the *missio Dei*. Though not the originator of the term *missio Dei*, no twentieth-century figure was more influential in shaping the church's understanding of God's sending nature than one of Stott's contemporaries, the British missionary, pastor, author, and theologian Lesslie Newbigin (1909–1998). Newbigin was among the early advocates of God's sending character and had been one of the most influential drafters of the 1952 Willingen statement.[4] For Newbigin, as for Barth, mission was not simply something God did; it was part of the triune God's very nature.

As the 1960s wore on, however, Newbigin became concerned that many in the ecumenical movement were misusing the concept of the *missio Dei* in such a way as to actually marginalize the church. In their effort "to get out into the world, find out 'what God is doing in the world' and join forces with him," many were overlooking

---

[2]John Stott and Christopher J. H. Wright, *Christian Mission in the Modern World*, updated and expanded ed. (Downers Grove, IL: InterVarsity Press, 2015), 21.

[3]Stott and Wright, *Christian Mission in the Modern World*, 21-23.

[4]For a succinct overview of the creation of the Willingen Statement, see Michael W. Goheen, "A Missional Reading of Scripture for Theological Education and Curriculum," in *Reading the Bible Missionally*, ed. Michael W. Goheen (Grand Rapids: Eerdmans, 2016), 302-3.

the role of the church. The problem, in Newbigin's assessment, was that "'what God is doing in the world' was generally thought to be in the secular rather than in the religious sectors of human life." In practice this led both to the marginalization of the church in the world and to the church's acceptance of cultural movements that Newbigin found "bizarre" and sometimes even anti-Christian.[5] As a case in point, he noted that for some "even Chairman Mao's 'little red book' became almost a new bible."[6] For Newbigin this was a misuse of the idea of *missio Dei* that needed to be challenged if the church hoped to keep its bearings in the world.

Newbigin found time to set himself to the task of salvaging the idea of the *missio Dei* after he retired from active missionary work in India and returned to the United Kingdom in 1974. Newly confronted with the reality of a rapidly secularizing West, Newbigin dedicated himself to confronting misuses of the *missio Dei* and to exploring and propagating the implications of a mission-based theology in a culture that had lost its spiritual moorings. His 1978 book, *The Open Secret: An Introduction to the Theology of Mission,* explicitly rejected the freewheeling handling of the *missio Dei* that had defined the church's use of the concept in the 1960s. Instead, Newbigin again argued that the church needed to root any concept of the mission of God in the Trinity, specifically in the authority of Jesus, who was "sent by the Father, anointed by the Spirit to be the bearer of God's kingdom to the nations."[7] For Newbigin, the church's duty in any context was "to go back to the original biblical sources of this [trinitarian] faith in order to lay hold of it afresh and state it in contemporary terms."[8] Newbigin's emphasis on this basic understanding of the sending God as the source of mission offered Western Christians a means for thinking in new, post-Christendom ways about engaging Western society. It also pointed to a renewed role for the church. In a secularizing culture, the church could not simply open its doors and wait for people to stream in. Rather, the church's only viable option was to live into its primary calling as a *sent* community following the lead of the sending God. In future books like *Foolishness to the Greeks* (1986) and *The Church in a Pluralistic Society* (1989), Newbigin would further explore what it meant for the church to point to and engage in God's great mission.

In raising the profile of the *missio Dei* as a concept for mission, Newbigin pointed the way for the following generation of scholars who sought to further explore the basis and implications of a theology rooted in the nature of the sending God. Of these scholars none was more influential in shaping the conversation around

---

[5]Lesslie Newbigin, *The Open Secret: An Introduction to the Theory of Mission* (Grand Rapids: Eerdmans, 1995), 18.
[6]Newbigin, *Open Secret*, 19.
[7]Newbigin, *Open Secret*, 24.
[8]Newbigin, *Open Secret*, 27.

mission than the South African missiologist David J. Bosch. By virtually all accounts, Bosch's *Transforming Mission: Paradigm Shifts in the Theology of Mission* (1991) lived up to its title by reshaping the way the church understood mission. Among the most notable aspects of Bosch's work was his ability to demonstrate that the church's call to participate in God's mission did not hinge on a select few proof texts like the Great Commission, which appears at the end of Matthew and the beginning of Acts.[9] Rather, Bosch convincingly demonstrated that the entire New Testament pointed to God's mission in the world.

At the same time, Bosch's emphasis on God's missionary action throughout the New Testament also helped underscore the importance of thinking about mission in terms of the *missio Dei*. For Bosch the church's discovery of the *missio Dei* was one of the greatest of all the paradigm shifts that had occurred in the modern understanding of mission. "The recognition that mission is God's mission" represented what Bosch described as "a crucial breakthrough." Indeed, to Bosch's mind it was "inconceivable" that the church could ever again revert to a church-centered understanding of mission.[10] The Rubicon had been crossed. Theology had arrived at a first cause permitting no deeper delving. "Mission has its origin in the heart of God," Bosch declared. "It is impossible to penetrate deeper still; there is mission because God loves people."[11]

MISSIONAL CHURCH

But what did this mean for the church and for church planting? This was the question a group of scholars led by Princeton Theological Seminary missiologist Darrell Guder took up in the late 1990s. It was one thing to state that all mission pointed back to the work of a triune, sending God, but it was another to translate this into a practical way of being the people of God. Drawing on the legacy of Newbigin and Bosch, Guder's team from the Gospel and Our Culture Network worked to chart a trajectory for the church to live into this calling. The result of their effort was the 1998 publication of *Missional Church*.[12]

The edited volume did more than simply offer a new language for talking about the church as *missional*; it also explored concrete ways in which the church was called into the sending nature of God. As Guder noted in the book's first chapter, if the church followed a "missionary God" who carried forth his mission by sending

---

[9]Craig Van Gelder and Dwight J. Zscheile, *The Missional Church in Perspective: Mapping Trends and Shaping the Conversation* (Grand Rapids: Baker Academic, 2011), 36.

[10]Bosch, *Transforming Mission*, 393.

[11]Bosch, *Transforming Mission*, 392.

[12]Darrell L. Guder, ed., *Missional Church: A Vision for the Sending of the Church in North America* (Grand Rapids: Eerdmans, 1998).

himself and his followers into the world (Jn 20:21), it made sense that the church understand itself as "God's sent people."[13] For the Western church, still struggling to find its bearings in a society where secularism was increasingly displacing Christendom's cultural consensus, these efforts found a ready hearing. Whereas Newbigin's earlier reflections on the theme of a church sent into the world had been influential in scholarly circles but had made fewer inroads in popular practice, Guder's volume helped move the concept of the *missio Dei* from the ivory tower to local churches.[14] In the next decade, the term *missional* took on a life of its own and became one of the most popular catchwords among North American church leaders. Within fifteen years of the book's publication, *missional* had come to have what Timothy Keller later described as "a dizzying variety of different and sometimes contradictory definitions."[15] As Craig Van Gelder and Dwight J. Zscheile note, by 2011 the term *missional* had developed into four broad streams that understood missional to primarily denote either an (1) evangelistic, (2) incarnational, (3) contextual, or (4) reciprocal and communal church movement.[16]

While there is certainly overlap among proponents of these diverse understandings of missional theology, the fact that the term has come to mean different things to different people points to the potential for misunderstanding and confusion.[17] Perhaps now, two decades out from Guder's *Missional Church* and four decades out from Newbigin's *The Open Secret*, it is time for church planters and missional leaders to reemphasize the basis of missional church as being found in the mission of the triune God who has sent his Son, his Spirit, and his church into the world as part of his cosmic plan of redemption. This basis in the ongoing mission of the triune God is the touchstone that a missional people must return to again and again, perhaps even daily, as a way of ongoing formation. We are *sent ones* who minister and plant churches in the power of the *sending God*. We do not wait for people to come to us; we, being the sent ones, go to them. We do not go in our own power or the strength of our ideas. Like the disciples, we follow the lead of Jesus, trying to stay close enough to hear his voice, close enough to pick up some of the

---

[13]Guder, *Missional Church*, 6.

[14]In less than fifteen years Guder's book sold thirty-eight thousand copies; see Gelder and Zscheile, *Missional Church in Perspective*, 41, who note that three to ten thousand copies would have been good sales for a book of this type.

[15]Timothy Keller, *Center Church: Doing Balanced, Gospel-Centered Ministry in Your City* (Grand Rapids: Zondervan, 2012), 256; chap. 19 provides a succinct and helpful overview of the major trends in the missional movement.

[16]Gelder and Zscheile, *Missional Church in Perspective*, 10, 71-98. Keller offers a succinct summary of Gelder and Zscheile's work in *Center Church*, 256-57. The labels I use here for these overlapping missional approaches are Keller's rather than Gelder and Zscheile's original designations of discovering, utilizing, engaging, and extending missional approaches.

[17]For examples, see Keller, *Center Church*, 259-60.

dust he kicks up as he walks the city sidewalks and country roads of the places we call home.

FOLLOWING THE SENDING GOD

If we are honest, it's at this point we arrive at a dilemma. It is one thing for first-century disciples to follow closely enough to be covered in the dust from their rabbi's feet; it's another to apply this analogy to our lives today in a post-ascension world in which Jesus is no longer *physically* present.[18] How do we *follow* someone who is not here? Fortunately for us, Jesus himself offered some clues.

At the beginning of the book of Acts we catch some of Jesus' final interactions with his disciples before his ascension. We see Jesus, the sent one of God, preparing his disciples for (1) the sending of the promised Holy Spirit and (2) the sending of God's Spirit-empowered church into the world. How does Jesus prepare his apostles for these coming realities? Luke gives us Jesus' method at the end of his first volume, the Gospel of Luke.

The first way Jesus prepared the disciples for what was to come was through meeting them in their humanity by offering them a chance to personally *experience* him. "Look at my hands and my feet. It is I myself! Touch me and see" (Lk 24:39). The disciples needed to experience Jesus for themselves. They needed to hear his voice, see him with their eyes, and touch him with their hands. We get down on doubting Thomas, but Jesus did not. He met him in his humanity. But experience was not all Jesus offered his disciples. Experience, as important as it was, was not enough. Jesus supplemented the disciples' experience of his presence by turning their attention to *Scripture*. "He said to them, 'This is what I told you while I was still with you: Everything must be fulfilled that is written about me in the Law of Moses, the Prophets and the Psalms.' Then he opened their minds so they could understand the Scriptures" (Lk 24:44-45). This was nothing new. Jesus had already spoken many times about the ways in which Scripture pointed to him, but this time the disciples really got it. It was a lesson that would help sustain them as they participated in God's mission.

Together, an experience of Jesus and an ability to see Jesus as the sent one of God testified to in the entirety of Scripture were the foundation the disciples needed to participate in the next chapter of God's unfolding mission. The same holds true for

---

[18]The image of a disciple being covered in dust from his rabbi comes from the Mishnah, *Avot* 1:4: "Let thy house be a meeting house for the wise; and powder thyself in the dust of their feet; and drink their words with thirstiness." See Lois Tverberg, "Covered in the Dust of Your Rabbi: An Urban Legend?," *Our Rabbi Jesus* (blog), January 27, 2012, www.ourrabbijesus.com/covered-in-the-dust-of-your-rabbi-an-urban-legend/. For our purposes, it is enough to emphasize the extreme proximity stressed by this image.

us today. In order to discern how we can participate in God's mission as a sent people, we need both real experiences with the triune God and a deep appreciation and knowledge of the ways in which the missional God has revealed himself through Scripture. In short, we need a both *a missional pneumatology* (i.e., a missional understanding of the person and work of the Holy Spirit) and *a missional hermeneutic* (i.e., a missional framework for understanding Scripture).

Developing a missional pneumatology. What does following a missional God look like when God leaves the scene? That is the reality the disciples faced immediately after Jesus ascended to the right hand of the Father in Acts 1:9. They did not have to wait long for an answer. In the second chapter of Acts, the disciples stepped into the full reality of the promise Jesus made over and over again as his time drew short: "Nevertheless, I tell you the truth: it is to your advantage that I go away, for if I do not go away, the Helper will not come to you. But if I go, I will send him to you" (Jn 16:7 ESV). One can imagine the disciples hearing this in the Upper Room and thinking "How could that possibly be true? How could anything be better than actually *being* with Jesus?"

Then the day of Pentecost came.

The sending of the Spirit came with wind and fire that must have been impressive enough in themselves, but the Spirit also brought a personal connection to God and greatly expanded ministry and boldness. Thus we see Peter, only weeks after denying he even knew Jesus, filled, emboldened, and sent by the Spirit to preach a sermon in the very streets where he had previously cowered before a servant girl. In addition to boldness, the Spirit also brought cultural sensitivity and missiological tools that rejected a mechanistic, one-size-fits-all approach. When God first sent his Spirit to his church and his church to the world, he did so by speaking the language each person in the crowd needed to hear. Indeed, God launched the church into the *missio Dei* in a way that pointed to the creation-wide scope of his mission. The events of Pentecost were a foretaste of the *telos* (end goal) of God's cosmic redemptive plan that Israel's prophets pointed toward and that the book of Revelation describes in sweeping fashion in passages like Revelation 7:9, where John is shown a vision of people from every tongue and nation worshiping the Lamb.

This is the heart of the sending God, a God who calls and sends the particular for the sake of the many. It is a calling that we see unfolding in the book of Acts as the fledgling Christian community works through ethnic and social divides. It is a calling that God's sent church still symbolizes in the world. Like Abraham, who was sent from his home in Genesis 12 in order that God might bless him and thereby make him a blessing by which God would bless "all the peoples on earth" (Gen 12:3), so the church is called to follow the Spirit of the living, sent, and sending Christ as a participant in God's great mission.

The fact that the mission is God's and not ours means that the most important thing we can do as people called to participate in God's mission through planting and working to sustain communities of faith is to cultivate in our own hearts an ability to hear, see, and sense the presence and the hope of God's Spirit. It is impossible to be missional in our communities without knowing the One who invites us to participate in his mission and who gives us wisdom and power for mission. Jesus is alive, but he is at the right hand of God. We can only experience him through the ongoing presence of his Spirit. Our ability to discern God's mission requires that we *experience* the One, the Spirit of God, who is sent to us. This is why the whole second section of this book is devoted to developing a missional spirituality that cultivates Spirit-centered discernment.

Developing a missional hermeneutic. As essential as an experience of God through his Spirit is to our participation in the *missio Dei,* experience alone is never enough of an anchor to hold us steady in our missional task. Our experience of God is more like the chain that holds the anchor to a ship. The chain is an essential part of the whole apparatus. Without a chain the anchor is simply one more piece of sea litter. Conversely, a chain without an anchor, though it might give the impression of stability (if one does not look below the surface) leaves us at the mercy of whatever wind catches our sails.

For two millennia Scripture has been the anchor that has helped the church hold fast to its identity. This is certainly not to say that the church has always interpreted Scripture well or actually obeyed the truth of Scripture even when it was correctly understood. But even when the church has missed the mark and fallen short of utilizing Scripture well, Scripture endures and contains within itself the potential to point the church toward repentance and healing. In American history perhaps no issue bears this out more than the practice of slavery during the centuries preceding the Civil War. In antebellum America, folks on both sides of the issue used the Bible to underscore their opinion. At first, a literal reading of the Bible that seemed to condone slavery appeared to have won the day. Eventually, however, the Bible played a major role in undercutting the false biblical argument used to condone the evil of slavery.[19]

For modern Christians, it may be surprising to hear that the Bible's use in relationship to the church's engagement in mission has a somewhat similar history,

---

[19]For a good discussion of the way both slave holders and abolitionists argued their case from the Bible, see Mark A. Noll, *America's God: From Jonathan Edwards to Abraham Lincoln* (New York: Oxford University Press, 2002); and Charles F. Irons, *The Origins of Proslavery Christianity: White and Black Evangelicals in Colonial and Antebellum Virginia* (Chapel Hill: University of North Carolina Press, 2008).

especially in the Protestant world. While Reformation principles like *sola Scriptura* (Scripture alone) emphasized the authority and primacy of Scripture for the church, this did not mean that the church always managed to read Scripture well or as a whole. It certainly did not entail that the church picked up on the Bible's missionary impulse. Within the Protestant world, a focus on particular parts of the biblical narrative related to salvation, the sacraments, and theological concepts like election took up much of the church's attention from the time Luther penned his Ninety-Five Theses in 1517 until 1706, when Bartholomew Ziegenbalg and Henry Plutschau began missionary work in India.[20] Other Protestant efforts soon followed the work of these Danish pioneers. In 1731 Nikolaus von Zinzendorf's Moravian movement launched its first missionary. Only a few years later a group of Moravians on a boat to the British territory of Georgia deeply influenced two brothers named Charles and John Wesley, thereby playing a part in the later rise of Methodism.[21]

As missionary efforts gained momentum throughout the eighteenth century, these efforts derived their impetus for mission from a variety of sources. For some like Zinzendorf's Moravians, the motivation for mission stemmed from the influence of German Pietism, a renewal movement that stressed the importance of cultivating deep feeling for God. For many, mission was linked to global trade as chaplains accompanied European traders around the world. For a few, such as the Puritan settlers in New England, missionary work was a secondary feature of their efforts to avoid religious persecution.

What all these groups lacked, however, was a systematic, biblically based way of thinking about their missionary practices. For modern readers who take for granted the importance of biblical texts like the Great Commission found in Mark 16, Matthew 28, or Acts 1, it may come as a shock to learn that a biblical rationale for missionary work did not emerge until 1792, when an English cobbler named William Carey penned a short volume (with a long title) called *An Enquiry into the Obligation of Christians to Use Means for the Conversion of the Heathens*.[22] With Carey's biblically reasoned approach, which stressed that Christ's Great Commission applied to all Christians and not simply the apostles, Protestant involvement in cross-cultural mission turned a corner.

---

[20]Scott W. Sunquist, *Understanding Christian Mission: Participation in Suffering and Glory* (Grand Rapids: Baker Academic, 2013), 79-80.

[21]Dale T. Irvin and Scott W. Sunquist, *History of the World Christian Movement* (Maryknoll, NY: Orbis, 2012), 2:356-58.

[22]This was only the first portion of the title, the rest of which read: *In Which the Religious State of the Different Nations of the World, the Success of Former Undertakings and the Practicability of Further Undertakings, Are Considered.* For more on Carey's tract, see Andrew F. Walls, *The Missionary Movement in Christian History: Studies in Transmission of Faith* (Maryknoll, NY: Orbis, 1996), 245-47, and Sunquist, *Understanding Christian Mission,* 80-81.

Following Carey's groundbreaking *Enquiry* and the subsequent formation of independent missionary societies like the London Missionary Society, Protestant missions—and the church planting that almost always accompanied it—experienced a century of dramatic growth.[23] But even as Protestant missionary efforts expanded, the rationale for mission remained tied to a handful of proof texts, the most notable of which was always the Great Commission. This remained the case for over a century following Carey's groundbreaking work. The entire missionary task of the church hinged on a handful of biblical texts pulled from their context and lumped into a list.

It was only the church's discovery of the *missio Dei* in the second half of the twentieth century that propelled a more sustained, more holistic approach to identifying traces of God's mission throughout all of Scripture. As noted above, while British voices like Newbigin and Stott initially pointed toward this type of hermeneutic, or way of reading the biblical text, it was David Bosch who provided the most important early work in this direction. Yet as influential as Bosch's mission-centric reading of Scripture was, it came with significant shortcomings. Most notable among them was his relative neglect of the Old Testament as a missional document. In 2006 the British Old Testament scholar Christopher J. Wright published a massive text that addressed this glaring lacuna in Bosch's work head on. Wright's *The Mission of God: Unlocking the Bible's Grand Narrative* provided a nearly six-hundred-page defense of the centrality of the *missio Dei* in *both* the New and Old Testaments. Wright's background as an Old Testament scholar enabled him to place the major emphasis of his book on God's missional nature and Israel's missional call in the Old Testament. For Wright it was not simply the imperatives (commands) like the Great Commission that pointed toward the mission of God; the indicative (narrative) portions of Scripture also gestured toward God's unfolding mission.[24] Israel was a called-out people, sent out as a priestly nation for the sake of the world.

Like Bosch's earlier work, Wright's missional reading of Scripture provided a new landmark in missional theology. The idea that the entire Bible was a missionary text inspired by a missionary God raised the stakes by making the *missio Dei* and the missional church movement it inspired not merely a biblical side story but the centerpiece of the entire narrative. Since then a widening circle of scholars including N. T. Wright and Joel B. Green have weighed in in favor of a missional hermeneutic. What stands out about this hermeneutical approach is its ability to make sense of the diversity of the canon within the unity of the *missio Dei*. In a

---

[23]On Carey and the rise of missionary societies, see Walls, *Missionary Movement*, 241-54.

[24]Christopher J. H. Wright, *The Mission of God: Unlocking the Bible's Grand Narrative* (Downers Grove, IL: IVP Academic, 2006), 61.

fragmented, sound-bite age, this coherence makes for a welcome and empowering approach. Most importantly, the idea of a Scripture-encompassing hermeneutic actually seems to fit well within the approach of the resurrected Jesus, who supplemented the apostles' post-resurrection experience of him with a biblical hermeneutic that demonstrated how the entirety of Hebrew Scripture pointed to the fact that Israel's God had planned all along to send himself, *via* his Suffering Servant, to his people. By emphasizing the Bible's holistic focus on the centrality of the *missio Dei,* modern advocates of a missional hermeneutic are doing much the same thing.

MISSIONAL SENSIBILITIES, MISSIONAL STORIES

So far, this chapter has focused on exploring the historical, theological, and scriptural basis for grounding our efforts as church planters in the *missio Dei.* As essential as this theological orientation is, theology—even good theology—divorced from action is not enough. Time and time again Scripture directs God's people to *know* God and then *live* in light of that knowledge (e.g., the Shema, Ten Commandments, Great Commandment). These twin imperatives still apply to us as twenty-first-century church planters. Orthodoxy (right belief) and orthopraxy (right practice) go together. To return to our earlier agricultural analogy, sustained growth and reproduction take good soil (theology) but also require good gardening practice. Weeds grow without cultivation, but good things usually take more intentionality. In light of this we are left with two primary questions: How do we intentionally cultivate the eyes, ears, and hearts that can *discern* the ways in which God is carrying out his mission in our communities, and then how do we equip ourselves and the communities we are leading to *participate* in what we see God doing?

On a basic level, answering these two questions is the project of the rest of this book. Each of the coming chapters builds on the theological foundation of the *missio Dei* by pointing to ways in which church planters and church communities can practically discern and intentionally participate in the unfolding mission of God. The scope of this chapter cannot possibly encompass the wide variety of ways in which an understanding of God's missional character informs and undergirds all our efforts to follow this sending God as individuals and local churches. What it can do is point to the importance of some *missional sensibilities* that prepare us to discern and participate in the mission of God in our community.

Missional sensibilities. Over the years I have found myself drawn time and time again to the story of Jesus' healing of the demon possessed boy in Mark 9:14-29. From the goodness and power of Jesus to the father's heartfelt plea, "I believe; help my unbelief" (ESV), there is a lot to love in this story. I have always had a deep appreciation for the plight of the disciples as they struggle in the face of desperate need. While Jesus is up on the Mount of Transfiguration with his inner circle, the rest of the disciples are trying desperately to help a boy in the throes of demonic possession. It is loud and chaotic, and a crowd is gathering. The disciples have experienced success in similar circumstances before (Mark 6:7-13), but this time their efforts fall flat. The boy is not healed, and the crowd takes note. Eventually, Jesus comes and saves the day, and the disciples are left asking what went wrong. I have always had a lot of sympathy for their question: "Why could we not cast it out?" Jesus answers by saying, "This kind cannot be driven out by anything but prayer" (Mark 9:28, 29 ESV).

Easy enough, right?

No way! If you've ever been in a situation in which you felt you were completely in over your head, you can identify with the disciples here. You know that nothing drives us to prayer like emergencies, especially when a crowd of people is watching. My guess is that quite a few prayers were offered up in that moment as the crowd pressed in and the boy's condition remained the same. What it seems the disciples lacked was a lifestyle of prayer—the kind of lifestyle of connection and intimacy with the Father that Jesus embodied. When Jesus showed up he did not have to drop to his knees in that moment because he was steeped in prayer. Prayer was the fabric of his life, a habit of the heart built intentionally over a long time.

Sports offer an analogy that can help us understand what seems to be the difference between the disciples and Jesus in this account. I love sports and spent much of the first twenty years of my life playing sports, especially basketball. As a young athlete, I always wanted to get through the portion of practice that involved drills as fast as I could in order to get to the "real" practice, the end-of-practice scrimmage. Growing up I always assumed that as one advanced to higher levels of competition at some point practices would pretty much consist entirely of scrimmage time. Imagine my surprise when I stepped into my first collegiate basketball practice and found we did *more* drills than in high school! Time and time again my college coach used the term *muscle memory* to emphasize that we did repetitive, sometime very basic drills to train our bodies to do the right thing by habit. By building intentionality into our everyday practice lives, we were actually freed up to live in the moment during the game. Our bodies knew what to do. Good habits had become second nature. If I had been free to follow my own inclination to downplay drills and devote all my time to playing games of pick up, or even an organized scrimmage, I never would have been ready for the real game. One cannot develop muscle-memory on the spot or by focusing only on the big picture or the end result. Developing muscle memory requires that we devote sustained, repeated attention to the small things.

A spiritual version of muscle memory is what we are aiming for in our Christian lives and in our work as church planters. We want the ways of Jesus to become second nature. This means that we work to make things like the fruit of the Spirit (Gal 5:22-23) or traits like mercy, justice, and humility (Mic 6:8) habitual practices that shine through even in our knee-jerk reactions. Similarly, we prepare ourselves to participate in the mission of God by developing missional sensibilities based around what we see first in the life of Jesus and the testimony of Scripture, but also in the lives of those who have learned to follow in the way of Jesus. We can start developing this sensibility by asking a question like, What traits does Jesus develop to help him stay firmly grounded within his Father's mission? We've already mentioned prayer. Jesus spent a great deal of time communicating with his Father, both talking *and listening*, so that he learned to hear and clearly recognize his Father's voice. This was a practice that he, the Good Shepherd, then urged his followers to develop too—"his sheep follow him because they know his voice" (Jn 10:4). Jesus also cultivated eyes capable of *seeing* the ways in which his Father was going about his mission in the world. Jesus then turned this act of seeing into practice. "Very truly I tell you, the Son can do nothing by himself; he can do only what he sees his Father doing" (Jn 5:19). Jesus saw what his Father was doing and then he joined in.

By listening to his Father's voice and watching what his Father did Jesus also developed a heart capable of feeling what the Father would have him feel. Sometimes this meant that Jesus' heart felt anger in the face of blatant injustice and corruption (Lk 19:45-48; 20:45-47). More often, however, having a heart shaped by the concerns of his Father entailed feelings of compassion and mercy. With a heart attuned to his Father's loving, missional heart Jesus could extend mercy to social outcasts in one moment (Lk 19:1-10) while weeping over the city that would soon prosecute him unjustly (Lk 19:41-42) or praying for the forgiveness of the very people who murdered him in the next (Lk 23:34). Jesus had seen his Father in action and heard his Father's voice for years. All of this shaped his heart, conforming his sensibilities and his actions to those of his Father. When the moment of decision, crisis, or opportunity came he was ready.

If we are going to be missional church planters who can help the communities God has called us to lead into discernment of and participation in the *missio Dei*, we have to develop missional sensibilities that become the disciplines of our individual and community lives. There is no better place to look for these sensibilities than in Jesus. So what do we see Jesus doing?

Jesus cultivated a lifestyle of prayer. Everything starts with prayer. As noted above, prayer was not simply something Jesus did from time to time. Prayer was a practice that made up the fabric of Jesus' life in a way that the Gospel writers wanted to be sure no one would miss. Time and time again they highlight Jesus' practice of retreating into silence and solitude (e.g., Mk 1:35; 6:46; Lk 6:12). By repeatedly emphasizing this, they demonstrate that prayer was not an occasional retreat from the real world or a threat to building the momentum of a successful ministry. What we see instead is an emphasis on prayer as the source of Jesus' connection with the heart and mission of his Father and the source of his fortitude in the face of temptation and looming despair. A key part of Jesus' prayer life was his ability to take time not just to talk to God but also to *listen*. When he had to choose his twelve disciples, he stayed up all night praying, listening for God to tell him whom to choose (Lk 6:12-16).

This type of sustained, listening prayer is essential for us as missional church planters. So often we develop good missional theologies that emphasize God's ongoing mission in this world and then act as if God does not want to communicate with us about it. We have a fully formed trinitarian theology and pneumatology, but we easily become practical deists with what amounts to a clockmaker God who winds the clock and then walks away. A deistic God is not a sending God. We cannot afford to transform the living and active God into a benign, unknowable force. When we neglect a life of listening prayer, this is exactly what we do. Discerning and participating in God's mission in the on-the-ground realities of our local context requires that we cultivate ears to hear the voice of God's Spirit in our midst.

Jesus was at home in Scripture. Jesus did not only hear the voice of God in prayer. Throughout his ministry Jesus demonstrated that his ability to understand the mission of his Father also stemmed from his deep knowledge of Scripture. Throughout the Gospels Jesus constantly made reference to Scripture, often, as in the Sermon on the Mount or during his temptation or crucifixion, he even quoted portions of the Hebrew Bible by heart. During his moments of deep testing, Scripture functioned as his compass for discerning the truth in the midst of the enemy's lies. When Jesus was seeking to define his mission, it was Isaiah's account of God's servant that he turned to. Even as a young boy, Jesus confounded the religious leaders of his day with his knowledge of Scripture. When he was on the verge of death, Jesus quoted from Psalm 22. The soundtrack of Jesus' life and ministry was Scripture. From the first to the last, Jesus' life and ministry were defined by his familiarity with God's story and God's voice as recorded in the Torah and the rest of the Hebrew Scriptures.

If Jesus, the one human being who had a perfect connection with God, relied heavily on Scripture in times of trial and in the framing of his participation in God's mission, how could we expect to be able to really hear God and understand his mission in the world apart from a deep knowledge of Scripture? It is Scripture that helps us learn to recognize the Shepherd's voice in our prayerful listening and the Shepherd's ways as we discern how God is carrying out his mission in our world. Through stories, poetry, commands, and direct teaching, Scripture builds our missional sensibilities by alerting us to major themes that have defined God's mission from the beginning. Scripture presents us with a God who models covenant faithfulness, compassion, grace, and righteousness, a God who draws near by sending his Son and his Spirit. Scripture gives us stories to fuel our missional imagination. Scripture gives us words to speak that are founded on a rock that is higher and more secure than we'll ever be.

Thus, like listening prayer, regular engagement with Scripture is essential if we hope to develop the ability to discern the ways the unchanging God adapts his mission to a dizzying array of contexts. We should not only read Scripture but sit with it, even memorize large passages of it, so that it is woven into the fabric of our hearts. This is the way of Jesus. Jesus did not pull out his scroll or concordance (or iPhone!) when he was tempted in the desert or as he languished on the cross. No, Scripture had made its way into Jesus' heart. This scriptural awareness made all the difference as Jesus discerned the contours of his Father's mission and then participated confidently in what his Father was already doing.

Jesus walked the streets. And participate he did! Jesus' life was lived in total and perfect participation with the mission of his Father. We see this especially in the three years of his life and public ministry that are documented in the Gospel accounts. Like Jesus' intentionality in the area of prayer and scriptural awareness, Jesus' actions provide us as church planters with a helpful example of how we might set about the process of discerning what God is doing in our communities and how we as individuals and congregations might meaningfully join in. As with the first two points, this is not really new, but it is often deemphasized or simply neglected in favor of canned strategies or less time-intensive means.

As simple as it sounds, walking the streets was one of the missional practices that Jesus seems to have used to both discern and participate in his Father's mission. At this point you may be thinking, Give me a break. Jesus walked the streets because he lived in the first century, not because walking has some inherent value. Perhaps you are right. Maybe today Jesus would have a car or even a private jet (?!) to carry his rabbinical entourage. But it is not just the fact that Jesus walked that matters. The *way* he walked is also significant. That walking was more than simply a means of transportation for Jesus can be seen in his willingness to be interrupted. Jesus' journeys were full of interruptions of all kinds. From a Roman centurion and chronically diseased people to religious rulers, hungry crowds, faith-filled mothers, and annoying (at least to the disciples) children, Jesus chose most frequently to travel in a way that kept the realities of life before his eyes, in his ears (and nose, I might add), and sometimes directly in his path. This practice helped him translate what he heard in prayer and read in Scripture into tangible participation as he joined in the kingdom-centered mission his Father was working on the ground.

Jesus knew his context. Walking the streets also helped ensure that Jesus, like any good sent one (i.e., missionary), knew his context. What motivated people in first-century Palestine? What fears plagued their imaginations? What thoughts fueled their hopes? How did they see themselves in relation to their neighbors both next door and across the border? What hardships did they face? By refusing to sequester himself in a quiet corner (or rabbinical study), Jesus opened himself up to experiencing the real condition of the places and people he encountered as he journeyed. What first-century Jewish man would spend time talking to a Samaritan woman? Jesus (Jn 4). What rabbi would make time for a late-night chat with a member of a religious group that hated him? Jesus (Jn 3). What rabbi would let a ceremonially unclean woman touch him and offer healing and grace rather than rebuke? Jesus (Mk 5:25-34).

Being out among the people his Father had called him to serve allowed Jesus to know their hearts and participate in God's mission among them in a way they were able to understand. His parables referenced agriculture, family, indebtedness, and other realities of their lives. His teachings were geared to the religious and political context of his times. He who had been forced to flee Herod's wrath knew the weight of Roman oppression and unjust rulers first hand. He who had been in the temple among the moneychangers and sectarian feuds of the religious elite knew the corruption of the systems that dominated first-century Jewish life. He knew the way all these realities fueled the people's messianic hopes—hopes that could work both for or against God's mission depending on how they were turned. If God's people could discern and participate in God's mission, these hopes could bring life. If God's people got impatient or failed to discern God's plan correctly, the results could be devastating.

Jesus trusted in God. In the face confusion, oppression, and violence, Jesus drew on the missional sensibilities that had defined his entire life to discern what his Father was doing and then participate in that action with faithfulness and clarity. Even then Jesus did not get the immediate results many of us would hope for or even expect if we successfully managed to discern God's mission in our communities and act accordingly. This is at once a freeing, sobering, and sometimes perplexing reality. As church planters in twenty-first-century contexts, success often seems to mean fast results and more seats filled every week. Success for Jesus meant something different. It meant faithfulness, faithfulness to God and faithfulness to persevere in our call as ministers of his gospel. Jesus demonstrated and called his disciples to cultivate "a long obedience in the same direction" because of one primary fact: He knew and trusted his Father.[25] Even with perfect discernment of and participation in his Father's mission, Jesus' ministry did not seem to meet with sustained success. Indeed, the major stage of his public ministry ended with a trusted friend betraying him, his right-hand man denying him, and his own people handing him over to be killed by an oppressive foreign regime. Nothing pointed to success—at least not before Easter, and even then some, like Thomas, had doubts. Jesus, however, was able to keep his bearings because his hope was in his Father, the only one who could truly measure success.

Missional stories. Of course, Jesus' apparent lack of immediate success is relatively easy to talk about now, over two thousand years removed from the events that shaped the life of God-made-flesh. But the story still matters. It still has power to orient our efforts. Now after two millennia of church history we have a treasure chest of stories of others who have followed the story of Jesus' participation in God's mission. People like Paul, who called the church to imitate him as he imitated Christ by cultivating a life of prayer, a deep Scriptural awareness, a willingness to mingle with people on the streets and thereby understand his context, all the while trusting himself and his success to God alone. Church history is full of stories like this. From Francis of Assisi's missionary trip across Crusade battle lines to the throne of the sultan in 1219, to the efforts of missionaries like Matteo Ricci (1552–1610) in Imperial China, Jean de Brebeuf (1593–1649) in Canada, and Sadhu Sundar Singh (1889–1929) and Amy Carmichael (1867–1951) in India. Of course, this only hints at the great "cloud of witnesses" (Heb 12:1) that have lived lives defined by long-term faithfulness to God and compassion for the cultural sensibilities and individual needs of those they met. How many more have lived faithful lives attuned to the sensibilities of a missional God in their local churches, villages, and daily lives? Their stories seldom register on our modern scales of success, but their faithfulness is not lost on God or those their lives touched. Whether known by many or few, their missional stories continue to ripple out, impacting eternity in a myriad of ways.[26]

---

[25]Eugene Peterson introduced this phrase to the English-speaking Christian world in 1980. He got it from Friedrich Nietzsche and applied it Christian discipleship; see Eugene H. Peterson, *A Long Obedience in the Same Direction: Discipleship in an Instant Society*, 20th anniversary ed. (Downers Grove, IL: InterVarsity Press, 2000), 17.

[26]For instance, colonial missionary David Brainerd could never have imagined that the biography Jonathan Edwards wrote about his brief but faithful and passionate missionary experience would never go out of print and would influence an English cobbler named William Carey, who would eventually be known as the father of modern mission.

As church planters, part of our calling is to know, tell, and add our own local narratives to these stories. Building on a theology that takes into account the triune, sending God who remains actively committed to carrying out his mission in the world, we move forward by committing ourselves to discerning God's mission in our local communities and then participating in it. We are sent people. We are Spirit-empowered people. We are listening people. We are scriptural people. We are people who walk the sidewalks and country roads where we live and take time to know the names, needs, and hearts of our neighbors. In it all we entrust ourselves to God. It is his mission, not ours. May his kingdom come, may his will be done on earth as it is in heaven.

DISCUSSION QUESTIONS

1. In what ways have we sensed God moving in our community?

2. What practices can we develop to help us better discern the heart of God for our context and the local needs?

3. Do we balance a missional hermeneutic with a missional pneumatology? If not, which comes more naturally to us?

4. What stories have shaped our individual lives, worshiping community, and local context?

WHAT WOULD GOD'S REIGN LOOK LIKE IN OUR NEIGHBORHOOD?

JESUS, THE KINGDOM, AND THE CHURCH

JR WOODWARD

ONE OF THE MOST COMMON QUESTIONS that church planters ask (and one which was primary for me in my first plant) is: What do I need to do to grow my church? I asked this question in earnest. I had a genuine desire to see more people come to know Jesus, who had become my hero and Savior. I wanted more people to go to heaven. At that time, I didn't think much about what it meant to join God in seeing more of heaven become visible on earth.

After more theological reflection (such as the previous chapter's insights into the *missio Dei*) and more practice and experience in ministry, the primary question in my second church plant had changed. I was asking: What would God's reign look like in our neighborhood? This second question helped our community live into the Lord's Prayer more vibrantly. Asking what would be different if God's reign were more fully realized in our neighborhood shaped the entire mission of our church.

So why is the second question a better primary question than the first? Let's answer that together as we journey through this chapter.

THE IMPORTANCE OF REFLECTION

While I love to take risks and live for things that outlast me, reflection hasn't always come easily to me. If you are starting a church or are on the journey of church planting, you probably don't mind taking risks. But how are you in the practice of reflection? Having planted churches

A church that lives its life under the kingdom of God cannot help but provoke questions.

GRAHAM TOMLIN

The kingdom of God is at hand; repent and believe in the gospel!

MARK 1:15 ESV

on the east and west coasts, I have learned the necessity of deep reflection. The more time I take to reflect as a practitioner, the more centered I become, leading to wiser living. Reading and reflecting have become a regular rhythm of my active life.

One benefit of reflection is learning to ask better questions. Our educational system tends to reward answers more than questions, so very few of us are nurtured in the art of asking good questions. Too often we think answers gain respect while questions simply display our ignorance. But asking questions assumes a curiosity and hunger to learn. The doorway to discovery is entered through asking good questions. Asking questions was one of the fundamental ways Jesus shaped his disciples for the work of the kingdom. Jesus understands that questions help guide people to the beauty of truth, and that truth has a way of setting us free.[1] That is one of the reasons why each chapter title in this book starts with a meaningful question.

As a planter, teaching regularly has given me a growing hunger to learn. Knowing that teachers will incur greater judgment (Jas 3:1), I recognized the need to have some theological mentors in my life.[2] As I engaged in the rhythm of reading and reflecting more, I started to realize that the gospel I was sharing was reductionistic. In the early 1990s, for me the gospel was all about my relationship with God and helping others have a relationship with him. It was a good start, but it was not the full good news that Jesus taught. I started to realize that a gospel focused on getting people to heaven was actually an escapist gospel that tended to minimize the real-life issues our world faces—senseless violence, ecological disasters, extreme poverty, and racial injustices, to name just a few. I came to understand that a gospel that only addresses the forgiveness of sins through the death of Christ on the cross, without addressing systemic injustice, creation care, and our own brokenness and wound-edness, is an inadequate, shallow gospel. It's a gospel that starts in Genesis 3, instead of Genesis 1. It also comes off as self-serving to those outside the faith, and rightly so, because it is not the holistic gospel that Jesus preached.

THE KINGDOM OF GOD IS AT HAND

In the opening chapter of Mark's Gospel, we hear Jesus proclaiming, "The kingdom of God is at hand; repent and believe in the gospel!" (Mk 1:15 ESV). There is a widespread understanding among theologians that Jesus' central message is the kingdom of God. Though currently and historically there has been debate about the nature of the kingdom of God, "most scholars agree that it has to do with God's reign

---

[1]These thoughts are adapted from the foreword I wrote for Dan White Jr., *Subterranean: Why the Future of the Church Is Rootedness* (Eugene, OR: Cascade, 2015).

[2]Some of my early and current theological mentors include N. T. Wright, Eugene Peterson, René Padilla, Henri Nouwen, Lesslie Newbigin, Marva Dawn, Stanley Hauerwas, and Leonardo Boff.

breaking into history and into our world in a decisive and new way to bring resto-ration" to all creation.[3] This idea of the kingdom of God did not originate with Jesus. The central hope of the Hebrew prophets pointed to a time when God would in-tervene and restore the people of Israel and all creation. The word *shalom* best cap-tures this idea of complete restoration.

While shalom is translated as "peace," it means much more than that. Through imagery and story, the prophets painted a picture of how life was supposed to be. They expressed their hope for the day when justice would reign, when love, joy, and peace would characterize life on earth. In the place of poverty, there would be abun-dance. In the place of violence and war, there would be peace. Isaiah writes often about this day (e.g., Is 11, 40, 52, 61), which is why Mark's audience took notice when he began his Gospel with words from Isaiah, "I will send my messenger ahead of you, who will prepare your way, a voice of one calling in the wilderness, 'Prepare the way for the Lord, make straight paths for him'" (Mk 1:2-3). The faithful longed for the day when God would finally establish his rule on earth.

While theologians agree that the central message of Jesus is the kingdom of God, many have struggled with how to articulate this theme in the context of America, where king and kingdom are largely foreign concepts. But all that changed with the HBO series *Game of Thrones*.

Game of Thrones has become a cultural phenomenon, garnering record-breaking viewing for paid-subscription television in the United States and other countries, as well as holding a record number of primetime Emmys for a scripted television se-ries.[4] Created by David Benioff and D. B. Weiss, *Game of Thrones* is based on the bestselling book series A Song of Ice and Fire by George R. R. Martin.

This epic fantasy series, made to feel like historical fiction, takes place on the fictional continents of Westeros and Essos, a world of kings and kingdoms, queens and lords, violence, sex, domination, making allegiances, bending the knee, new and old gods, gods of nature, gods of the elements, dragons, and armies of the dead. While our Western world, shaped by the Enlightenment, has become victim to a progressive disenchantment of the world, shows like *Game of Thrones* feed a hunger for a reenchanted world filled with surprise and a sense of wonder.

One of the overarching themes in *Game of Thrones* centers on the Iron Throne, the seat of the Lord of the Seven Kingdoms. Aegon the Conqueror had the throne made from a thousand swords surrendered by his enemies. The Iron Throne represents the

---

[3] Allen M. Wakabayashi, *Kingdom Come: How Jesus Wants to Change the World* (Downers Grove, IL: InterVarsity Press, 2003), 29.

[4] Eliana Dockterman, "Game of Thrones Now Has the Most Emmy Wins Ever," *Time*, September 19, 2016, www .time.com/4498870/emmys-2016-game-of-thrones-most-wins/.

authority of the ultimate ruler of the seven kingdoms—the King of kings, if you will. Unsurprisingly, there is a constant battling and building of alliances among the noble families in the attempt to claim the Iron Throne, as well as fighting for independence from it.

Undoubtedly, people resonate with this TV series for various reasons. Might one reason be the yearning inside each of us for a true and just king? *Game of Thrones* replays the familiar story we see all around us, the vying for power to have ultimate reign. Violence, wars, and power plays stretch from the time of Cain and Abel all the way to our present day. So it feels real. We live in a world that is characterized by economic disparity, sexual abuse, gender inequality, racial injustice, oppressive politics, and the use of violence to maintain the status quo in each of these areas.

When Jesus was born, King Herod was so insecure and threatened that he had all boys in Bethlehem who were two years old and younger killed. We live in a world where narcissism and nationalism run rampant. The cry of our souls is for another kind of king and another kind of kingdom. The truth is that if God is not the King of kings, something or someone else will need to take his spot. The alternatives are less than desirable. So we pray, "Your kingdom come, / your will be done, / on earth as it is in heaven" (Mt 6:10).

Jesus is a different kind of king who represents a different kind of kingdom. When we read the Gospels, it doesn't take long to realize this. Jesus is the Prince of Peace who did not buy into the myth of redemptive violence, and his kingdom is in deep contrast to the kingdoms of this world. As Lesslie Newbigin wrote,

> The Christian gospel has sometimes been made the tool of an imperialism, and of that we have to repent. But at its heart it is the denial of all imperialisms, for at its center there is the cross where all imperialisms are humbled and we are invited to find the center of human unity in the One who was made nothing so that all might be one. The very heart of the biblical vision for the unity of humankind is that its center is not an imperial power but a slain Lamb.[5]

Communities being formed through the Spirit of Christ and living under the reign of his kingdom exist to serve others instead of dominate, forgive others instead of holding grudges, suffer instead of inflicting suffering, and cross barriers instead of creating walls. Stop and think a moment with me. Does the gospel we share with others help cultivate these kinds of people? Is the gospel shaping me in this way? Do I have a life worth imitating? These questions are central to the health of our soul and the fruitfulness of our mission.

---

[5]Lesslie Newbigin, *The Gospel in a Pluralist Society* (Grand Rapids: Eerdmans, 1989), 159.

OUR MESSAGE

The message that we have the opportunity to share with a troubled world is about a king and a kingdom. Yet, as we look at the current landscape, I've noticed that on the one hand, some planting networks and denominations emphasize the kingdom by focusing on social justice issues important to them, while deemphasizing a personal relationship with the king. Others, however, emphasize a relationship with the king but consider the kingdom as an afterthought, or maybe more accurately, they look suspiciously at the kingdom as the "social gospel" and not actually a part of the good news itself.

A holistic gospel involves a king *and* a kingdom.

A holistic gospel is also about the *life*, *death*, and *resurrection* of Jesus.[6] Some groups emphasize the atoning death of Christ as the gospel key and place much less significance on the life and resurrection of Jesus. Others emphasize the life and give less thought to the death of Christ. Both approaches are incomplete and reductionistic.

The gospel is not just centered on the *death* of Christ but also his *life* and *resurrection*. Jesus, through his life, taught us what it means to live as humans amidst the fall.[7] The Sermon on the Mount was not just a nice message, it is how Jesus taught us to see reality and how to live like him. Jesus died so that we might know how to live. Through his death he broke the power of him who holds the power of death so that we might enter into kingdom life. As we die to ourselves, we learn to live as a sign, foretaste, and instrument of his coming kingdom.[8] When we trust Christ, we become the fruit of resurrection life, living the future in the present, which is a theme we will take on shortly.

Activist and author Mark Scandrette has a good relationship with a Zen Buddhist priest in his San Francisco neighborhood. They share tea and long walks together. One day Scandrette asked him, "What is the way of Buddhism?" In five minutes the priest was able to explain to him the four noble truths and the eightfold path—what he believed about reality and an explanation about his way of life. This prompted Scandrette to wonder if he as a Christian had language to adequately explain *the way* of Jesus. How would he summarize *reality* and *the way* of Jesus?

Recently, Scandrette has been working with Steve Bassett, the creative director of SGM Lifewords, on a project called the Nine Beats Collective. They are developing a language to explain how Jesus saw reality and lived his way of life, using the ancient

---

[6]While emphasizing the life, death, and resurrection is more complete than just focusing on the death of Christ, one could certainly be more exhaustive. David J. Bosch explores how mission is shaped by incarnation, cross, resurrection, ascension, Pentecost, and Parousia in *Transforming Mission: Paradigm Shifts in Theology of Mission* (Maryknoll, NY: Orbis, 1991), 512-19.

[7]A phrase I adapt from William Stringfellow.

[8]The language of *sign, foretaste,* and *instrument* comes from Lesslie Newbigin, one of my favorite authors.

wisdom of the beatitudes in the Sermon on the Mount.[9] In a video he made in London, he gives fresh language to the beatitudes, referring to them as the "nine beats," to inspire various artists to develop songs, instrumentals, and spoken words for this project.

Scandrette talks about how in the beatitudes Jesus is waking us up to the possibilities of a new world where we have these strange blessings, which are like whispers that describe a better way of seeing and living. Jesus invites us into this better reality. We feel we live in scarcity, but what if we really live in a world of abundance? We experience the world as competition and difference, but what if we all belong to one another? We feel like we have to hide who we really are and feel shame, but what if we could step into the light and tell the truth about ourselves? It may seem to us that the world is stuck—that it doesn't work and can't change—but what if we have the potential to be agents of healing and wholeness? We do everything we can to avoid pain, but what if suffering is part of the mystery and paradox of how life comes through death? What if we could live unafraid to die?[10]

What I love about this project is that it focuses on the life of Jesus. It invites us to enter into kingdom living. The good news that we have to share is about a *king* and a *kingdom*. The good news is that the comprehensive divisions created by the Fall—between us and God (theological), between each other (sociological), within ourselves (psychological), and with creation (ecological)—have all been reconciled through the life, death, and resurrection of Christ. The good news is also cosmic in nature. We may live in a fallen world, shaped by the god of this world, in enemy-occupied territory, but because of the life, death, and resurrection of Christ, the enemy has no property rights, and he is not the legitimate lord.

A BETTER QUESTION

This holistic gospel is about a different kind of king and kingdom, and it has led me to ask better questions. Instead of asking what I need to do to grow my church, I'm asking: What would God's reign look like in our neighborhood?

When I use the word *neighborhood*, I'm talking about a particular geographical part of the city that is walkable and often has its own name, history, and culture. For example, Los Angeles County has anywhere from 272 to 472 distinct neighborhoods.[11] My neighborhood, East Hollywood, is very different than Westwood or

---

[9]See Nine Beats, "Mark Scandrette—Introducing the Ninefold Path," YouTube Video, 2:15, August 23, 2017, www.youtube.com/watch?v=HXYaEuGIbYk&t=13s.

[10]Nine Beats, "Mark Scandrette—Introducing the Ninefold Path."

[11]The *Los Angeles Times* divides Los Angeles County into 272 distinct neighborhoods: "Neighborhoods," *Los Angeles Times*, accessed February 3, 2018, maps.latimes.com/neighborhoods/neighborhood/list/, while Eric Brightwell maps 472 different neighborhoods in the county: Tim Loc, "Check Out This Amazing Map That Features Every L.A. Neighborhood," July 27, 2017, www.laist.com/2017/07/27/neighborhood_maps.php.

even West Hollywood. Beverly Hills is quite different than Watts. Each neighborhood has its beauty and brokenness and needs an expression of church that lives for the good of that particular neighborhood with all its nuances. When we focus on the entire city as opposed to a neighborhood within the city, we tend to live above place, instead of living incarnationally *in* a place. Living above place is when we don't give concrete thought to how our actions shape the people and place where we physically live. As my friends at the Parish Collective explain, each particular neighborhood or parish "is a relational microcosm that helps bring many cause-and-effect relationships back together again."[12] A neighborhood is an area of space large enough to live life and small enough to be a known character.[13]

So the question we need to ask is, If God's kingdom became more visible in our neighborhood, what would be different? This then becomes the mission of the church. It's a better question because it treasures a holistic gospel. Graham Tomlin, after studying the New Testament pattern of evangelism, makes a strong case that evangelism works best in the context where it's an answer to a question. In other words, when we live out our calling as the people of God under the reign of God—when we become the church in which the poor find riches, the lonely find community, the sick find healing, the broken find wholeness—then our words about the person and work of Christ become meaningful, and people are provoked to ask why we are doing this.[14]

Before we can answer this question well, we first need to learn to live under his reign. For if we don't know how to live in God's presence under his reign as a sent community called *out* of the world, it will be difficult for us to live *in* the world *for* the world, without falling to the principalities and powers that seek to devour us (Rom 8:38; 1 Cor 2:8; 15:24-26, Eph 1:20; 2:11; 6:12; Col 1:16; 2:15; 1 Pet 5:5-9). In other words, our community needs to be formed by Christ as a new social order before we can hope to transform the larger social order around us.

While Jesus gives us several ways to practice his presence so that we might be shaped for mission, I'd like to anchor this chapter in the Lord's Prayer, or what some appropriately call the "kingdom prayer," as it will help us learn what it means to live under his reign so that we might be agents of transformation in our neighborhood and world.[15]

---

[12]Paul Sparks, Tim Soerens, and Dwight J. Friesen, *The New Parish: How Neighborhood Churches Are Transforming Mission, Discipleship, and Community* (Downers Grove, IL: InterVarsity Press, 2014), 24.

[13]Christiana Rice, "Starting New Churches from Scratch," lecture, Inhabit Conference, Seattle, April 26, 2018.

[14]Graham Tomlin, cited in JR Woodward, *Creating a Missional Culture: Equipping the Church for the Sake of the World* (Downers Grove, IL: InterVarsity Press, 2012), 144.

[15]David Fitch works through the practices of the Lord's Table, reconciliation, proclaiming the gospel, being with the least of these, being with children, the fivefold calling, and the kingdom prayer in *Faithful Presence: Seven Disciplines That Shape the Church for Mission* (Downers Grove, IL: InterVarsity Press, 2016).

THE KINGDOM PRAYER

One of the most meaningful practices we can engage in as a community is to pray the Lord's Prayer together, until we start to live into it fully. This kingdom prayer can be used as a catechism that teaches us what it means to live under a different kind of king and kingdom. This prayer is Jesus' response to the disciples asking him how to pray. The prayer is in the plural (our) because we have been wounded by others in our communities of origin, and we need to find healing through a new way of being community under the reign of Christ. This kingdom prayer, when prayed and lived out in faith, allows his kingdom to become more visible in our lives and neighborhoods, witnessing to our neighbors that God has not abandoned this world, but is present in our problems in a special way through his people.

> Our Father who art in heaven,
> Hallowed be thy name.
> Thy kingdom come,
> Thy will be done,
>> On earth as it is in heaven.
> Give us this day our daily bread;
> And forgive us our debts,
>> As we also have forgiven our debtors;
> And lead us not into temptation,
>> But deliver us from evil
>
> [For thine is the kingdom and the power and the glory, for ever. Amen.] (Mt 6:9-13 RSV)

While I will reflect on this kingdom prayer in five parts—communion, co-mission, community, conflict, and consummation—I will give more focus to the co-mission and community sections, since they relate more directly to the theme of this chapter.

Our Father in heaven (communion). When planting a church in East Hollywood, the primary question I asked was, If God's reign were to be more fully visible in our neighborhood, what would be different? This question, along with the prompting from some neighborhood friends, led me to run for an elected, but unpaid office in our newly formed neighborhood council. As a newcomer, I wanted to have as many connection points in our neighborhood as possible so I could understand both its beauty and brokenness. It didn't take long for me to feel overwhelmed by the need that was visible, let alone the chaos that remained hidden from sight. As our church plant was becoming aware of the brokenness of our neighborhood—homelessness, hunger, loneliness, people struggling to pay rent, street violence, conflict exasperated by a lack of parks, and so on—we, like the disciples, wanted to know how to pray, and so we started to pray this prayer together. When we prayed it together publicly, it became more than just a rote exercise for us. It gave us a framework for how to think about and build a communal prayer life, as well as how to live in and for our neighborhood in the way of Christ.

Praying to and knowing God as Father helped us remember that our central role in this journey of life is that of his beloved children. I feel fortunate that on the whole my childhood years were good ones. But I've ministered to enough people to know that is often not the case. Some have experienced an absentee or abusive father. If that is the case, Jesus and Scripture remind us that this God we call "Abba, Father" is a good God, a Father that is present to us and knows how to give good gifts to his children. That's why Jesus taught us to pray, "hallowed be thy name," for the nature, person, and heart intentions of our Father are only and always good. Jesus knew this because he experienced it. Even in his suffering, he was able to remember the goodness of his Father.

One of the reasons our community loves to pray this prayer is that in the midst of our ministry responsibilities and opportunities, in the midst of overwhelming needs, we know that we can call out to our Father. Calling him Father reminds us of his closeness to us as well as the fact that family has been redefined in the kingdom. Ultimately our family is not about where we are born (geography) or the family we were born into (genealogy). True family consists of people from all around the world who do the will of the Father (Mk 3:35). Having had the opportunity to travel to forty-three countries, I've been blessed by our global family. Praying "Our Father" reminds us that the church isn't *like* family, the church *is* family.

While the title Father lets us know how close God is to us, the fact he is *in heaven* reminds us of his transcendence, and thus when we spend time with him, we are able to get perspective, energy, and nourishment from a source that transcends our current situation. Jesus was able to remain faithful to his calling because he learned to ground himself in the Father, so that even his words were not his own, but his Father's (Jn 12:49). As we imitate Christ, we as a community will also ground ourselves in God and let the Father embrace us as his children. As we understand our identity as children, we will live in greater dependence on what flows from the mouth of God and hold a humble approach to hermeneutics. We will gladly grab hold of our Father's hand and as a community of children trust him to help us discern how to be present in the neighborhood, as well as trust him to provide the necessary provisions (spiritual and material) for the journey on which he has sent us. God is not just our destination, he is our Father, whose hand we can hold as we seek to *join him* in the renewal of our neighborhood, knowing that full renewal (new creation) is around the corner, upon the return of the king.

But until Christ's return, we are to continue to pray this transformative prayer, including this next line, which reminds us that while Jesus calls us out of this world (the ways of the world), he has sent us back to live *in* this world, immersed and grounded in our Triune God, seeking the good of our neighbors and neighborhood. So we pray, "*Thy* kingdom come, *Thy* will be done, *on earth* as it is in heaven" (Mt 6:10 RSV).

Thy kingdom come (co-mission). These verses remind us of the larger narrative of Scripture that starts in a garden ends in a city, the New Jerusalem. The good news that we proclaim is not a gnostic gospel reserved for another time and place but an incarnational gospel about how the inbreaking kingdom of God transforms the here and now in light of the renewal of all things (Rev 21:1-5). Our prayer that his kingdom would come *on earth* as it is in heaven is the hope of the prophets and involves both a king and kingdom.

In other words, prayer is a political act of resistance, protest, and hope. For when we bend our knee to the true king of the world and live as transforming servants in the way of Christ, the Prince of Peace, we confound the "god of this world" and his victims, who are under the lie that they are in charge. The fact is that God reigns (Ps 47:6-8; 103:19). In his co-mission to the disciples (and to us through them), Jesus says, "*All* authority *in* heaven and *on earth* has been given to *me*" (Mt 28:18). God reigns. Hallelujah!

But when we look out at the evil being unleashed in the United States (let alone in the entire world!)—kids getting gunned down at school, innocent African Americans victimized by police brutality, a lack of care for the environment, the sexual abuse named in the #metoo and #churchtoo movements—the evidence of God's reign over heaven and earth seems lacking. So, like the early disciples, we ask God, When will you restore your kingdom (Acts 1:6)?

The now and not yet. When observing the empirical realities of our world and examining the Scriptures, one of the more common ways of understanding the kingdom of God in its most basic framework is the *now* and *not yet* aspect of the kingdom. George Ladd was an early advocate of this framework. In Ladd's *Gospel of the Kingdom*, two of the chapters are "The Kingdom Is Today" and "The Kingdom Is Tomorrow," where he exegetes Scripture's talk about this age (*aiōn*) and the *aiōn* to come.[16] While in *the age to come* we qualitatively experience the fullness of the kingdom, in *this age*, before the second coming of Christ, we are going to see and experience hostility to God's reign, for the "god of this age"

---

[16]While Ladd looks at this idea through many different passages, some that expressly mention "this age and the age to come" are Mt 12:32; Mk 10:29-30; Lk 20:34-36; Eph 1:21. George Eldon Ladd, *Gospel of the Kingdom: Scriptural Studies in the Kingdom of God* (Grand Rapids: Eerdmans, 1959).

through various ideologies, has blinded the minds of those who reject God's reign (2 Cor 4:4). And while the life, death, and resurrection of Jesus have disarmed the principalities and powers (Col 2:15), the time is coming when the God of peace will crush the enemy under our feet (Rom 16:20). The principalities and powers claim ultimate relevance in history, and the signs of death are evident in every place. Yet Christ exposes their false claims and reveals that he is the Lord of history. Through Pentecost, the powers of *the age to come* have broken into *this age* in which evil and rebellion runs rampant. So the kingdom is now *and* not yet, which is why Jesus teaches us to pray for a little more of heaven to become visible on earth.

While the kingdom of God remains the dominant message of Christ, there have been different understandings of the kingdom throughout the history of the church. Howard Snyder maps out eight different models of the kingdom and how they seek to resolve six different tensions in Scripture. He concludes:

> If we take Scripture seriously, we must affirm that the kingdom is *both* heavenly and earthly; *both* present and future; *both* individual and social. That is the nature of God's reign because of who God is and because of the nature of the created order. The kingdom comes *both* by divine and human action, yet without compromising God's sovereignty. The kingdom comes gradually, but there are those crisis points, those critical moments of powerful in-breaking or revelation of the kingdom. The Bible consistently presents the day of the final coming of the Son of Man as the crowning cataclysm. Finally (as we have seen), the kingdom is not the church but is closely linked with the church because Jesus Christ, the one under whose sovereignty all creation is being gathered together, is also Head of the church (Eph 1:9-23). The church, to the degree that it is faithful to Jesus Christ, is the first fruits of the kingdom, of the general reconciliation God is bringing to fullness.[17]

How do we live into this? The question then becomes, what does this look like on this side of the new heavens and the new earth (Rev 21:1-5)? What does it mean to live into this prayer, so that the reality of God's reign would be more visible on earth, in the concrete realities of our neighborhood?

We need to approach this question with the posture given to us in the first part of the prayer. We come as a community of kids, humbly learning what it means to imitate Christ, who while on earth lived in communion with the Father by the power of the Spirit. For when it comes to living out this part of the prayer, too often the church seeks to bring about the kingdom of God by mimicking the methodology of the world and unwittingly imitating the powers in submission to the god of this

---

[17]Howard Snyder, *Models of the Kingdom: Gospel, Culture, and Mission in Biblical and Historical Perspective* (Eugene, OR: Wipf and Stock, 1991), 121.

world. But light does not come through darkness. The ends never justify the means, no matter how noble the ends. In fact, the means will always define the ends. Doing evil in the name of good is a significant moral problem in our day. What are some ways this is happening today?

Whether by crusades or colonization, historically the church has used means that have not and cannot bring about the kingdom of God. This is why Jesus told his own people to repent and follow him. The people of God in Jesus' time sought to see the reality of the kingdom become more visible, but in *their own ways*: the Pharisees through spiritual piety, the Sadducees through political power, the Essenes through separatist societies, and the Zealots through brute force. But none of these ways would bring about the kingdom.

Even today we try to manage and manipulate the image of how God's kingdom comes to earth: We portray a cherished baby, born to a virgin, on a silent night, under the nativity star. Raised by well-regarded parents, he grew up in a safe middle-class neighborhood, regularly attended synagogue and was compliant to synagogue leaders. He then became a master rabbi who knew all the right people, never drank, and was liked by most everyone. He rode into Jerusalem on a white stallion, was eventually recognized for who he was, and crowned the king of Israel. Is this not the script we want for Jesus and therefore for our own lives?

But in truth the kingdom came through a bastard child (no human father), born in a barn, raised in a ghetto (Nazareth), with a common name (Joshua). It came through a blue-collar worker (carpenter), who was introduced to the world by a crazily dressed, organic-food-eating man (John the Baptist). The kingdom came through one who as a full-time minister had nowhere to lay his head (was poor and warned against the worship of money), who rides into the capital city of Jerusalem on a donkey (moped) and was crowned with a crown of thorns and nailed to a cross. This is the one who said, "I am *the way* and the truth and the life" (Jn 14:6, emphasis mine). If God came into the world in this way, and students are not greater than their teacher, what might we expect for our lives and what ought to be our posture in mission?

The missional church. The missional church, with a heightened awareness of past failures in which the church looked more like *Game of Thrones* than the way of Jesus, has moved from crusades and colonialism to thoughtful contextualization. Richard Twiss, in his powerful book *Rescuing the Gospel from the Cowboys,* gives a devastating account of colonization in the past and present. As a First Nation man, he seeks to lead Native Americans in the work of *decolonizing* the gospel: "We must progress beyond the narrative of Euro-American imperialism, conquest and assimilation via Christian missions—and move forward as prophetic advocates seeking guidance from our very present Creator made known among us in Jesus, who is the Christ."[18]

While some have moved forward and seek to engage in contextualizing the gospel, too often the reigning ideology of the day holds us in bondage to idolatry, leading to dehumanizing others. Sometimes we are held captive to egotism, clericalism, consumerism, or pragmatism. As Richard Rohr has said, "Most people do not see things as they *are*, rather, they see things as *they* are."[19] In other words, our perceptions of reality are shaped by where we are emotionally, mentally, spiritually, economically, geographically, biologically (race, gender), sociologically, and autobiographically. The point at which we stand shapes our point of view. Thus, if we want to know how to best live into this prayer, we need to learn from a variety of God's people, from different denominations, ethnic backgrounds, genders, places around the globe, and time periods. Amos Yong, Allen Yeh, Veli-Matti Kärkkäinen, Henning Wrogemann, and Graham Hill are scholars who have served us well in this endeavor, introducing us to missional ecclesiology from ecumenical, historical, and global perspectives.[20]

Writing on the mission of the church, Ruth Padilla DeBorst articulates an integral transformational approach to mission, developed by Samuel Escobar, Orlando Costas, René Padilla, Vinay Samuel, Britton Chris Sugden, and others. Birthed from a Latin American context, the questions they encountered and that we need to ask in our context are: "Is faith relevant to the human condition? Is there truly good news for a world racked with injustice and pain? What is the role of those who claim to believe and experience the good news of God's love for the world? And what, then, is the mission of the church?"[21] This movement, along with others, have helped the global church better understand that "the mission of the church can be understood

---

[18]Richard Twiss, *Rescuing the Gospel from the Cowboys: A Native American Expression of the Way of Jesus* (Downers Grove, IL: InterVarsity Press, 2015), 46.

[19]Richard Rohr, *Everything Belongs: The Gift of Contemplative Prayer* (New York: Crossroad, 2003), 104.

[20]Amos Yong, Vinson Synan, and Miguel Alvarez, eds., *Global Renewal Christianity: Spirit Empowered Movements: Past, Present, and Future,* vol. 2, *Latin America* (Lake Mary, FL: Charisma House, 2016); Vinson Synan, Amos Yong, and J. Kwabena Asamoah-Gyadu, eds., *Global Renewal Christianity: Spirit-Empowered Movements Past, Present, and Future,* vol. 3, *Africa* (Lake Mary, FL: Charisma House, 2016); Allen Yeh, *Polycentric Missiology: Twenty-First Century Mission from Everyone to Everywhere* (Downers Grove, IL: IVP Academic, 2016); Veli-Matti Kärkkäinen, *An Introduction to Ecclesiology: Ecumenical, Historical and Global Perspectives* (Downers Grove, IL: IVP Academic, 2002); Henning Wrogemann, *Intercultural Theology,* vol. 1, *Intercultural Hermeneutics,* Missiological Engagements (Downers Grove, IL: IVP Academic, 2016); Graham Hill, *GlobalChurch: Reshaping Our Conversations, Renewing Our Mission, Revitalizing Our Churches* (Downers Grove, IL: IVP Academic, 2016); Graham Hill, *Salt, Light, and a City: Ecclesiology for the Global Missional Community,* vol. 1, *Western Voice,* 2nd ed. (Eugene, OR: Cascade, 2017).

[21]Ruth Padilla DeBorst, "An Integral Transformation Approach," in *The Mission of the Church: Five Views in Conversation,* ed. Craig Ott (Grand Rapids: Baker Academic, 2016), 44.

only in light of the Kingdom of God."[22] Indeed, "this mission is carried out between the times, between the already inaugurated kingdom and its coming in fullness."[23]

N. T. Wright talks about the importance of a hope-shaped mission; the mission of the church ought to be shaped in light of the narrative arc of Scripture.[24] Thus, if the story of God were broken down into six acts, we have been given the first five acts (creation, Fall, Israel, Jesus, church) and the last chapter of the sixth act (new creation). Now as people who live in these in-between times, we are called to know these acts so well that we live improvisational lives that are faithful to the God of this story.

Thus, a good way for us to live into this kingdom prayer, understanding the *now* and *not yet* of the kingdom of God, is to reflect on God's future—the fullness of his kingdom (new creation) and let it shape our sense of calling in the neighborhood. Then we can join God in writing a new future for our neighborhoods, cities, and world, by *anticipating his future* in the present. Let me explain.

Hunger for beauty. John the seer in Revelation 21:11-21 describes the beauty of New Jerusalem. The foundations of the city were not made of cement but precious stones like jasper, sapphire, and emerald. The streets were made of pure gold, and each of the twelve gates was made from a single pearl. John is using imagery to describe how, when the fullness of the kingdom arrives, our hunger for beauty will finally be satisfied—no more smog, no more water pollution, no more gang graffiti on new windows and newly painted walls.

If life *in the coming age* is a place of beauty that takes our breath away, how should we foster and sustain artists and environmentalists *in this present age*, anticipating the beauty of new creation?

When speaking of the mission of the church and how it should be shaped by our future hope, N. T. Wright mentions the importance of justice, beauty, and evangelism. In regard to beauty, he says,

> The message of new creation, of the beauty of the present world taken up and transcended in the beauty of the world that is yet to be—with part of that beauty being precisely the healing of the present anguish—comes as surprising hope. Part of the role of the church in the past was—and could and should be again—to foster and sustain lives of beauty and aesthetic meaning at every level, from music making in the village pub to drama in the local primary school, from artists' and photographers' workshops to still-life painting classes, from symphony concerts to driftwood sculptures. The church, because it is the family that believes in hope for new creation should

---

[22]René C. Padilla, *Mission Between the Times: Essays on the Kingdom* (Grand Rapids: Eerdmans, 1985), 200.
[23]Ruth Padilla DeBorst, "Integral Transformation Approach," 57.
[24]N. T. Wright, *Surprised by Hope: Rethinking Heaven, the Resurrection, and the Mission of the Church* (New York: HarperCollins, 2008), 194.

be the place in every town and village where new creation bursts forth for the whole community, pointing to the hope that like all beauty always comes as a surprise.[25]

Living in Hollywood, a city filled with budding artists, we wanted to think of a way to appreciate the artists in our neighborhood. While we did this in various ways, one of our mid-sized groups was connecting with students at the Musicians Institute on Hollywood Boulevard. I befriended a Japanese student there by the name of Daichi Kimera. We became good friends and eventually roommates. Through many conversations with Daichi, I came to realize how difficult the road of being a musician in LA was. Unlike other cities, a number of bars in Hollywood have a policy that when bands play there, the band is expected to bring in a certain amount of people. If they don't, they need to pay instead of getting paid. Because Daichi was leading his own band, I was able grow in greater empathy with musicians facing these challenges.

In one of our late-night conversations, Daichi and I came up with an idea that we later persuaded our mid-sized community to get behind. We would host a monthly artist event in our gathering space, which was perfectly suited for events like this. We called these events "Artist at the Fountain" because the building where we gathered was on Fountain Avenue, just a block south of the famed Sunset Boulevard. We would invite a local band, often from the Musicians Institute, to play a benefit concert for some local and global social justice initiatives we had either started or were participating in. We charged ten dollars per ticket, and the money we made for the tickets and during the silent auctions all went to our justice causes. We often surprised the band members with gift certificates from local restaurants we frequented. The restaurant owners were as glad to provide these gift certificates as the bands were to receive them. Because these events drew a decent crowd, the bands would grow a larger fan base by playing at them.

Many of the bands that played did not self-identify as Christians, so they were curious about why we did this. God gave us many opportunities to build relationships and share the good news with them. When a community of faith prays for God's kingdom to come and God's will to be done on earth as it is in heaven, and anticipates it in the present, that community becomes a sign and foretaste of the coming kingdom.

Lesslie Newbigin puts it this way:

The question which has to be put to every local congregation is the question of whether it is a credible sign of God's reign in justice and mercy over the whole of life, whether

---

[25]Wright, *Surprised by Hope*, 194.

it is an open fellowship whose concerns are as wide as the concerns of humanity, whether it cares for its neighbors in a way which reflects and springs out of God's care for them, whether its common life is recognizable as a foretaste of the blessing which God intends for the whole human family.[26]

In other words, what would God's reign look like in our neighborhood? And in light of the passions and calling of our group, what concrete way is God calling us to join him?

Our daily bread and debts (community). If we have forgotten the first part of this prayer, we might be tempted to use the next part of the Lord's prayer to simply feed our consumeristic tendencies individually or collectively—according to our country of birth—by translating "us" to "me." But the prayer is, "Give *us* this day *our* daily bread, / And forgive *us* our debts, / As *we* also have forgiven *our* debtors" (Mt 6:11-12 RSV). This is a communal prayer. When we pray that God's kingdom would be more visible in our neighborhood and in our world, we ought to expect this would challenge and undermine the current social order (Lk 1:46-55). This kingdom prayer proposes alternative social, economic, and political practices, by which we invite *all* to enjoy God's banquet *in this age,* as we anticipate his banquet in *the age to come.* When we pray to "Our Father," we remember that our mother, brother, and sister are those who *do* God's will (Mk 3:32-35).

There are many images of the kingdom of God, but perhaps the most pronounced is the concept that the kingdom of God is a Jubilee. Leviticus 25 lays out how the Jubilee was supposed to work (though the jury is out on whether it was actually carried out in Israel). Besides observing the Sabbath on the seventh day, the seventh year was to be a sabbath for the land—the idea of environmental responsibility. Finally, after seven time seven years, the fiftieth year was the year of Jubilee, the year of the Lord's favor, where they were to announce the Jubilee with a ram's horn and "proclaim liberty throughout the land" (Lev 25:10). This Jubilee was to be particularly liberating for the poor, those on the margins, and those thrown in jail due to debts they couldn't pay. "The Jubilee aimed to dismantle structures of social-economic inequality by releasing each community member from debt (Lev 25:35-42), return encumbered or forfeited land to its original owners (vv. 13, 25-28), and freeing slaves (vv. 47-55)."[27] It was basically a reset, a restart, another chance for those who ended up on the negative side of economic well-being. Can you imagine what this would mean for generational sin that is perpetuated through systematic injustice?

---

[26]Lesslie Newbigin, *Sign of the Kingdom* (Grand Rapids: Eerdmans, 1981), 64.
[27]Shane Claiborne, *The Irresistible Revolution: Living as an Ordinary Radical,* 10th anniversary ed. (Grand Rapids: Zondervan, 2016), 180.

When the disciples prayed for daily bread, the forgiveness of debts, and forgiving debts, I wonder if they thought back to Jesus' inaugural address in his hometown. We are told that Jesus was handed the scroll of Isaiah and read to the congregation:

> The Spirit of the Lord is on me,
>> because he has anointed me
>> to proclaim *good news to the poor.*
> He has sent me to proclaim freedom for the prisoners
>> and recovery of sight for the blind,
> to set the *oppressed free,*
>> to proclaim *the year of the Lord's favor.* (Lk 4:18-19)

After reading this, Jesus said, "Today this scripture is fulfilled in your hearing" (Lk 4:21). In other words, the kingdom of God is at hand. Today is the acceptable time to share the love and justice of God. These words set the trajectory for Jesus' ministry, which we see fleshed out in Luke through Acts, first in his life, then in the life of the church. For as the Father sent Jesus, Jesus has sent us into the world (Jn 20:21), to see his reign become more visible in our neighborhood and on our planet.

As we think about what God's reign looks like in our neighborhood, we need to give significant thought to economics, for it is often in this area that we find a need to be forgiven and the place we need to extend forgiveness.[28] Throughout Jesus' ministry, he disturbed the comfortable and comforted the disturbed. The early church struggled to live out the Jubilee in the midst of empire, and we need to struggle to live it out in our local and global context.

Two guys from Romania. In the mid-1990s, I took a trip with some leaders through Eastern and Western Europe. While I was in Budapest, Hungary, I met a couple of guys from Romania. Some friends from Ball State University were in Budapest for the summer and were hosting a few public events in the town square. The day I was there, they had a band playing to a large crowd of people. They would alternate between playing music and proclaiming the gospel. I was glancing around the crowd to see who was attentive to the preaching, as I assumed that God was preparing people to respond to the good news. All of a sudden, my eye caught two twenty-year-old guys who seemed to be engrossed in what the speaker was saying.

I walked over to where they were standing so that I could more easily strike up a conversation with them. After the message was preached and the music started up again, I asked the guys their thoughts about the speaker's message. I can't remember exactly what they said to me, but I realized rather quickly that these guys were

---

[28]See Sparks, Soerens, and Friesen, *New Parish,* chap. 5, where they deal with the neighborhood holistically by looking at it from a perspective of social, economic, environmental, educational, and civic well-being.

overwhelmed by feelings of extreme guilt. As I took the time to listen to their story, I realized *why* they were feeling guilty. They told me that over the last couple of days they had been stealing from a lot of people, and it seemed that God was convicting them of this.

As I sat and listened to their longer story, my eyes welled up with tears. I discovered that these young men had come from Romania to Hungary in hopes of finding employment so that they could send money back home to their families, who were suffering from severe hunger. If I recall properly, at the time the Romanian economy was in shambles with unemployment hovering around 35 percent. Most people were struggling to find enough food to survive.

As they shared their story, it was apparent they hadn't had a full meal in some time. They were just skin and bone. Struck with compassion, I invited them to join me for lunch and told them I would like to treat them. But they said no. I asked a second time. Again, they refused. I gently asked them, "Why won't you let me treat you to lunch?" They told me they didn't deserve such a gift after all they had done. I began to share with them about the grace and love of God, about the story of Jesus and the kingdom of God, and about how much they are loved by God. I could visibly see God at work in them. They finally accepted my invitation to lunch.

We talked all the way until dinner, where we met up with a pastor friend of mine from Columbus, Ohio, and a few other people. By the time we had finished dinner, God had allowed them to see what the good news of Jesus was all about, what it meant to enter the kingdom and join God in seeing his kingdom become more visible on the earth. So they asked God to forgive them of their debts.

After dinner, I talked with them about what it meant to trust God in hard times. It was one of the most difficult discussions I've ever had. I was thinking to myself, who am I to tell them to trust God for their needs? Knowing their circumstances, how could I share with them that if they put God and his kingdom first in their life, that God would take care of their needs (Mt 6:23), and that they didn't need to worry if they prayed (Phil 4:6)?

What would you say to them if you were in my shoes? I could only do what I sensed that God was prompting me to do, and that was to read through Matthew 6, and then put them into the hands of a mighty God whom I had learned to trust. As we read through the passage about how they don't need to worry anymore about their provision if they seek first God and his kingdom, through their facial expressions I could sense the Spirit helping them to trust.

That evening, my pastor friend and I drove them back to where they were staying. It was then that I experienced one of the most unforgettable moments in my life. I can still picture the scene as clearly in my mind as if it happened yesterday.

We prayed together and we prayed for them. Then they reached into their pockets and gave pens to both my friend and me. Then one of the guys took off his watch and gave it to me. It looked as if these were the only possessions they had. We didn't want to take the pens and I didn't want to take the watch, but they kept insisting, saying, "Please remember us. Please remember us." We said our goodbyes and as we drove away, they stood at the side of the road and waved until we were out of sight. I left thinking that these guys completely understand what it means to depend on God daily for their survival.

Yet, while I rejoiced in their newfound faith and felt compassion for their needs, the reductionistic gospel that I had adopted at that time didn't cause me to reflect on my complicity in the global economy that resulted in these guys and countless others to turn to stealing just to survive. It wasn't until I learned about a holistic gospel of a king and kingdom (in the late 1990s) that I realized my great need to ask forgiveness of many debts in which I was complicit without being aware. It wouldn't be until years later, when I met a bishop from Kenya, that I grew in my sense of responsibility for and understanding of economic justice, to the point that our congregation in Hollywood, led by a businessman and myself, started a foundation that provided micro-grants to help launch small businesses in the poorest part of Kenya.

Darrell Guder, a professor at Princeton Theological Seminary, shared a story about a man who had come from a poor region in Africa and had a full scholarship for his MDiv at Princeton. One day this African man came into Guder's office and said, "Professor Guder, I need to go back to my country." Guder asked him why. He said, "Because I'm losing my faith." Guder asked him to clarify, so he explained, "Back home, I had to trust God every day for the meal I was going to eat. Living in America has changed all of that. With my scholarship, I realize that all my meals are taken care of for years to come, and I have no need to rely on God for my daily bread." When I heard this story, the proverb that came to my mind was,

> Give me neither poverty nor riches,
> but give me only my daily bread.
> Otherwise, I may have too much and disown you
> and say, "Who is the LORD?"
> Or I may become poor and steal,
> and so dishonor the name of my God. (Prov 30:8-9)

John the seer writes about the day when there are no longer any people who live with hunger or thirst for something to drink (Rev 7:16)—a day when people don't have to leave their homes to try and find work so that their families can survive, a day when no one is desperately scrounging for food to feed their children.

So, if the life of the *age to come* is the elimination of hunger and thirst and in their place is abundance, how are our economic practices as the church *in this age* anticipating the reality of abundance and the elimination of hunger and thirst? When the Spirit of God came upon the early church, God moved in them in such a way that those who had a lot of resources helped others who didn't have much; the mission of the early church was shaped by their understanding of God's future:

> They devoted themselves to the apostle's teaching and to fellowship, to the breaking of bread and to prayer. Everyone was filled with awe at the many wonders and signs performed by the apostles. All the believers were together and *had everything in common. They sold property and possessions to give to anyone who had need.* Every day they continued to meet together in the temple courts. They broke bread in their homes and ate together with glad and sincere hearts, praising God and enjoying the favor of all the people. And the Lord added to their number daily those who were being saved. (Acts 2:42-47)

This may be the first time that the people of God actually celebrated the heart of Jubilee.

This past week I was sharing with a group of church planters on the topic of caring for your soul. One of the practices I encouraged these planters to live into was sabbath. After talking about the importance of sabbath and how to practice it, one of the leaders in the room politely interrupted me, asking, "It seems easier for me to practice sabbath, but what about the poor in our neighborhood? Isn't this just a privilege that some of us have the opportunity to experience?"

And sadly, that is the case for many living in urban areas, who often work two jobs to survive. This is why we need a larger picture of sabbath, one that includes the Sabbath of sabbaths, the Jubilee, where there is a redistribution of resources that allows all to share in God's rest. The beauty of the good news is that it leads to generosity, where those who have much will help those who don't have enough. As a community we should find ways to make sure everyone in the community can enter into God's rest. This is what we see happening in Acts 2; these events were not driven by an ideology with some salvation narrative, whether it be conservatism, liberalism, communism, or unbridled capitalism. Ideologies created and perpetrated by the god of this age deform our desires and dehumanize others. Communism seeks to replace God and downplay competition, often creating apathy or slothfulness. Capitalism, on the other hand, has a rival salvation story that emphasizes competition and tends to create greedy people who fail to look out for the common global good. Ideologies are today's idols, to which too many are enslaved. Here is where we can learn from the early church. Shane Claiborne writes,

> It's important to understand that redistribution comes from community, not before community. Redistribution is not a prescription for community. Redistribution is a

description of what happens when people fall in love with each other across class lines. When the Bible tells the story of the early church in the book of Acts, it does not say that they were of one heart and mind because they sold everything. Rather, they held all in common precisely because they were of one heart and mind, as rich and poor found themselves born again into a family in which some had extra and others were desperately in need. Redistribution was not systematically regimented but flowed naturally out of a love for God and neighbor. I am not a communist, nor am I a capitalist. As Will O'Brien of the Alternative Seminary here in Philly says, "When we truly discover love, capitalism will not be possible and Marxism will not be necessary."[29]

When we start to seek the economic well-being of neighborhoods, we will need much discernment. We don't come to a neighborhood as saviors, but as ones who follow the way of our Savior. We first come to detect and discern what God is doing.

Walking with the poor locally. In East Hollywood, we have a number of people who would be considered poor, some who are legal citizens and others who are undocumented. Let's take José as an example of the life of far too many. José made his way to LA in hopes of finding opportunity, with the goal to send back some money to his relatives in his home country.

José waits outside the Home Depot in hopes that someone will come by and offer him a job for a day or even a half day. Sometimes when I drive up to the Home Depot, José and his friends run up to my car hoping that I have some work for them. Often I and others do not, so many days José stands with his friends just waiting. Some days he waits and waits until the sun starts to set, then returns home only to come back again the next day. Repeating this activity daily adds to a deep sense of rejection that often penetrates his soul. In a country where people talk about their rights, he fights to imagine that he is a person who is worthy to have any rights.

José lives with multiple fears—the fear of not being picked up and the fear of being picked up. Living in the land of plenty only adds to his lack of self-worth. No wages to low wages begin to take their toll on his psyche. And doing the kind of work that no one else desires to do makes him feel undesirable. Yet José continues to wake up and make his way to Home Depot in hopes that things might be different for him and his future.

We learn from José's story that at the heart of poverty is a "web of lies that results in the poor internalizing a view of themselves as being without value, and without a contribution to make, believing that they are truly god-forsaken."[30] If our desire for the common good of the neighborhood doesn't transform the identity and

---

[29]Claiborne, *Irresistible Revolution*, 154.

[30]Bryant L. Myers, *Walking with the Poor: Principles and Practices of Transformational Development* (Maryknoll, NY: Orbis, 2011), 177-78.

WHEN PRESENCE IS UNRESOLVED

ROHADI NAGASSAR

What happens when a church joins the kingdom in their midst even when it takes them beyond programs and ministry plans?

My first church plant gathered in an eclectic inner-city neighborhood along with two other small church communities. Being in an urban area had unique advantages. For one, we didn't have to talk about the poor; they were literally in our midst. This is how we first encountered Matt.

Matt was homeless and hung out near our gathering space. His disheveled appearance made him look older than he really was. A stringy grey beard and unwashed hair matched his tired expression and bloodshot eyes. The flat of beer he drank a day probably had something to do with it.

As a small church we didn't have resources to run an outreach ministry or food program. However, we had the people to work with Matt. What if Matt was a part of our community rather than someone we served from the community? So that's what we did. The church committed to Matt in the most important way—to be present as he rebuilt his life. For his part, Matt slowly found a new family that offered him love and care.

The presence of the community along with the tireless hours many in the church offered Matt in the form of phone calls, company, and help, had no direct agenda other than to love. Over the years we loved without condition, and through his own revelation, Matt had a transformational encounter with Jesus. He started to see the light, both physically and in his spiritual life. But the kingdom reached even further.

He started to pull away from his addictions, managed to find transitional housing, and started reconciling with his estranged family. This is the kind of goodness we pray for. It wasn't easy, but seeing his transformation was worth it. We experienced the kingdom at work in the present! This is what happens when a church joins the kingdom unfolding in their midst.

But there's a tension at play. The fullness of the kingdom on earth is incomplete. There's still evil in our world. Final restoration has yet to come.

I wish I could say that Matt kept getting better and better—that he found a job, permanent housing, and reconciled with his family. He certainly did all these things, but as of now he's back on the street. In many ways he's a living testament to a liminal kingdom. He's found spiritual renewal and transformation yet continues to struggle with the power of flesh and past pain. Although this is the end of this story, it's not the end of God's. In the kingdom story we rest assured that our work of love matters even if we can't see all the pieces.

vocation of the poor, where they see themselves as loved by God and capable of contributing to the well-being of the neighborhood, then we unintentionally add to the poverty of those we seek to help. Too often, as planters, we suffer from a savior complex and an ego, which frequently lends itself to a triumphalist approach to mission in the neighborhood, where we seek to "serve" the poor, instead of live in community together, allowing them to set the agenda.

When thinking about the complexities of poverty, I have come to realize that not only is it helpful to have a holistic approach, but if we want to walk with the poor wisely, we need to work with other organizations who are called to tackle issues we don't have the gifting or ability to tackle. I found the five metaphors that Frances O'Gorman uses to analyze responses to the poor helpful: band-aid (handouts and relief), ladder (providing information and skills), patchwork (self-help projects), beehive (grassroots movements), and beacon (confronting society and constructive action).[31] Every form of relief is helpful, and different groups are called to attend to different areas and find partners who are willing to work in the other areas of need.

Not only that, but when it comes to people like José in East Hollywood, and other people in our neighborhood, as a planter there is one place and practice that I have found the inbreaking of the kingdom taking place, possibly more than any other. It's the place we come when we are hungry and thirsty. It's the place where we experience laughter and tears, where we share stories, surprises and secrets. It's the place where families are formed and community is deepened. It's the place where there is opportunity for honest conversation, where words that are shared shape who we are and who we are becoming.

It's the place that church planters need to be—*the table*. I find it fascinating that the story of God starts with a picnic and ends with a feast. The climax of the story is Jesus. The table is the most used piece of furniture in his life. Jesus taught at the table. He trained the Twelve at the table and he extended the table to those whom religious leaders and society dismissed and damned. In addition, he turned over the table in the temple because of the unscrupulous economic practices of the ruling elite. This is why Len Sweet says, "Jesus was killed because of his table talk and his table manners—the stories he told and the people he ate with."[32] Even near the end of his life, Jesus is at the table for the Last Supper. I like to ask church planters, Are you spending more time preparing for the pulpit or being present at the table?

The table is where we ask God to give *us* our daily bread, the place where we receive forgiveness and learn to forgive others. As we break bread together, we

---

[31] Myers, *Walking with the Poor*, 190.

[32] Leonard Sweet, *From Tablet to Table: Where Community Is Formed and Identity Found* (Colorado Springs, CO: NavPress, 2014), 6.

remember he was broken so that we might become one whole new humanity. As we drink from the cup, we remember his blood was spilled, so we don't need to spill more blood, but seek the peace of our neighborhood. But often peace does not come without economic justice. When people are unable to meet their basic needs, there is no peace.

Deliver us from evil (conflict). As we pray the Lord's Prayer and start to live into this upside-down kingdom, we will face the fury of the god of this age, which is why we need to put on the helmet of hope (1 Thess 5:8), take up the shield of faith (Eph 6:16), and remember that the only thing that counts is faith working through love (Gal 5:6). We need to pray "And lead us not into temptation but deliver us from the evil one."

As planters, we need to be aware that our enemy seeks to subvert our attempts to see God's reign become more visible in our neighborhood through *the way of Jesus*. The principalities and powers desire us to imitate *their ways* to bring about the kingdom. But this just leads to death. As Jesus began his ministry, he was tempted by the devil to fulfill his Father's mission by bowing down to the powers and ways of the world. But Jesus remained faithful to his calling. His approach to leadership was counterintuitive. He didn't follow the religious approaches of his day, and he sought to subvert the political and cultural approaches that had captured the desires of most, including his own disciples. He sought to deliver and heal people who were possessed by the spirit of the day. Jesus never bowed to the powers; he resisted them and sought to imitate and reflect the heart of his Father. But the powers did not stand idly by and allow Jesus to break their spell on the world. The powers crave ultimate devotion. They have developed rules, systems, structures, and institutions that speak to the longings we each have, so that we are tempted to give ourselves over to them. They are not satisfied until they have our ultimate devotion. The *way* we go about seeing the reign of God more fully realized is just as important as the desired ends.

We need the Spirit to help us resist the temptation to try and make the kingdom of God visible *in our own way*. It can be easy to fall to the ideology of pragmatism, where if it works, it must be good and it must be true. We need to ask, Do our ways demonstrate the fruit of the spirit or do they reveal the fruit of the flesh (Gal 5:19-26)? When we pray to be delivered from temptation and from the evil one, we recognize that we are not capable of facing the onslaught of evil on our own. We must rely on the Holy Spirit, through whom the church was constituted and called into being. The gift of the Spirit is the authority and victory over every power of death. As we live in the Spirit we can discern, identify, and expose the work of the evil one, instead of imitating his ways. The Comforter can help us do the uncomfortable.

As we join God in the renewal of our neighborhood, we will experience suffering, doubt, and discouragement, as well as see and experience God's power in new ways. As I examined and reflected on the highs and lows of my life in the area of my physical, emotional, financial, and vocational needs, I realized that the first five years of my church plants have often been the roughest. One of the highs was that God blessed me by giving me an apartment for a low price, on Hollywood Blvd close to the metro, which met all my prayer requests. One of the low parts in regard to my physical well-being was that I was involved in a significant car accident. In addition I had my computer stolen from my apartment when I was out meeting needs in Africa; there was a flood in my bedroom where my desktop computer was ruined along with a number of prized books; an anonymous threatening letter was sent to me after an article came out in the *LA Times* about our church; someone smashed the driver's side of my car window with a crowbar and stole some important items from my car; on a day trip to the east coast I was rear ended in my rental car. That same day I fell through a trap door scraping my back pretty hard. To top that day off, I ran out of gas. Later that year a rash was developing on my leg and the doctors said it was shingles.

I coach a number of church planters around North America and was recently talking with a young planter, just thirty years old, who within the last month of our conversation discovered he had an ulcer, high blood pressure, and six cracked teeth, because at night he dealt with the stress he encountered in the day by grinding his teeth. As Dan Allender has said, "Leadership is far from a walk in the park; it is a long march through a dark valley. In fact, leadership has been described as wearing a bull's-eye on your chest during hunting season."[33] The emotional hits that we face in planting come hard and fast and hurt like crazy. How do you deal with the expectations, the financial need, the unsafe people, and the ministry crises? How do you keep going when you feel overwhelmed, confused, and sometimes even wonder if you are actually making a difference? How do you keep going when the very people you are trying to bless just stab you in the back?

Developing an inner life that can match the demands we face as we join God in this mission is vital. There is no single answer to this question. There isn't a magic formula or four quick steps. I have had to learn a way of life where I get refreshed physically, recharged emotionally, and renewed spiritually. I have learned to live the punctuated life. If we are going to last in ministry over the long haul, we need to live punctuated lives. In other words, life can become one long run-on sentence. But life was not meant to be lived that way.

---

[33]Dan Allender, *Leading with a Limp: Take Full Advantage of Your Most Powerful Weakness* (Colorado Springs, CO: WaterBrook Press, 2006), 3.

We need commas in our lives, times where we pause, reflect, have long lunches, take afternoon naps. At the end of each day we need to put a period, where we take ten minutes to reflect on the day and think about where we walked with God and where we failed to and on what gave us life and what drained life from us. The period also stands for sabbath, where we just stop once a week from our work, to pay attention to God and recharge ourselves emotionally.

We need exclamation marks in our lives. We need to know what stirs our passions. We need to learn to play in our neighborhood and with our community. The question mark reminds us to have an ongoing curiosity about God, the world we live in, our neighborhood, and life in general. The hyphen between words reminds us of our need to be connected to soul friends—people who we practice intimate space with. People with whom we can be completely unfiltered. So, let me ask you as a planter, is your life a run-on sentence, or are you living a punctuated life?[34]

Thine is the kingdom (consummation). This brings us to the final phrase of the Lord's prayer. While this last part is not found in the early manuscripts, I think it may have been added because it expresses the primary temptation that we will have as people and as planters. The temptation is for us to build our *own kingdom*, by our *own power*, for our *own glory*. As planters, we need to know that the *telos*, the end goal, is God's kingdom not ours. The church exists for the kingdom of God, not itself. We need to recognize the various ideologies that seek to captivate and control us by having us rely on our own power. This relates to our methodology. Not every method is equal. Some methods require us to bow down to the powers, and if we bow to them, we will never arrive at the *telos* of God's kingdom. And finally, we will be tempted to fall into egotism, our own glory and status, which is why we need to imitate Christ in making ourselves nothing, even being willing to lay our life down for the gospel, for the sake of his kingdom.

CONCLUSION

When the primary question is, What do we need to do to grow our church?, the church tends to be more concerned about its own interests than about being a sign and foretaste of the coming kingdom. The neighborhood might think that the church cares more about itself. But when the primary question is, What does God's reign look like in our neighborhood?, we seek first his kingdom and his righteousness and look out for the common good of the neighborhood. In this case, the neighborhood is blessed by the presence of the church, and the church is a faithful witness to the good news.

---

[34]Inspired by Randall Jenkins, *The Punctuated Believer* (Nashville: CrossBooks, 2012).

As we pray and live into the Lord's Prayer, by the power of the Spirit, we will seek to live in *communion* with the Father, who is close to us, but also transcendent, so he can give us fresh perspective as we join him on the *co-mission* to see the kingdom become more visible in our neighborhood. It is not an individualistic journey that we do alone; we are a sent *community* guided by the incarnation, rooted in our neighborhood and linked to neighborhoods across the world, as our mission and family is global. We recognize that students are not greater than their teacher, so we too will encounter *conflict* with the god of this age. We need to live punctuated lives and live in light of the *consummation*, where every knee will bow and tongue confess that Jesus is the King of kings and Lord of lords. This will provoke people to ask why we are living this way and sets us up to invite others to join us in God's mission of love to all creation.

DISCUSSION QUESTIONS

1. What are the hopes, dreams, fears, and stresses of people in our neighborhood?

2. When reflecting on God's future, what part is our team most passionate about?

3. In light of the needs of our neighborhood and the passions of our team, what concrete ministry does God want us to start or join to better reflect what our neighborhood would look like if God were in charge?

4. How do we share the good news about the king and kingdom when people ask us?

3

HOW DOES GOD'S STORY SPREAD?

THE GOSPEL, EVANGELISM, AND REPRODUCTION

JOHN LO

Just as the true fruit of an apple tree is not an apple, but another tree; the true fruit of a small group is not a new Christian, but another group; the true fruit of a church is not a new group, but a new church; the true fruit of a leader is not a follower, but a new leader; the true fruit of an evangelist is not a convert, but new evangelists. Whenever this principle is understood and applied, the results are dramatic.

CHRISTIAN SCHWARZ

Then Jesus said to them, "Don't you understand this parable? How then will you understand any parable?"

MARK 4:13

WHY DID JESUS COME TO EARTH?

Recently I began a section called "Mandate to the Nations" in my Perspectives on the World Christian Movement class with a question: "Why did Jesus come to earth?" One student said, "To save us from our sins" (the perfect Sunday School answer), and I responded, "Great answer—but insufficient!" In response to the ensuing slack jaws, we turned to John 17:4, where Jesus says, "I have brought you glory on earth by finishing the work you gave me to do."

"Jesus says he has brought glory to God by finishing the work he was given to do, but he hasn't died on the cross yet! What does he see as his work?"

No answer.

"Well, what else did he do?"

"Teach people." "Disciple Peter, James, and John." "Heal the sick and cast out demons." "Dismantle the powers of darkness." Of course!

I then explained that because the end of all time is revealed in Revelation 7:9-10, where we see people from every people group,[1] tribe, people, and language singing "Salvation belongs to our God, / who sits

---

[1] The Greek word *ethnos*, normally translated as "nation," does not refer to modern nation-states but to ethnic or people groups, as Dr. Ralph Winter discovered. Recent scholarship has defined it as "a large group of people based on various cultural, physical, or geographical ties." Luis Bush, "The Meaning of Ethnē in Matthew 28:19," *Mission Frontiers*, September 1, 2013, www.mission frontiers.org/issue/article/the-meaning-of-ethne-in-matthew-2819.

on the throne, / and to the Lamb," then all the things Jesus did must be pointed toward this end. That's when the lights went on in the room!

Simply put, Jesus began a missional movement that was meant to help every people group know and worship God in their own tongue. Jesus began with the end in mind: to see the gospel preached as a testimony to all nations (Mt 24:14). Jesus knew his time on earth was short; the only way this could ever happen was for him to start a movement of disciples which would continue until the intended objective was reached.

In chapter one we looked at the importance of locating the missional heart of God that sends us into our community and discerning his heart working in us as part of that story. Chapter two focused on prayerfully reflecting on Jesus' kingdom prayer as a guide to understanding what the kingdom might look like in our neighborhood.

In this chapter we're going to trace the contours of what Jesus, followed by the apostle Paul, taught and did to form the DNA of what we now understand as the church. What's significant is how important the reproduction of disciples, groups, and churches is to the genetic code of what Jesus began. Jesus didn't start a church; he started a movement. And as we follow the master, this must also be the end vision of any church planter today.

HOW WOULD GOD'S STORY SPREAD?

A helpful place to begin is Jesus' parables of the kingdom. Jesus often taught in parables and "did not say anything to them [the crowds] without using a parable" (Mk 4:34). Jesus told parables to teach the disciples something about which they had no knowledge (the growth of God's kingdom) through something they did under-stand (everyday life analogies). This is the reason the kingdom parables were the center point of his preaching.

Of course, the first question is, What exactly is the kingdom? As we saw in the chapter two, the church sits squarely between two aspects of the kingdom of God: the present and the future, or what George Ladd defined as the *now and the not yet* of the coming fullness of the kingdom of God.[2] Its ministry and cause is to see the rule and reign of God come.[3] John the Baptist and Jesus both proclaimed the nearness of the kingdom of God at the outset of their ministries, indicating that what was once far away was now close (Mt 3:2; 4:17). In his initial instructions to both the Twelve and the seventy-two in the first and second short-term missions, Jesus teaches them to proclaim this same nearness, indicating that the proclamation

---

[2]George Eldon Ladd, *Gospel of the Kingdom: Scriptural Studies in the Kingdom of God* (Grand Rapids: Eerdmans, 1959), 25.

[3]Ladd, *Gospel of the Kingdom*, 53.

of the nearness of the kingdom accompanied by a demonstration of that nearness (healing, deliverance, and raising people from the dead) was the primary calling of his followers (Mt 10:7; Lk 10:9).

Ladd reminds us that the church must never be equated with the kingdom of God: "The Church therefore is not the Kingdom of God; God's Kingdom creates the Church and works in the world through the Church. Men cannot therefore build the Kingdom of God, but they can preach it and proclaim it."[4] While this is the case, it's also true that the growth of the kingdom only comes because the church grows—not necessarily by creating huge megachurches which could single-handedly reach whole nations, but by churches being planted, neighborhood by neighborhood and people group by people group. The coming of the kingdom is intimately tied to church planting. Shenk and Stutzman note, "Church planting is the most urgent business of humankind. It is through the creation (or planting) of churches that God's kingdom is extended into communities which have not yet been touched by the presence of the kingdom of God."[5] This is the *missio Dei*, where the church is seen as essentially missionary in nature.[6] Furthermore, movements of church planting must be associated with the expansion of the kingdom. H. Richard Niebuhr writes, "Christianity, whether in America or anywhere else . . . must be understood as a movement rather than an institution or series of institutions. . . . The true church is not an organization but the organic movement of those who have been 'called out' and 'sent.'"[7]

Traditional dating of the Synoptic Gospels puts them in the mid-60s to mid-80s CE.[8] Thus Matthew, Mark, and Luke write with the knowledge of the beginning of the church, Paul's missionary journeys, and the church planting which resulted. The history, experience, and issues of the early church—more specifically, the initiation of the church and the churches that were planted—shape the narratives of the New Testament, especially the construction of the Gospels. The Gospel writers constructed their narratives to highlight the importance of the kingdom parables for the church planting movements they saw and experienced.

From this perspective, the parables can be seen not only as stories Jesus told to the crowds during his ministry, but as prophetic descriptions of the actual growth of the kingdom through the early church in the first century. Parables describing

---

[4]Ladd, *Gospel of the Kingdom*, 117.

[5]David W. Shenk and Ervin R. Stutzman, *Creating Communities of the Kingdom: New Testament Models of Church Planting* (Scottdale, PA: Herald, 1988), 23.

[6]David Bosch, *Transforming Mission: Paradigm Shifts in Theology of Mission* (Maryknoll, NY: Orbis, 1991), 381.

[7]H. Richard Niebuhr, *The Kingdom of God in America* (New York: Harper & Row, 1937), xiv as quoted in Smith, 13.

[8]D. L. Bock, "The Gospel of Luke," 500; R. A. Guelich, "The Gospel of Mark," 514; S. McKnight, "The Gospel of Matthew," 528, in Joel B. Green, Scot McKnight, I. Howard Marshall, eds., *Dictionary of Jesus and the Gospels* (Downers Grove, IL: InterVarsity Press, 1992).

the growth of the kingdom narrated what had already taken place, and parables about the character of kingdom workers described the kinds of people through whom the kingdom grew.

As such, the parables continue to speak to us today about the movement and growth of the kingdom in and through a person and the church. Three particular foci of Jesus' parables stand out: (1) how the kingdom grows, (2) the fact that something is amiss when this type of growth does not occur, and (3) the role of Jesus' followers as workers in the kingdom.

The kingdom is meant to grow. The kingdom is meant to grow like seeds which are sown and yield "a hundred, sixty or thirty times what was sown" (Mt 13:23). It is natural for a tiny mustard seed to be "the largest of garden plants and becomes a tree" (Mt 13:32). It was Jesus' teaching and his expectation that the kingdom would grow like yeast "until it worked all through the dough" (Mt 13:33). Jesus paints these pictures to illustrate the inevitable and relentless (if temporarily unseen) manner the kingdom is to grow. "The seed of the gospel has innate power to accomplish what God desires."[9] Even more specifically, in these parables growth often takes place through multiplication. Seeds multiply thirty, sixty, or one hundred times; yeast continues to reproduce within the dough.

Jesus spoke not only parabolically but descriptively and prophetically. Jesus not only described what he was doing with the disciples (and how they felt about themselves) but what would happen in the book of Acts: the movement began through the unschooled, ordinary disciples (Acts 4:13) who became the yeast that eventually worked all through the dough of the Roman Empire and turned the world upside down (Acts 17:6).

And because these parables of the kingdom apply to the church in this in-between age, we must assume these same growth dynamics still apply today, whether it's in Bakersfield, Bangalore, or Beijing.

When growth doesn't occur, something is amiss. "This is what the kingdom of God is like. A man scatters seed on the ground. Night and day, whether he sleeps or gets up, the seed sprouts and grows, though he does not know how. All by itself the soil produces grain—first the stalk, then the head, then the full kernel in the head. As soon as the grain is ripe, he puts the sickle to it, because the harvest has come" (Mk 4:26-29). In this simple passage, Jesus reveals a kingdom truth: all life reproduces. Reproduction is a defining character of life. Animals reproduce. So do plants. And when a seed is planted and properly cared for, harvest is inevitable.

---

[9]Stephen Robert Smith, "A Study of the Dynamics of Developing Sustained Church Planting Movements in Asian Nations" (master's thesis, University of South Africa, 2009), 18, in reference to Mk 4:26-29.

When something is alive, it grows and reproduces. Conversely, when that doesn't happen, something is wrong, either with the environment (like poor water or toxins in the soil) or because somewhere along the way, the original DNA has been compromised. Of course, Jesus tells parables about growth not taking place: seeds find poor soil; there are thorns in the ground which preclude the seed from taking root; weeds have been sown by the enemy (Mt 13:19-30). When a tree does not bear fruit, it should be cut down (Lk 13:6-9). The owner expects a gain from his investments, and when this is not the case, the servant is punished (Mt 25:14-30).

This basic kingdom dynamic is likewise illustrated in the story of the early church. As a whole, the soil of the Jews was not receptive to the gospel. Examples of tares that were planted by the enemy include Judas, Ananias and Sapphira, the Judaizers and Hymenaeus (1 Tim 1:20), Phygelus, Hermogenes (2 Tim 1:15), Philetus (2 Tim 2:17), Jannes, Jambres (2 Tim 3:8-9), and Alexander (2 Tim 4:14).

When the kingdom does not grow and expand today, one must assume there is something wrong. However, the problem does not lie in the seed of the gospel. Perhaps the church has not sown the seed, or perhaps there is something wrong with the soil—perhaps something has been added to the soil or some aspect of the kingdom has not been properly understood. When the church does not see the growth that Jesus taught about in the parables, it must look for what is amiss.

One of the great inventions of history is seedless watermelon. Children born recently would never be able to imagine a past when eating watermelon meant carrying around a spittoon to spit seeds into. Imagine that! The interesting thing about seedless watermelons is that while they're great for consumers, they're terrible for farmers. The lack of seeds makes for great eating, but this require farmers to buy fresh seed each time they're planted. They're bred for consumption but not for reproduction.

Is the twenty-first-century church a seedless watermelon?

When we find a Christian who is leading others to faith, we assume they have an evangelistic gift. When we find a small group leader who grows a group, we think they have a leadership gift. When we find a church that is not only growing but planting other churches, we assume there's something special about that church or its leader.

This tells us something about our basic assumptions concerning the church and the Christian: namely, that it's not normal for them to reproduce—and that any time this happens, something is exceptional. We don't actually expect Christians and the church to grow and multiply, so when they do, we look for something special or unique. Because our basic assumption is lack of growth, we see growth and reproduction as anomalies. This line of thinking reveals defective

DNA. Post-industrial America has bred a strain of the church that is great for consumers but does not reproduce.

We know it shouldn't be like this. We often grieve with couples who have the deeply sensitive and painful condition of being unable to get pregnant and have children, which we call infertility. Many such couples spend untold months, years, and dollars trying to rectify this condition. Specialized reproductive technology and processes have now been created to assist couples in what for the majority of people is natural. We intuitively know this is not how life is meant to be. Human life was created to reproduce.

Is there something amiss in the waters of Christianity that has rendered its churches unable to conceive or reproduce, and then made this the expectation for what is normal?

I remember visiting Morris and Beverly, a young couple our church sent to Asia as kingdom professionals. In this nation, they had helped many like-minded professionals learn to be salt and light. But after seven years, neither they nor their friends had led anyone to faith. When I asked about this, they were a little defensive.

But God had other plans. We visited them with the desire to help them understand the reproducing DNA of the gospel. While there, we met a waiter who, after being asked a few questions, turned out to be quite spiritually hungry. In the course of the next few days, they led him to faith and baptized him. And this did amazing things for them, because they realized what life in the kingdom could look and feel like.

We helped change their perception of the gospel of the kingdom, taught them how to engage in conversations that helped them sense spiritual hunger, gave them tools to lead people to faith, and then equipped them to disciple these new followers to do the same. Just two months later, their work sent them to another part of the country where they ended up leading scores of college students to faith, who then led others to faith. They had rediscovered the true DNA of the gospel, and it led to a reproducing movement.

Every follower of Jesus is a worker in the kingdom. Of the thirty-three kingdom parables, nearly half deal with servants or workers in the kingdom. As a whole, these workers and servants of the kingdom are meant to serve the master in bringing in the harvest.

Yet there are many instances where the kingdom does not grow because sons called to work in the field are not obedient (Mt 21:28-32), or because servants entrusted to bring in a return are lazy and wicked (Mt 25:26), or because they have forgotten who is the master (Mt 21:33-45), or because they have not counted the cost (Lk 14:28-33), or because they have forgotten their calling (Mk 13:33-36; Lk 12:35-38; 17:7-10).

In contrast, when an individual understands the kingdom, he or she sells everything to gain this treasure in the field (Mt 13:44) and this pearl of great price (Mt 13:46). He who leaves the ninety-nine sheep rejoices when the lost one is found (Lk 15:1-7), as does she who finds the lost coin (Lk 15:8-10).

In the New Testament, Jesus calls the disciples to be fishers of people (Mk 1:17). Jesus later calls them to make disciples (Mt 28:19-20) to the ends of the earth (Acts 1:8). And so Stephen, Cornelius, Paul, Timothy, and many others demonstrate the decision making and the life of those who understand they are workers for the kingdom (2 Tim 2:15).

Church planting is premised on the understanding that making disciples is central to our call as Christians. When Jesus gave the Great Commission, his audience was just the eleven disciples (Mt 28:16). Jesus' clear intention was for each of these followers to take this commission as a personal mandate. These clear instructions were Jesus' call, meant for each of his followers, and intended to define the course of their lives. Those who heeded the call became the foundation of the church.

The simplicity—and the personal mandate—of Jesus' words have largely been lost today. Most Christians in America do not feel equipped or ready to engage in Jesus' personal mandate. Believers often say: "Evangelism is scary," "I've never been discipled," or "Mission is for those who are specially called." The disparity between Jesus' original call and what Christians say today is striking.

Among typical Christians today, the lack of personal ownership of Jesus' mandate results in the unspoken expectation that a believer's job description might be boiled down to listening to someone preach and giving some money. In this scenario, the institutional church has taken over the work of the Great Commission: mission committees focus on "go"; "making disciples" is delegated to Christian education classes or a few hardy individuals; "baptizing" is handled in baptism classes; and "teaching them to obey" is assumed to be taken care of by the preacher or lumped in with someone else's responsibilities. Believers do not live out the Great Commission because they think that it's someone else's job.

This unwitting takeover of the personal mandate by the institutional church leaves believers unclear as to what their role is, disempowered from believing they can be world changers, and ill-prepared to attempt to do what Jesus said. The joy every believer was meant to experience—in praying for nonbelievers, seeing them come to Christ, discipling them to obey what Jesus says, watching their lives change as Christ increasingly becomes Lord of their lives, and seeing them reproduce this with others—has been stolen by the church, leaving individuals disillusioned, unchallenged, and uninterested.

The church must regain the understanding that its primary work is not to do the work of ministry, but to equip its people, the priesthood, to become workers in the harvest, living a life of rejoicing as the harvest is reaped (Eph 4:12; 1 Pet 2:9; Jn 4:36-38). At our church, we tell people that the church is Ephesians 4 for Matthew 28 to see Revelation 7: We equip our people to do the Great Commission so that all peoples can hear and worship Jesus.

THE NECESSITY OF BROAD AND FAITHFUL SOWING

The parable of the sower and the seed, found in all three Synoptics, is foundational to understanding how the kingdom grows: "Then Jesus said to them, 'Don't you understand this parable? How then will you understand any parable?'" (Mk 4:13). This astounding statement, that understanding this parable is critical to understanding any of the parables, is Jesus' invitation for disciples to go beyond a superficial reading of the sower and the seed. Their response of asking Jesus for deeper understanding is noted in each Synoptic (Mt 13:10; Mk 4:10; Lk 8:9).

Jesus' parable about the sower and the four seed-in-soil responses provides an insightful foundation for the growth of the kingdom in church planting movements and gives practical instruction to those who endeavor to start them.[10] The growth and spread of the kingdom is based on sowing the seed, that is, the proclamation of the gospel of the kingdom (Mt 13:19). It is incumbent on sowers to find ways to clearly proclaim the gospel to those who hear it and help them understand. Equipping sowers for this task in simple, understandable, and winsome ways is a critical first step not only to help a seeker become a follower of Jesus but to planting a church.

There is a second, hidden variable in the parable: whether the sower actually sows the seed. The clear emphasis in the parable is that sowers must sow the seed of the gospel faithfully. Scholars have spilled a fair amount of ink worrying about the carelessness of the farmer and his wasted seed, something Jesus does not address.[11] This is because one cannot predetermine the response of a person from the outside. Aside from the first soil, the problems with the second (rocky) and third (thorny) soils could not be seen from the surface. In much of Palestine, a layer of limestone is covered by a thin layer of soil. Seeds that are sown would spring up immediately, but because their roots had to grow sideways, these plants would wilt when the sun came up. Similarly, thorny soil looked fine from the surface, but the fibrous roots of the couch grass and bishop weed, both perennials, lurked beneath the surface waiting to choke out any other seed planted.[12]

---

[10]David Wenham, *The Parables of Jesus* (Downers Grove, IL: InterVarsity Press, 1989), 44.

[11]Wenham, *Parables of Jesus*, 42.

[12]William Barclay, *The Gospel of Matthew,* vol. 2, *Chapters 11-28,* rev. ed. (Philadelphia: Westminster, 1975), 58.

Thus, what might initially look like careless sowing was, in fact, necessary to grow the crop. The reason the farmer might not be concerned about wasting seed is because she knows that the seeds that find good soil will reproduce thirty, sixty, or one hundred times. Having done this in the past, she realizes that with such percentages, good seed stewardship required broad sowing. Every last seed must be sown.

The responsibility of the gospel sower is, as church planter and missiologist Stephen Smith observes, "to proclaim the gospel widely," rather than attempt to predetermine the type of response. One only finds good soil by broadly and frequently spreading the seeds of the gospel. Sowing sparingly or scattering only a handful of seeds might mean never finding good soil. However, sowers must keep the flip side of this truth in mind: the more negative responses that take place, the higher the probability that good soil is right around the corner.

One must not be discouraged by poor response. Whenever there is a clear presentation of the gospel, there will always be a response. The parable of the sower gives four possibilities, only one of which the farmer is ultimately seeking. The first soil is hard, and the gospel never sinks in at the level understanding. Initially, the second and third soils seem to offer a more hopeful response; however, in the end, the long term response of both types of soil is also ultimately negative: the farmer does not sow seed so he can grow stunted plants.

As Jesus' description makes clear, the rocky soil represents those who fail to count the cost of following Christ. When times get hard they fall away because the seed of the gospel is not able to penetrate the deeper parts of their heart, because Jesus is not truly Lord in their lives. While these people might believe the right things and say the right things when asked about Jesus, they ultimately desire to grow their own kingdom, not God's.

Frequently, the proclamation of the gospel results in a joyful response. This is especially the case in pioneering contexts when many jump on the bandwagon of faith. However, church planters know that this initial response is not necessarily one that will produce a return. Stephen Smith notes that unless the gospel message challenges followers to true repentance and results in costly obedience, "There will be many casualties and shallow movements that do not last."[13]

The thorny soil represents those whose hearts are not ultimately aimed at eternity. Because they do not really see themselves as servants of the master, working for an eternal return, the short-term lures of wealth and the cares of this world divert them from the pearl of great price. Only those who understand their calling as servants and are willing to pay the price to continue to follow Jesus at great cost are chosen

---

[13]Smith, "Study of the Dynamics," 14.

(Lk 9:57-62). Church planters must be clear in the articulation of these costs. Not doing so prevents these third-soil people from revealing the condition of their hearts. Church planting movements will not begin with third-soil people—they yield nothing (Mt 13:22).

Pastorally, the Gospel writers included this parable as an encouragement to sowers who might otherwise be discouraged by all the initial positive responses in their church that end up bearing no fruit. To them Jesus' word is, Don't be discouraged; this is natural. Just keep sowing. As surely as there are bad responses, if you endure, you will see a great harvest.

The significance of fourth-soil people. In contrast, the fourth soil bears great results. This is not because there is anything special about the soil. As a matter of fact, the defining quality of this soil is that it simply does not have any growth-inhibiting rocks or thorns in it. An absence of something amiss in the soil results in kingdom growth. This is why it is so important to understand the nature of the soils and their resultant effects. Stephen Robert Smith writes, "Such responses will not usher in the fullness of God's kingdom or lead to church planting movements. Only responses characterized by the good soil will usher in the kingdom of God."[14] Not understanding this point has proven deadly for the church in America, as Neil Cole laments:

> I am convinced that we have made a serious mistake by accommodating bad soil in our churches. When we see people come to Christ, then slip away, we assume a responsibility that is not ours. We would not take it on if we truly listened to this parable. We assume that we must be doing something wrong . . . and search for other ways to keep people. The results are devastating to the local church. Because we think that the number of people is a sure sign of success, we do everything we can to keep people. We try to woo people to come and keep coming. What we end up with is an audience of consumers shopping for the best "services." We cater to this sort of thinking by trying to compete with other churches with a better show. We compromise the life of the church if we keep bad soil in our membership . . . our churches are full of bad, unfruitful soil. A common refrain of pastors is that eighty percent of the work in church is done by twenty percent of the people. Reread this parable and you will understand why.[15]

This is the key to understanding the parables and the growth of the kingdom because this parable not only instructs the disciples on the initial importance of sowing seed, but tells them that of all the kingdom responses, they are to focus on the fourth-soil response. Fourth-soil people are the key to kingdom growth. Church planters must relentlessly be on the lookout for fourth-soil people, because without them, the

---

[14]Smith, "Study of the Dynamics," 16.

[15]Neil Cole, *Organic Church: Growing Faith Where Life Happens* (San Francisco: Jossey-Bass, 2005), 69-70.

harvest will not come. And they must not be discouraged when the first-, second-, or third-soil people are revealed. This also is the way the kingdom grows.

The disciples are fourth-soil people. Looking more deeply at this parable reveals that the disciples are fourth-soil people. Throughout the Gospels, a key theme is the tension between Jesus' ministry to the crowds and to the disciples. Stanley Hauerwas notes that Matthew's Gospel is constructed to draw a distinction between the crowds and the disciples.[16] Jesus issues calls for deeper commitment to himself from the crowds, but not everyone responds. Those who do, however, become his disciples. This is why the specific structure of the parable is so critical:

1. Jesus tells the parable to the crowds (Mt 13:1-8; Mk 4:1-8; Lk 8:1-8).

2. Jesus issues an invitation to discipleship: "Whoever has ears, let them hear" (Mt 13:9; Mk 4:9; Lk 8:8).

3. The disciples respond by asking him about the parable (Mt 13:10; Mk 4:10; Lk 8:9).

4. Jesus quotes Isaiah 6:9 to tell them that parables can hide the truth from the crowds: "The secrets of the kingdom of heaven [have] been given to you, but not to them" (Mt 13:11; Mk 4:11; Lk 8:10).

5. Jesus affirms that the disciples are blessed because they asked for more (Mt 13:12-17; Mk 4:10-12; Lk 8:10).

6. Jesus then explains the parable to them (Mt 13:18-23; Mk 4:13-20; Lk 8:11-15).

There is a parable within the parable at work here. Jesus' telling of the parable was sown among the crowds and ended with an invitation for listeners to move beyond simply being a part of the crowd to becoming disciples or followers. But in fact the crowds mainly represented first, second, and third soil. The disciples' response showed that they alone received the invitation-only word and responded by going deeper with Jesus. This is why Jesus says, "The knowledge of the secrets of the kingdom of heaven has been given to you, but not to them" (Mt 13:11). The disciples were the fourth soil. And, of course, in due time they became sowers themselves. They proved themselves to be the ones who bore thirty, sixty, and one hundredfold.

REPRODUCTIVE LOOPS IN THE GOSPELS AND ACTS

The amazing results of sowing and finding fourth soil are limited to one season. But taking those seeds and resowing them is even more amazing. If a farmer sowed four seeds in the first season, and one seed fell in each soil type, and then took the thirty

---

[16]Stanley Hauerwas, *Matthew*, Brazos Theological Commentary on the New Testament (Grand Rapids: Brazos, 2006), 58. Significantly, the focus of Matthew's Great Commission is "making disciples" (Mt 28:20), while Mark and Luke emphasize "preaching" (Mk 16:15; Lk 24:47).

to one hundred seeds that he reaped and resowed in the second year, by the third year his yield from those first four seeds would range from 16,880 to 62,500 seeds. This is when the mathematics move from multiplicative to exponential. This sort of reproductive loop, where disciples make other disciples, who make other disciples, generation after generation, is at the heart of a church planting movement, and it is found in numerous places in the New Testament.

It is also the heart of the personal mandate of the Great Commission (Mt 28:19-20). Jesus tells the disciples to go and make other disciples and teach them to obey "everything I have commanded you," which includes teaching these new disciples to go and make other disciples. Jesus' Great Commission assumes that faithful, fourth-soil people continue to sow seeds broadly everywhere they go. This is the New Testament pattern.

The reproductive loop of Mark 4 is also embedded in John 15, where the main goal of abiding in the vine and enduring necessary pruning is that ultimately each disciple has been "appointed to go and bear fruit—fruit that will last" (Jn 15:16). While one might assume that this fruit is simply the fruit of the Spirit (Gal 5:22-23), Jesus' words to his disciples that he has chosen and "appointed" them to "go" and "bear fruit" indicates that he is not simply speaking of transformation of character but of evangelism and mission as well.[17]

But how does that fruit last or remain? In the natural world, no fruit lasts forever. But one can always have fruit if one takes the seed from one's fruit and from it plants a new tree, which can happily be illustrated in the aphorism, "Anyone can count the number of seeds in an apple, but no one can count the number of apples in a seed." Jesus calls the disciples to bear fruit in others' lives, who will bear fruit in still others, and this is what is found in Acts.

This same sort of multiplicative return on investment is also present in the Parable of the Talents, where the man with the one talent is upbraided for not at least putting the money in the bank where it would have gained interest (Mt 25:14-30; Lk 19:11-27). In this parable, "Everyone who has will be given more and he will have an abundance. Whoever does not have, even what he has will be taken from him" (Mt 25:29). He who sowed five talents gained six back. Kingdom servants are to seek after reproductive growth in their endeavors.

The amazingly multiplicative and reproductive nature of first-century discipleship is illustrated in 2 Timothy 2:2. Jesus' second generation protégés (the Twelve) discipled Barnabas, who represented the third generation, who in turn discipled Paul

---

[17]D. A. Carson, *Jesus' Sermon on the Mount and His Confrontation with the World: An Exposition of Matthew 5-10* (Grand Rapids: Baker, 1987), 523.

(Acts 4:26-27; 11:25-26). This fourth-generation leader, Paul, tells his fifth-generation disciple, Timothy, to find reliable sixth-generation leaders who could teach others, who would then be the seventh generation of Jesus' disciples.

This is the key to the explosive growth of the New Testament church. The parable of the sower and the seeds, Jesus' foundational parable, focuses on the reproductive nature of the seed. He gets the disciples to look for reasons why this growth is not taking place, and then gives them an understanding that all disciples are workers of the harvest field. But by focusing their eyes on fourth-soil people, he gives vision and sets expectation for what is about to take place. What we know—and they didn't—was that Jesus was actually describing what they themselves would do in becoming the apostolic founders of the church. By beginning here, Jesus encourages the disciples to expect multiplicative growth, and teaches them how to begin. This pattern, which Jesus taught and practiced and which the apostles lived out, is the underlying growth dynamic of the New Testament church.

Jesus first made disciples. The Gospels tell us that immediately after returning from his confrontation with Satan in the wilderness, Jesus proclaims that the kingdom has come and begins to call disciples to himself. In his classic book *The Master Plan of Evangelism*, Robert Coleman writes, "His life was ordered by his objective. Everything he did and said was part of the whole pattern . . . that is why it is so important to observe the way Jesus maneuvered to achieve his objective. The Master disclosed God's strategy of world conquest . . . weighing every alternative and variable factor in human experience, he conceived a plan that would not fail." Coleman continues by describing the plan: "Men were his method . . . Jesus' plan was to enlist men who could bear witness to his life and carry on his work after he returned to the Father." While Jesus clearly ministered to the masses, because he had his disciples with him all the time, he effectively "staked his whole ministry on them."[18] Jesus' method for reaching Revelation 7:9 was by discipling.

Looking for persons of influence. As it turns out, Jesus has some fascinating missiological insights on this matter (Mt 10; Lk 10). In the first short-term mission trip in history, Jesus teaches his disciples, who are about to have their initial experience doing the stuff of ministry in Jesus' bodily absence, what to do. If we understand the Gospels and Acts not only as the beginning of the New Testament but as actual descriptions of the first church planting movement in history, this helps us see Matthew 10 not simply as a description of what Jesus taught his disciples, but as a pattern, process, and means for Jesus' discipleship movement to culminate at Revelation 7:9.

---

[18]Robert Coleman, *The Master Plan of Evangelism* (Grand Rapids: Revell, 1993), 17-18, 21, 25.

In Matthew 10, Jesus sends out the disciples two by two, grants them authority to drive out impure spirits and heal every disease and sickness, indicating the basic mode by which pioneering church planting would take place. Jesus not only equips the disciples attitudinally (Mt 10:16-42) with apostolic fortitude but gives them missiological strategy for starting church movements. In Luke 10, Jesus takes the next step by sending out the seventy-two likewise to continue their mission.

Note the sequence of the narrative: Before sending the disciples out on this mission, he goes through all the towns and villages and concludes that "the harvest is plentiful but the workers were few" (Mt 9:37). As a result, the disciples are told to pray for God to send out workers into his harvest field (Mt 9:38). Then, when Jesus sends the disciples out, he tells them to not take food or provisions with them (Mt 10:9-10) but instead forces them to look for a "worthy person" (Mt 10:11) or a person of peace (Lk 10:6) in the towns they're about to go. If they don't find them, there's no place to eat or sleep. Now that's focus! But who are these worthy people of peace?

> They are people of receptivity—to the person and plan of Christ;
>
> They are people of reputation, either good or bad—when things happen with them, everyone knows;
>
> They are people of relational connections who, when their lives are changed, spread the good news of Jesus and his transforming power to those around them.[19]

When they find these God-prepared people, they are told to not move around from house to house (Lk 10:7). Once you find them, stay put. Live in their house.

While there are many valuable insights recent church planters have discovered in these texts regarding the initial stages of church planting, here are the key points.

First, discerning which fields are ripe for harvest is crucial. When Jesus says that the harvest is plentiful and the workers are few (Mt 9:38), he does not indicate that all fields are ripe for harvest, but that there are always ripe fields. The way for the disciples to find the ripe fields is to look for the people of influence. And if no one receives them, they are to shake the dust off their feet (Mt 10:14) and move on, assuming that this is not a ripe field.

Second, discipleship of the person of influence is the key. When the disciples find the person of influence, why does Jesus instruct them to stop? It's so that the person of influence they found they can be discipled and trained. This is the God-ordained worker for the harvest field. God prepares a harvest field by priming church planters from within that field to be receptive to the gospel and to become influencers for the gospel. The disciples are looking for first dominoes to fall and create momentum for the new church planting movement in the towns they are visiting.

---

[19]Cole, *Organic Church*, 182.

As we might expect, we can see many such first dominoes in the New Testament, each of whom had a distinct reputation, receptivity to the gospel, and relational connections which were harnessed for the first gospel movements in history:

- Matthew, who holds a Jesus party for the sinners in his relational orbit (Mt 9)

- The woman at the well, who shares with everyone in her village such that "many of the Samaritans from that town believed in him because of the woman's testimony" (Jn 4:39)

- The Ethiopian eunuch, whose baptism is believed by Ethiopians to be the formation of the church which still exists to this day (Acts 8)

- Cornelius the centurion, whose friends experienced the coming of the Holy Spirit at their initial gathering (Acts 10)

- Lydia, a businesswoman from Asia whose household became the first believers in Philippi (Acts 16)

Third, this is evangelism by multiplication, not addition. By taking this approach, Jesus teaches the disciples to lead and disciple households of new believers, not simply individuals. In each of these cases—and there are many more in the Gospels and Acts—the persons of influence and either their households or those within their relational networks become Jesus followers. And this results in an approach that leads to church multiplication movements.[20]

Finally, because these new groups of believers are led by someone they know, churches can start immediately. The discipling of these individuals, who have standing in their communities prior to being saved, is probably what allowed churches to be formed in Lystra and Derbe by the apostle Paul in less than three weeks.

Jesus teaches the disciples to find fourth-soil people because once they are discipled, they will continue to share the gospel; this is the key to finding a ripe field. Thus the discipler's practical tool for working apostolically with the Holy Spirit today is to find persons of influence who will be the tomorrow's church planting disciplers. Jesus taught his disciples to do what he did: sow broadly, then find and disciple fourth-soil people and teach them to do the same.

---

[20]On multiplication movements, see Roland Allen, *The Spontaneous Expansion of the Church and the Causes Which Hinder It* (Eugene, OR: Wipf and Stock, 1962); Ralph W. Neighbour, *Where Do We Go From Here? A Guidebook for the Cell Group Church* (Houston: Touch, 1990); David Garrison, *Church Planting Movements: How God Is Redeeming a Lost World* (Midlothian, VA: WIGTake Resources, 2004). This approach is resulting in historic numbers of multiplying movements in the Muslim World, as seen in David Garrison's *Wind in the House of Islam: How God is Drawing Muslims Around the World to Faith in Jesus Christ* (Midlothian, VA: WIGTake Resources, 2014). Currently, movement thinking is championed in the US by Exponential (www.exponential.org) and globally by NoPlaceLeft (www.noplaceleft.net).

A fascinating example of this occurs in Acts 16. Paul has the desire to enter the province of Asia, and later Bithynia, but is hemmed in by the Holy Spirit, who re-routes Paul by giving him a dream of a man inviting him to Macedonia. Paul responds at once, concluding that God was calling them there. When Paul arrives in Philippi, the main city of Macedonia, he immediately comes upon Lydia, who not coincidentally was from Thyatira (of the province of Asia!). Her response and that of her household show her to be a person of influence—and the first church of Philippi was planted.

Paul continues to stay in the city, and by being arrested and beaten, meets the Philippian jailer, whose household also comes to faith through Paul and Silas's witness. After they are baptized, Paul then leaves Philippi, concluding that his work in the city is complete: he had met the God-ordained man who appeared in his dream, led his household to faith, and begun a church there. Twelve years later, Paul notes that the church which started in these homes had been partners in the gospel from the first day until now (Phil 1:15).

Jesus teaches his disciples to pray for, find, disciple, and empower fourth-soil people. This is what Paul does in his missionary journey. These are the cornerstones of the churches which are planted in the New Testament.

Paul and his disciples. While it is clear that Jesus chose disciple making as his primary strategy, one might not notice that this was Paul's as well. His missionary journeys are focused not just on evangelism but in the discipling and equipping of church leaders. For example, while Paul's initial visit to Lystra was quite short (Acts 14:8-20), it evidently led to the formation of a church. He visits this church on his return to Antioch and appoints elders (Acts 14:21-23), and visits again two years later on his way from Syria to the province of Asia (Acts 16:1-3). At this point, he recruits Timothy as a coworker so he can continue to train him in the work of the gospel.

Paul takes those who prove themselves faithful in the local church along with him in order to disciple them further in the work of a church planter. This is because a critical component of exercising leadership in the local congregation is doing the work of an evangelist. Eckhard Schnabel writes, "The leaders of the congregations are called upon to proclaim the gospel, evidently before people who have not yet heard the message of Jesus Christ. The congregations are not to wait for traveling missionaries who pass through. Rather, they are to make sure that people hear the gospel."[21] Paul chooses persons of influence who have proven themselves as fourth soil. This is critical to his strategy.

---

[21]Eckhard J. Schnabel, *Paul the Missionary: Realities, Strategies, and Methods* (Downers Grove, IL: IVP Academic, 2008), 247.

While it does not appear that Paul chose twelve disciples for a set period of time like Jesus did, it is clear that he intentionally chose fourth-soil people from each city. For example, in the middle of Paul's second missionary journey (Acts 16:1–18:22), Paul goes from Lystra to Derbe, Phyrgia, and Galatia, before moving on to Philippi, Thessalonica, Berea, Athens, and Corinth. In recounting Paul's third journey, some three years later, Luke parenthetically describes Paul's traveling companions: Timothy from Lystra and Erastus from Corinth were sent ahead to Macedonia, while Gaius from Derbe and Aristarchus from Thessalonica were still with him (Acts 19:22, 29). In addition, Sopater from Berea, Secundus from Thessalonica, and Tychicus and Trophimus from Ephesus were also with Paul (Acts 20:4). It appears that Paul chose men from seven of the nine cities he visited during his second journey. After they had established themselves as fourth-soil people, Paul took them with him for additional training and discipling.

The scope of Paul's discipling is amazing.[22] Of the approximately one hundred names connected with Paul in Acts and the Pauline letters, thirty-eight are co-workers of the apostle and eight of these are women. As a result, when he is subsequently jailed, Paul has a standing group of coworkers who can continue the work of the ministry: Timothy spreads the gospel through Asia; Titus does work in Illyricum (2 Tim. 4:10) and Crete (Titus 1:4-5); and Epaphras works in Colossae, Hierapolis, and Laodicea.

Alex and Michelle. This biblical pattern of sowing seeds broadly, finding persons of influence, and then discipling them so multiplication takes place is meant for today too.

Alex and Michelle, a Mandarin-speaking Chinese couple who had been in the United States for a number of years, arrived at our church shortly after it was planted in 2003. Though they had been Christians for a number of years, their reason for coming seemed pedestrian: we were closer to their home and our services started later!

However, the Holy Spirit began to prompt me to invite Alex into a discipling relationship. When he said yes, I began to meet him at his home, helping him to begin to read the Bible, pray, and reach out to those in his circle of relationships who didn't know Jesus. Over the next year, he and Michelle (who was discipled by my wife, Evelyn) began to see nearly everyone on their prayer lists come to faith. We'd found persons of influence! As we began to teach them principles of finding other persons of influence, praying, evangelizing, and discipling, their fruit began to grow.

Michelle led Lillian, the mother of one of her daughter's classmates, to Christ and then began to disciple her. In time, Lillian led Rachel to faith, who then led Cynthia

---

[22]Schnabel, *Paul the Missionary*, 249-54.

to faith. Cynthia was a mainland Chinese student studying English, so they started a new Bible study focusing on these students, and this is how Tao and Kitty then came to faith.

Alex met Oscar, who was serving on the board of a Chinese cultural club with him. Through friendship with Oscar, they met Oscar's wife Jennifer. When Michelle started an exercise class for her friends, Jennifer jumped in, and over the next year, she was eventually saved and baptized. As Jennifer began to grow in her faith, she began to get a heart for her neighbors. She began a prayer list of her neighbors and began to pray for healing for those on her street. She is now leading a small group of Chinese on her street who are studying the Bible (about half of whom are Christians).

Alex and Michelle eventually started a Mandarin-speaking church whose members have led friends and relatives to faith not only in Los Angeles, but in Asia as well. Alex and Michelle are apostolic, bivocational church planters who've learned how to work with the Holy Spirit in seeing the Great Commission take place: they look for persons of influence, teach them to lead others to faith and disciple them to do the same. And they've planted a church this way.

TAKING IT TO THE STREETS: THE FOUR FIELDS

One framework which church planters have found helpful in distinguishing between general principles and practical tools is called the Four Fields (see figure 2). It was developed by missionaries Nathan and Kari Shank, who actually learned it from a farmer they were working with in India.[23] It's based on understanding that in a church planting process, there are five main stages (or fields) of development, no matter the type or location of the church plant. Any church planter will encounter these fields (and, as a church or church movement grows, will encounter multiple fields simultaneously). The Four Fields simply help us understand each stage so that we can focus on the most critical question of all: What is the Holy Spirit-led tool for this field?

Field one is an empty field, where there is no gospel witness and where the church planter is just beginning. Here the key is developing an entry plan: How to reach people in this city (or people group) for the gospel. Who do I start with? How do I start a conversation? What tools will we develop—and then teach those who become new believers—to find out whom God is leading us to?

Field two is a seeded field, where I now am ready to share the gospel. Here the key is developing a gospel plan. How do I share the gospel clearly and simply, in a

---

[23]"The Four Fields of Kingdom Growth," *Church Planting Movements*, August 17, 2011, www.churchplanting movements.com/index.php?option=com_content&view=article&id=126:the-four-fields-of-kingdom -growth&catid=36:the-big-picture&Itemid=78.

manner that can be understood by the people I am trying to reach? This is where contextualization of the gospel and message are crucial. For the gospel to be able to be shared widely by the fourth-soil people of influence, the gospel must be simple, transferable, reproducible, and understandable (both in the content that is shared as well as the means by which it is shared). For example, one cannot expect a person without appropriate technology to share the gospel using *The Jesus Film*. Ultimately, this turns on developing a contextualized gospel tool which can be used by a brand-new believer as she shares her story with her non-Christian friends.

Field three is a growing field, where some have made initial responses to the gospel. Here the key is developing a discipleship plan. How do I begin to disciple the new believers so that they can grow into the fourth-soil church planters they are called to be? Practitioners have learned some important things along the way: Teach new believers the Great Commission (Mt 28:18-20), so that the key pieces of DNA are established from the beginning:

- Everyone is called to go and share the good news with others.

- Each of us is a disciple who disciples others.

- Baptism is an important marker for Christian identity.

- Obedience to the words of Jesus is the key to being a disciple.

The first lesson is that they must obey the Holy Spirit as revealed in the word of God. This is usually done by using some sort of simple, reproducible, inductive Bible study like a Discovery Bible Study, which is not dependent on a mature Christian to lead.[24] Here the focus is on obedience, not knowledge: Disciple in groups rather than one-on-one, so that disciples can learn from each other. This is key in developing indigenous discipling movements. Focus your time together in three equal segments of caring for one another, studying the Word, and practicing new skills or equipping each other to lead others. This is called the Three Thirds process.[25]

Crucially, we must disciple new believers in how to disciple others. When I sit down with brand-new Christians, I go through the Great Commission and explain how this is what a Christian is. I then ask them to take an index card and write down the names of non-Christians that they think need to know who Jesus is. After this I begin to dream with them about what it might be like to see these friends and family members follow Christ, and I tell them I am committed to discipling them in how to share their faith and baptize and disciple their friends, because this is what Christians do.

---

[24]International Project, "Discovery Bible Resources (DBS)," accessed June 8, 2018, www.internationalproject.org/discovery-bible-study/.

[25]T4T Global Missions, "Three Thirds Process," accessed June 8, 2018, www.t4tglobalmissions.org/the-three-thirds-process.

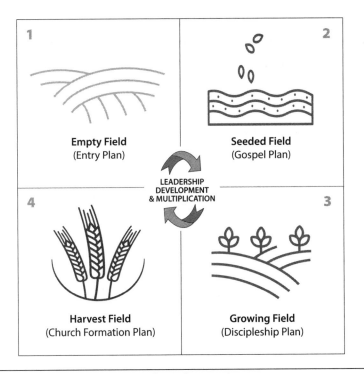

Figure 2. The four fields of kingdom growth (Mark 4:26-29)

Field four is a harvest field, where multiple groups of disciples are now meeting. Here the key is developing a church formation plan. How do I form a church and what is its definition? Once discipleship has been established the focus can now shift to the formation of churches. The definition and marks of church health based on passages like Acts 2:42-47 can be helpful.

At the center is the development and multiplication of leaders, where churches have been formed. Here the key is developing a leadership formation and multiplication plan. How do I grow and multiply leaders? Leaders' maturity is based on their hunger, responsiveness, obedience, and fruit, not their knowledge.

The way one answers each of these questions in one's context is the key to developing a church planting plan.

As a church planter, before you launch into the twenty-first-century church planting methodologies of budgets, launch teams, and preview services, start—and ground yourself—at the very beginning. Since Jesus was the first church planter and his aim was to start a missional movement that would result in Revelation 7:9, then we who've been handed the baton can find not only nuggets of inspiration but a baseline of missiological insight into how to find those whom God has prepared, lead them to faith, disciple them, and equip them to plant churches that plant other churches.

What we've looked at is not only the story of the emergence of the church but something that is meant to be a present reality for those of us who've been handed that baton. So it's also the key to our future. Let's plant with his beginning in mind!

DISCUSSION QUESTIONS

1. What would you expect the typical attender of your church plant to do in terms of sharing their faith and discipling others? What does that reveal about the DNA of your church?

2. Which of the kingdom parables regarding workers in the kingdom resonates with you and your situation and why?

3. How is God calling you to be a fourth-soil Christian? What kinds of attitudinal or behavioral changes might this entail?

4. What would the continuous sowing of seed look like in your life?

5. Think of a non-Christian or a new believer in your life. What might it look like to help them grasp that the Great Commission (Mt 28:18-20) is meant as a job description for them? What might it look like to equip them to go, make disciples, baptize, and teach others to do the same?

PART 2

HOW DO WE CULTIVATE A MISSIONAL SPIRITUALITY?

THE FORMATION OF A CHURCH PLANTER

AFTER JESUS SPOKE TO THE WOMAN AT THE WELL, he said something interesting to his disciples: "I have food to eat that you know nothing about" (Jn 4:32). What Jesus meant was that leading this Samaritan woman to trust in himself as the Messiah was like a deeply satisfying meal. To his clueless disciples who wondered if someone brought him a to-go order, Jesus had to explain what he meant: "My food is to do the will of him who sent me and to finish his work" (Jn 4:34). The Son of God was nourished and sustained by this interaction with the woman who became one of the first evangelists in the New Testament.

Missional spirituality is not about ruining a perfectly good word like spirituality by cramming the word *missional* in front of it. Rather, it is about seeing a deep and abiding connection between being sent to do God's will and being nourished and strengthened by the power of God. Many of us whose ministry was reared in Christendom "know nothing about" this food, for it is an acquired taste for a particular kind of meal that comes from interacting with and loving a post-Christian world. Rather than separating the sacred and the secular or divorcing our devotional life from mission, a missional spirituality strengthens God's people to embrace their calling as sent ones.

This section will look at ways in which the planter, the leadership team, and the whole congregation can enter into a missional spirituality that fills us just as it filled Jesus. The life of Jesus flows from the vine to the branches to the fruit, radiating outward in impact.

4

HOW CAN I SURVIVE, THEN THRIVE, IN THE MIDST OF THE STORM?

MISSIONAL SPIRITUALITY FOR CHURCH PLANTERS

TIM MOREY

THREE FAMILIES IN TWO MONTHS. In his mind's eye James looked around at his barely one-year-old congregation. People would feel this departure. One family leaving is sad, two makes people stop and take notice, but three? James couldn't help feeling like the remaining families would start to wonder if these people knew something they didn't: Should we all be getting out? Is this ship sinking? Is there something wrong with James or his leadership?

Ah, that last question. Along with James's grief over these departures, that last question burrows deep enough to reach another layer of fresh, more tender pain: Are they right? Is there something wrong with me or my leadership? Do I have what it takes to plant this church? Am I capable of navigating the complexity that comes with shepherding these people and reaching the lost?

Other fears surface: How long can I keep this going? If many more people leave, we won't be financially sustainable. How long can I keep putting on a Sunday smile when I'm riddled with my own doubts about myself and this church, and feeling so rejected on top of that? A painfully honest thought, long lurking in the background, makes its way to the front of James' mind: I feel like a fraud.

As his doubts and fears swirl, James allows himself a rare moment of honest introspection. His sleep was a mess. Exhausted as he was, his worries would wake him in the early morning and not allow him to fall

I am the vine; you are the branches. If you abide in me and I in you, you will bear much fruit; apart from me you can do nothing.

JOHN 15:5

The question is not: how many people take you seriously? How much are you going to accomplish? Can you show some results? But: are you in love with Jesus?

HENRI NOUWEN

back to sleep. Time with God was almost nonexistent. The bad sleep was part of it, but if he was really honest, James knew it was more than that. Being still before God forced him to feel the full weight of his fear, his doubts, his growing self-loathing. Most days it was just too painful and tiring for him to go there.

And he knew he was becoming increasingly critical and sharp with his family. Yesterday with his son, what should have been a mild correction came out as a too harsh, too angry rebuke. He could see in his wife's face that his reaction was way out of proportion to his son's offense. He knew it too but hadn't yet been able to bring himself to apologize. He thought about how preoccupied he was when at home, and how he was probably spending more time sulking in front of the television than enjoying his kids. Connecting with his neighbors was increasingly awkward and felt like yet another desperate attempt to get people to come to church.

James's thoughts went to his typical work day. Emails went unanswered because he didn't want to deal with them. Leading and hosting his missional community had become a joyless chore and was yet another reminder that he had failed to raise up another leader. And under the surface there was a low-grade anger at his congregation—or some of them at least—for not being better at reaching out, for not serving more, for not being more affirming of his gifts, for being so screwed up in so many ways. Multiple times during a day, James would find himself daydreaming about leading some other more successful, more appreciative church, or of working in another field altogether. And then there were the temptations. Areas that he thought were long since conquered were back, sometimes with almost irresistible strength.

For the first time, James allowed himself to see it—the problems in this church plant were real, but the problems in himself might be his most serious problem.

Here is the issue. What undermines church planters, more often than not, is not underdeveloped skills in preaching or vision casting. It isn't a lack of motivation or passion for the kingdom of God. No, it is a spiritual life that is not sufficiently robust to deal with the challenges that church planting brings.

Maybe it has to do with the personality types of those who are drawn to church planting. By temperament, most planters are activists, not monks, and would rather be doing than sitting, even if that means sitting in God's presence. Or maybe it's the never-ending list of tasks the planter has before them (and truly, it is never-ending). Maybe it is their love for lost people or desire to see their people grow as disciples that keeps planters perpetually on the go. Or on a less healthy level, perhaps it is the desire to be seen as a success, however one defines that. Whatever the reason, many planters struggle to take time to abide in the presence of Jesus and find refreshment for their souls.

For many, a life of sitting in the presence of Jesus is a challenge. Yet this, I would argue, is the single most important work a church planter can engage in.

FRUITFUL MISSION LEADERS

It is possible to be incredibly busy yet entirely unfruitful. Jesus said as much to his disciples, and to every mission-driven disciple that would follow the original twelve. His words are familiar, so read them slowly:

> I am the true vine, and my Father is the gardener. He cuts off every branch in me that bears no fruit, while every branch that does bear fruit he prunes so that it will be even more fruitful. You are already clean because of the word I have spoken to you. Remain in me, as I also remain in you. No branch can bear fruit by itself; it must remain in the vine. Neither can you bear fruit unless you remain in me. I am the vine; you are the branches. If you remain in me and I in you, you will bear much fruit; apart from me you can do nothing. This is to my Father's glory, that you bear much fruit, showing yourselves to be my disciples. . . . You did not choose me, but I chose you and appointed you so that you might go and bear fruit—fruit that will last—and so that whatever you ask in my name the Father will give you. (Jn 15:1-5, 8, 16)

Note that Jesus uses the words *fruit* or *fruitful* nine times in these few verses. The longing of our hearts as church planters—to lead lives that bear lasting fruit—is the longing of Jesus' heart as well. When our lives are fruitful, Jesus says, it brings glory to the Father and it shows that we really are his disciples. Or as we like to say in Fuller's church planting program, "Healthy roots lead to lasting fruit."

How does this fruitful life come about? Jesus tells us that two indispensable factors contribute to our growth in fruitfulness.

The first is the Father's pruning. Every branch that does not bear fruit will be "cleared off" (was Jesus looking at Judas when he said this?), and every branch that does bear fruit will be pruned or "cleaned up" so that it might be even more fruitful.[1] This pruning, commentators agree, comes primarily in the form of difficulties.

In my denomination, the Evangelical Covenant Church, the first words a new church planter hears in our training are "You will be broken." Adversity in church planting is a given. We will find ourselves taxed spiritually, emotionally, and physically—over and over again. We will have great joys but also great heartbreaks. We will enjoy deep camaraderie with cherished leaders, but also experience desertions and betrayals. This adversity, if we fail to recognize it for what it is, has the potential to destroy us.

---

[1]Lesslie Newbigin, quoted in Bruce Milne, *The Message of John,* The Bible Speaks Today (Downers Grove, IL: InterVarsity Press, 1993), 219.

Such pruning, we must remind ourselves, comes not because the Father is displeased with us, but precisely because we *are* fruitful, and he wants us to be even *more* fruitful. The Father's desire and our desire are in alignment: that we bear much fruit, to his glory, and that the fruit we bear would last (Jn 15:8, 16). This means that every faithful church planter will experience pruning—you might even say this is a given. And you might also say this is a gift. If we take Jesus at his word, we must acknowledge that the fruitful ministry we desire *cannot* come without the pain of being pruned.

The second factor in our fruitfulness is time with Jesus. Unlike the Father's pruning, this second factor is not a given. We have to *choose* it. And Jesus is blunt: if we do not abide in him we will not bear fruit. In saying this, Jesus is not being harsh. A branch which is no longer connected to the vine is simply incapable of bearing fruit. Similarly, apart from him, we can do nothing.

I should pause here to point out that when I use the word *fruitful*, I do not mean it as a euphemism for growing a big church. Far too often we equate size with success, when I believe we would do better to pursue faithfulness, and with that, rejoice in fruit appropriate to our particular call. As Paul reminds us, we can plant and water but only God can make things grow (1 Cor 3:5-9). How can we say that the planter who leads a church of forty vibrant, missional disciples in an incredibly challenging context is less fruitful than the one who leads a church of four hundred, or four thousand, in a completely different context? Each ministry, minister, and mission field is different. Size and fruitfulness are not the same.

PUT YOUR OWN FORMATION FIRST

My wife and I have a corny running joke when we fly. During the part of the safety instructions when the flight attendant tells parents that in case of an emergency they are to put their own oxygen mask on before putting a mask on their child, my wife can't help but subtly shake her head no, and I gently poke her in the ribs. The intent of the instruction is clear, much as it feels counterintuitive to a loving parent. If the parent passes out from lack of oxygen, they will be of no use to their child. In this circumstance, to care for oneself first is not an act of selfishness but an act of love.

The same might be said for us as pastors. If we are not first nourishing ourselves in Christ, we will be of no use to those we lead. Consequently, I would propose that our first and greatest vocation as church planters is to be men and women who are deeply connected to Jesus. A healthy, spiritually growing self is the greatest gift we can give to our churches and communities. As Parker Palmer says, proper self-care is "simply good stewardship of the only gift I have, the gift I was put on earth to offer to others."[2]

---

[2]Quoted in Peter Scazzero, *The Emotionally Healthy Leader: How Transforming Your Inner Life Will Deeply Transform Your Church, Team, and the World* (Grand Rapids: Zondervan, 2015), 51.

Consider why this is the case. Personal spiritual vibrancy is:

- Vital to pastoral health and longevity. When we think about our health, as well as that of our family if married or close friendships if single, nothing can be more important than staying closely connected to Jesus.

- Vital to the health of our church. While being healthy as a pastor does not automatically mean you will have a healthy church, being an unhealthy pastor almost always means you will have an unhealthy church.

- Vital to mission. In an increasingly post-Christian world, I am convinced that our best apologetic is not a well-reasoned argument but an embodied apologetic—a community of people who increasingly look like Jesus.[3] The pastor who desires to live missionally must be spiritually formed.

"But I'm so busy—I don't have much time to give to my own formation," we say. This sentiment is shared by all those in pastoral ministry, and maybe especially by church planters.

John Stott, unquestionably one of the most productive and influential Christian leaders in the twentieth century, was strategic and intentional in his self-care. His practice was an hour of solitude with Jesus daily, a three-hour period weekly, a full day once a month, and a week-long retreat once a year (and he quipped that his prolific writing was made possible by his daily "Horizontal Half Hour"—his daily post-lunch nap).[4] Similarly, it is said of Martin Luther that he prayed for two hours every day, except for very busy days, when he needed to pray for three hours if he hoped to get it all done.

While I don't expect to ever come near the level of a Stott or a Luther, I have found the principle they put forward to be true. When I take time to remain connected to Jesus—even time I don't feel I have—somehow it seems my work time multiplies like so many loaves and fishes. Sermons come together faster, meetings are more efficient, my decision making is more decisive and insightful, the counsel I give is wiser and clearer.

Of course, devoting time to our spiritual formation comes at a cost. Practically speaking, I find in my own ministry that putting my own formation first means that sometimes people and tasks have to wait. Because (barring crises) I will not do ministry more than three nights in a given week, for example, it is not uncommon for me to have to tell a person with only evening availability, "I would love to meet,

---

[3]For more on this theme, see Tim Morey, *Embodying Our Faith: Becoming a Living, Sharing, Practicing Church* (Downers Grove, IL: InterVarsity Press, 2009).

[4]Roger Steer, *Basic Christian: The Inside Story of John Stott* (Downers Grove, IL: InterVarsity Press, 2009), 15. We might also note that Stott made much use of his singleness in keeping a schedule with such healthy rhythms of rest.

but my slots are full this week. How is the week after next?" Or I might have to look at a given outreach I want to start and conclude that it would require more energy than I currently have. It might need to wait until other tasks are no longer on my plate, or better yet, until others step up to take the lead.

But costly as investing in my own formation is, the alternative is even more costly. Physical, emotional, and spiritual exhaustion, burnout, and poor health are serious issues. Even serious moral failures are often just reflections of poor self-care, compounded over time until a leader finally breaks under the weight, seeking relief in a sexual affair, substance abuse, or more acceptable vices like gluttony or shopping. Moral failure is often just burnout in disguise, left untreated for too long.

Even if I manage to avoid burnout, I have to ask, what kind of husband and father are my family getting? Or as a single person, what kind of friend are those closest to me getting? Am I perpetually stressed and cranky? Will my kids grow up loving the church or resenting her for what the work did to their dad? And for my own quality of life—am I able to minister from a place of deep joy and experience the Father's smile, or as Eugene Peterson memorably put it, has my ministry been reduced to merely "running this damn church"?[5]

As tempting as it can be to do it all and to do it now, I'm learning that this is not the best way to serve my church or my family, or to steward my long-term ministry viability.

THE CHURCH PLANTER'S RULE OF LIFE:
FIVE ESSENTIAL SPIRITUAL DISCIPLINES

Peter Scazzero, a lifelong New Yorker, sees a powerful parallel between building a leader's spiritual life and building a skyscraper. For a foundation to carry the enormous weight of a seventy-five or one-hundred story skyscraper, builders have to reinforce it with foundation anchors called "piles." These piles are made from steel or concrete and must be driven into the ground until they penetrate the solid rock beneath. For the tallest buildings, piles have to be driven as deep as *twenty-five stories* underground. Nothing less will be able to support the building's weight and keep it strong and stable.

His point: you have to build down before you can build up.[6]

Starting a church from scratch is akin to building a skyscraper. The weight it puts on a planter's soul, mind, body, and relationships is acute. If we are not committed to building down, we will certainly not be able to build up. Similarly, a tree needs deep roots if it is to withstand the storms without toppling over.

---

[5]Eugene Peterson, *The Pastor: A Memoir* (Grand Rapids: Eerdmans, 2011), 145.
[6]Scazzero, *Emotionally Healthy Leader*, 47-48.

In this section I want to propose five spiritual disciplines that, in my personal experience and my work with other church planters, I have come to believe are indispensable for a church planter.

What is a spiritual discipline? At its core, it is simply a means of being with Jesus—a way of abiding in the vine. The disciplines create space for prayer. As such, Dallas Willard reminds us that there are essentially a limitless number of disciplines, so what you find here is far from an exhaustive list.[7] No doubt you will need to employ some additional disciplines that are uniquely suited to how God has made you, and the ones listed here will need to be customized to fit who you are and your particular season of life. But these disciplines, in my observation, form a reliable assortment of "piles"—areas where we might begin to build down in order to build up.

Silence and solitude. "Without solitude," Henri Nouwen says, "it is nearly impossible to live a spiritual life." Similarly, Dallas Willard regards solitude (along with meditation on Scripture and fasting) as one of the three most important spiritual disciplines for the Christian leader, and Peter Scazzero considers solitude to be indispensable for any Christian leader aspiring to be healthy.[8]

It is clear from Jesus' example that he regarded solitary times with the Father as crucial, as the practice of getting away for quiet prayer is one his most frequent activities recorded by the Gospel writers. Mark 1:35 is representative of his pattern: "Very early in the morning, while it was still dark, Jesus got up, left the house and went off to a solitary place, where he prayed."

This episode is singularly instructive for us as pastors. It occurs after a day of ministry that lasted late into the evening. His disciples are looking for Jesus because the crowd is looking for Jesus. It appears they are enjoying their first taste of success, ready to build on the previous day's gains. But Jesus has sought out the Father and centered himself in his Father's will. He has clarity and is empowered to do good. So he and the disciples move on, ministering throughout Galilee.

The pull of the crowd is a near constant theme in the ministry of Jesus, as it is in yours and mine. Where do we find the strength of will and the clarity of purpose to do the will of the Father rather than cater to the whims of those we would lead? Answer: We find it in solitude, learning to listen to the Father's voice.

During critical moments in his life and ministry, we see Jesus making space to pursue solitary time with the Father. Before choosing the Twelve, Luke tells us that "Jesus went out to a mountainside to pray, and spent the night praying to God"

---

[7]Dallas Willard, *Spirit of the Disciplines: Understanding How God Changes Lives* (New York: HarperCollins, 1988), 156-57.

[8]Scazzero, *Emotionally Healthy Leader*, 40.

(Lk 6:12). After a busy time of ministry, then receiving the news that his cousin John the Baptizer had been murdered, Jesus tells his disciples, "Come with me by yourselves to a quiet place and get some rest" (Mk 6:31). And again, when the desire of the crowds threatened to steer him off course, Jesus deliberately withdraws "to a mountain by himself" (Jn 6:14-16). And the transfiguration, which strengthened Jesus for the coming cross, occurred when "he took Peter, John and James with him and went up onto a mountain to pray" (Lk 9:28).

What is the pattern we see in Jesus? He practiced silence and solitude before, during, and after times of ministry. In other words, it was constant. Solitude was part of Jesus' preparation for ministry and also part of his recovery time after ministry. And what did he gain? Jesus found strength, guidance, comfort, power for ministry, solace, rest. You and I will certainly find the same in our regular practice of solitude and silence.

Why is the discipline of silence and solitude so crucial for leaders, and particularly for the church planter? As noted above and experienced by all, church planting is hard. What we may not be immediately cognizant of, though, is that the most difficult challenges church planters face are not external but internal. The external challenges are difficult, yes, but far more taxing are our own internal responses to these challenges.

What happens *in me* when a beloved family leaves the church? What happens *in me* when it looks like the church may not have enough money to pay me? What happens *in me* when a Sunday service is poorly attended, when I can't seem to convince congregants to care about evangelism, when a key leader lets me down, when my spouse says he or she is getting worn out, when I find myself coming under caustic criticism, when we can't seem to find someone to fill a desperately needed leadership role?

Church planting has a unique ability to surface our insecurities, fears, weak places, and immaturities. Silence and solitude form a helpful counterweight to this, as they are unique among the spiritual disciplines in their capacity to force us to deal with our junk. It is for this reason that Nouwen referred to solitude as the "furnace of transformation."[9] In silence, apart from the distractions and protections afforded us by our lives of constant stimulation, we have to deal with who we are. That is why so many of us cannot stand being in a quiet house and need the background noise of the television or radio. In silence God shows us who we are.[10]

---

[9]Henri Nouwen, *The Way of the Heart: Desert Spirituality and Contemporary Ministry* (New York: HarperCollins, 2003), 20.

[10]For this reason, many find that they need to ease into the discipline of solitude.

Jesus longs to take us to that place. He does so not to harass and harangue us, but to show us his love—to burn away those places in us that are sinful and to shape the places that are yet unformed. God's goal is not just to bring us to heaven when we die but to see us transformed—"conformed to the image of his Son" (Rom 8:29). If we are to lead our people to that place, then we must be led to that place as well. And silence and solitude are a crucial part of that journey.

How do we practice silence and solitude? While this is one of the most challenging practices because of the work God does in us there, it is also among the simplest to practice.

In solitude, we withdraw to a place where we can be alone and be quiet. We remove ourselves from all stimuli—music, media, other people, our to-do list. Once there, we pray, we meditate on Scripture, perhaps we journal, or nap, or go for a run. Whatever we do in this space, the crucial ingredient is that we do it with Jesus, in conscious awareness of his presence.

If solitude is going to be a regular, ongoing practice for us, it is good to think about it in terms of our regular rhythms. In my practice of this discipline over the last fifteen years, I have tried to pursue solitude on a daily, monthly, and annual basis.

Daily, I find that my best time for solitude is in the early morning, before my family is up and about. Armed with a cup of coffee and the presence of the Holy Spirit, the fifteen to forty-five minutes I get at my kitchen table are a daily refuge. It's become like my food, where if I miss a day, it feels like I've missed a meal.

Once a month, I take a half (or sometimes a full) day of solitude. I find I have to plan for this or it doesn't happen. So on the first day of every month a reminder pops up on my calendar to schedule my solitude day. I look at the next four weeks and figure out which will be the best week for me to miss a day of work and I mark it on my calendar as an appointment.

Most recommend that when we can, we conduct this practice in nature. Go to the park, the beach, the mountains, the desert, or an outside patio or garden, as your circumstances allow. When weather or proximity doesn't afford us the opportunity to be outdoors, a place like a library or a quiet coffee shop will do. Wherever we go, the idea is to get away from our normal surroundings, and from the noise and distractions that provide the soundtrack for our busy lives.

In my solitude times, I head out with a beach chair and a large thermos of coffee to one of several especially beautiful, quiet outdoor spaces that are relatively close to where I live. I generally bring just my Bible and a journal. No other books, no headphones, and definitely no computer or phone (I can't keep from checking my emails if my phone is by me). I avoid making my reading for the day anything that

I will be teaching on soon, or my devotional time quickly becomes outlining passages and jotting down sermon notes. Frequently I find myself drawn to the pastoral epistles on these days, as Paul's counsel to his young protégés so often corresponds to situations where God needs to speak to me. I'll often read through all three epistles or choose one and read through it in several different translations. I intentionally try to read slowly, stopping to journal new insights or areas where I sense God is speaking to me. As I drive to and from my location, I listen to worship music in the car, or to classical music, or listen to my text for the day in my Bible app.[11]

My aim is to immerse myself in the presence of the Trinity. I used to go into these days looking to receive an answer to a specific question or develop a certain area, but increasingly I'm coming just to *be*, and to receive whatever the Father might have for me that day.

After time soaking in Scripture, I often go for a run, as I've found running to be a very conducive place for me to pray. As I do, I turn over in my mind the bits of Scripture that stood out to me that morning, asking the Spirit to teach me. Or other days, I find I'm tired and that my body is telling me I need rest. So I'll lie down and take a nap, still in the presence of Jesus, asking him to give me the rest my body needs, and to speak to me even as I sleep. On several occasions, I've gotten a massage as part of a time of solitude, all the while conversing with Jesus about bits of Scripture or giving God thanks for the restorative work the masseuse is doing for my body.

Many people like to combine fasting with solitude, but I prefer to conclude my solitude with a lunch I really enjoy, while I read or watch something for pleasure. This practice, which Richard Foster calls the "discipline of celebration," is simply doing something nice for yourself, with and in the presence of God, as a reminder of God's love for you.[12]

Annually, I try to get away for thirty hours or so for an extended time of solitude and silence. (I say "try" as I find this has become more difficult since having children. May God give us grace to adapt our practices, guilt-free, in each new season of life.) I am blessed to have a Christian camp several hours from my home which allows pastors to stay there for free during non-peak times (you will find many camps will do this if asked). My time there looks much the same as my monthly solitude, only longer.

Meditation on Scripture. One of the most frequently appearing verbs in the Psalms is the Hebrew *hagah*, which most English Bibles translate "meditate." Beginning with Psalm 1, we find that this practice is foundational to spiritual health,

---

[11]The YouVersion Bible app has free audio versions of the NIV, ESV, NLT, *The Message*, and more.
[12]Richard Foster, *Celebration of Discipline: The Path to Spiritual Growth* (San Francisco: HarperCollins, 2000), chap. 13.

as we learn that the blessed ones are those "whose delight is in the law of the Lord, and who meditate on his law day and night" (Ps 1:2).

Eugene Peterson introduces a memorable insight on biblical meditation when he stumbles upon the word *hagah* in an unexpected portion of Isaiah. The picture Isaiah paints is of a young lion who "growls [*hagah*] . . . over his prey" (Is 31:4). As Peterson envisions the lion meditating on its prey—gnawing, growling, chewing— and as he pictures his own dog and its delight when it gnaws, growls, and chews on a bone, he notes that the mental picture he (and I and maybe you) often have of meditation is much tamer than what the Bible envisions. In comparing Isaiah's picture with his own mental framework of, for instance, a person sitting quietly in a rose garden with an open Bible, he writes:

> When Isaiah's lion and my dog meditated, they chewed and swallowed, using teeth and tongue, stomach and intestines: Isaiah's lion meditating his goat (if that's what it was); my dog meditating his bone. There is a certain kind of writing that invites this kind of reading, soft purrs and low growls as we taste and savor, anticipate and take in the sweet and spicy, mouth-watering and soul-energizing morsels—"O taste and see that the Lord is good!"[13]

Meditation on Scripture is less a picture of a person in quiet contemplation than it is a lion gnawing away on a bone. Meditation causes the words of Scripture to sink deeply into a person—to be ingested, metabolized, and become a part of the meditator's being. This discipline too is indispensable for the church planter.

The idea that the Christian leader should be deeply shaped by the words of Scripture takes us back to Joshua, the first leader after the Law has been given. Following the famous command to be strong and courageous, we find these words as to how we might do so: "Keep this Book of the Law always on your lips; meditate on it day and night, so that you may be careful to do everything written in it. Then you will be prosperous and successful" (Josh 1:8). Every part of this verse is instructive. The word of God is to be right near us ("on our lips"), at all times ("day and night"), so that we might obey it (not just know it). Then (then!) comes fruit: we will be prosperous and successful, strong and courageous.

Joshua's *then* foreshadows Paul's famous words on meditation: "Be transformed by the renewing of your mind. *Then* you will be able to test and approve what God's will is" (Rom 12:2). Read together, we see that the leader who is able to act with wisdom and courage, and to see fruit in the process, is the leader who is habitually being shaped by prolonged engagement with God's Word.

---

[13]Eugene Peterson, *Eat This Book: A Conversation in the Art of Spiritual Reading* (Grand Rapids: Eerdmans, 2006), 2.

Between Joshua and Paul we find Jesus, ever shaped by the Scriptures. For Jesus, the word of God was indispensable. It was to be obeyed ("whoever practices and teaches these commands will be called great in the kingdom of heaven") and is eternally significant ("heaven and earth will pass away, but my words will never pass away") (Mt 5:19; 24:35).

We find that Jesus is utterly fluent in the Scriptures, able to recall at will the right passage when confronted with the devil's temptations, or when teaching the crowds or his disciples, correcting a friend, or rebuffing an opponent. He grasps them not just as a succession of proof texts but understands their meaning within the overarching story of God, which finds its culmination in him (Mt 22:41-46; Jn 5:39-47). The Scriptures were his native tongue, shaping his mind and heart and informing and powering his ministry.

As church planters, we find we are constantly in need of these resources. Where will we as planters develop the kind of heart and mind needed to be "strong and courageous" as we lead (Josh 1:6)? To lead with the "wisdom that comes from heaven" (Jas 3:17)? To develop ears to hear the voice of the Spirit as he directs us? Patient, intentional meditation on Scripture is a vital discipline for the church planter.

What's more, our conversation with God in the Scriptures will inform and shape the way we interact with the non-Christians around us. The Word working in us will allow us to relate to them from a place of deep centeredness. Likewise, our conversation with non-Christian neighbors will inform the way we read the Scriptures, as we carry their questions, longings, and concerns with us to the text.

How do we engage in a habitual, life-giving discipline of meditation? Thankfully, the Scriptures and church history gives us the wisdom of a great cloud of witnesses to guide us in our practice. I have found three steps in particular to be helpful.

First, commit to a time and place. Much like the practice of solitude (which naturally and fruitfully pairs with the discipline of meditation), it is important to put meditation on one's calendar. One cannot stumble into meditation—it requires that one make space for it, and therefore it must be planned into one's day. Find a quiet place, a quiet time, and make your appointment with God. For me, I am most tuned in to the Spirit during my day if I make a time of meditation and prayer my first appointment of the day, before my family is up and the bustle of the day begins.

Second, find one or more methods that work for you. Meditation takes many forms. Many resonate with the slow repetition of *lectio divina* or with the imaginative engagement of Ignatian meditation (which brings the added benefit of helping the preacher who desires to paint vivid mental pictures for her congregation). Virtually every tradition has taught the value of slowly, meditatively, praying the Psalms. Madame Guyon and Martin Luther also shared methodologies with their students that many continue to find useful today.[14] In the evangelical tradition, any number of methods of Bible study (manuscript study, outlining a passage, word studies, topical studies) are essentially means of meditation, as is the slow work of translating a passage from the Greek or Hebrew if one is proficient in the original languages. Dallas Willard recommends memorization of Scripture, particularly larger passages of Scripture, as his go-to method of meditation.

What do these methods share in common? Each is a different way of slowing us down—way down. They cause us to pay careful attention to every word, and to the Spirit speaking to us from within those words. With my particular personality, I find that I bore easily, so it is necessary for me to switch up my method every month or so. Each of us needs to experiment with one or more methods to find which ones help us best engage the Bible.

Finally, we need to approach meditation with a prior commitment to obey whatever the Lord shows us. As James says, to receive the word but not obey it is to be like a person who has to keep looking back at the mirror because they can't remember what they look like. "Do not merely listen to the word, and so deceive yourselves," he says. "Do what it says" (Jas 1:22). If meditation is to be fruitful for us, we need to make an ongoing commitment to obey what we read, wherever it may take us.

Sabbath keeping*.* Our church is now fourteen years old, and I can count on my fingers the number of times I've gone home having finished everything on my to-do list. The nature of church planting is that the needs are never-ending. You can always visit one more person, send one more email, follow up with that leader, put one more hour into your teaching prep. On top of this, in a new plant you are often the only paid staff person, leaders are few or nonexistent, and many of the structures which maintain good ministry are not yet built. Given these demands, the danger of overworking our way into burnout—for ourselves, our spouses, any volunteers we may have—is very real.

For planters who are earning all or part of their living from that work, we have the additional pressure that our livelihood is tied to our success. While most of us cringe at the thought of being financially motivated to succeed, we cannot deny that the need to provide for our families is never fully absent from our minds, particularly if the church is struggling.

---

[14]On *lectio divina*, see Peterson, *Eat This Book*, chap. 7. On Ignatian meditation, see Ignatius of Loyola, *The Spiritual Exercise of St. Ignatius* (New York: Doubleday, 1989). For helpful methodologies for praying Scripture, see Donald Whitney, *Praying the Bible* (Wheaton: Crossway, 2015); Madame Guyon, *Experiencing the Depths of Jesus Christ* (Christian Books Pub House, 1981); and Walter Trobisch, *Martin Luther's Quiet Time* (Downers Grove, IL: InterVarsity Press, 1975).

And what about the hyper-busyness that often comes when a church is thriving? A church that is fruitful or growing rapidly can be equally tyrannical as a pastor attempts to work faster and harder to maintain the church's momentum.

In addition to these dangers is the subtle temptation church planters face to over-identify with their work. For many of us, the job becomes our identity. "I am a church planter" can begin to subtly overshadow the deeper truth: "I am a child of God in the ministry of church planting." When the line blurs between who I am and what my ministry is, then I wander into that dangerous space where the prospect of the church doing poorly threatens my very conception of who I am: What does it say about me if this church fails? What would I say to those who believed in me, or who backed me financially? Will I become unhireable to other churches if I can't make this work?

These pressures can make the temptation to overwork simultaneously irresistible and unbearable. Physically, psychologically, and spiritually—we need to rest regularly and well if we are going to be able to sustain a lifetime of fruitful service. This is true even though the work may not be fully done (because, again, the work will never be fully done). We need to treat church planting as a marathon, not a sprint.

How do we avoid burnout, maintain a healthy separation between what we do and who we are, and hold up under the pressure of needing the church to do well enough to provide a living?

The primary answer the Christian tradition gives us is the spiritual discipline of sabbath keeping. Far from being a legalistic holdover from Old Testament times, sabbath keeping was one of Jesus' spiritual disciplines, was practiced in the early church, and has been commended to us by saints throughout the church's history.

We often associate Jesus with breaking the Sabbath, or so it was thought, by healing and doing other good works on the Sabbath. It can be easy within that framework to forget that Jesus was resolutely pro-Sabbath. "On the Sabbath day he went into the synagogue, *as was his custom*" (Lk 4:16). Jesus practiced sabbath. His intent in shaking up this practice was not to downgrade sabbath keeping, but to restore it! He wanted to make sure that the Sabbath remained as life-giving as God intended. "The Sabbath was made for man, not man for the Sabbath" (Mk 2:27). Or as Dallas Willard has said of the disciplines, "They are not laws. They are not righteousness. They are simply wisdom."[15]

Church planters, by nature, are doers. They venture out, inspired by a deep sense of mission and call, and create something where there was nothing. As sabbath keeping is the cessation of doing, it should not surprise us that sabbath keeping is one of the most difficult disciplines for church planters to practice.

---

[15]Dallas Willard, *Renewing the Christian Mind: Essays, Interviews, and Talks* (New York: HarperOne, 2016), 408.

Eugene Peterson writes, "The most striking thing about keeping the Sabbath is that it begins by not doing anything. The Hebrew word *shabbat* means 'Quit . . . Stop . . . Take a break'. . . . Whatever you are doing, stop it. . . . Whatever you are saying, shut up. . . . Sit down and take a look around you. . . . Don't do anything. . . . Don't say anything . . . Fold your hands . . . Take a deep breath."[16] For the average church planter such a command may very well be the most difficult part of their job description.[17] But this is truth we need to embrace: the regular, habitual practice of stopping is essential for the long-term health of the church planter, the church planter's family, and even the church they lead.

When I first began practicing sabbath, I was a full-time seminary student and serving nearly full time as a pastoral intern. I was so busy I would read at traffic lights and rarely had time for a full night's sleep. The thought of taking a whole day off, and thus cramming one-seventh more work into every other day, was ludicrous. But at the urging of a wise mentor I began practicing sabbath, and much to my surprise, I found my other six days were far more productive than they had been when I wasn't taking a day to rest. My mind was sharper, my body held less anxiety, and I found my study time was far more efficient. In addition, I was more present for the people I ministered to, my demeanor was calmer, and I was all around a more pleasant person to be around.

How do we practice sabbath keeping as a life-giving, soul-restoring spiritual exercise? Eugene Peterson offers perhaps the best shorthand formula available: "On the Sabbath we pray and play."[18] We refrain from work, and we spend time doing what gives us life, with people who give us life, in the presence of the One who gives us life. Here are a few simple suggestions on how we as planters might do this well.

First, select a regular, whole day you can make your sabbath every week. The temptation is to say, "I can't take a whole day off so I will cobble together some times of rest throughout the week." Granted, sometimes our circumstances dictate that this is the best we can do (particularly for those who are bivocational or even work full-time in addition to planting), but I would advocate that we avoid this at all costs. Find a day—a whole day—that becomes your sabbath every week. Put it on the calendar and fight to protect it.

My sabbath is Friday. Many pastors like to take Monday off, but I find I am too consumed that day with thoughts of what I need to do for my mind and body to

---

[16]Eugene Peterson, *Christ Plays in Ten Thousand Places: A Conversation in Spiritual Theology* (Grand Rapids: Eerdmans, 2005), 109.

[17]For denomination/movement leaders, I recommend making sabbath an explicit part of each new planter's job description.

[18]Eugene Peterson, *Working the Angles: The Shape of Pastoral Integrity* (Grand Rapids: Eerdmans, 1987), 75.

really rest. Friday, on the other hand, gives me two days off (usually) before Sunday. On these days I move slower. I walk slower, eat slower, drive slower. I don't accomplish much.

I will often (again) pair with these days the discipline of celebration—intentionally doing things I enjoy in the presence of God as an act of worship. I might do some reading, watch a movie or YouTube videos, spend time on my hobby, take a trip to the beach or a walk with my wife and daughters. Maybe I'll go for coffee with a friend (if I'm not peopled-out) or sometimes just spend time by myself. I might treat myself to a food that I like or drink a little nicer wine with my dinner than I do the rest of the week.

Second, make sleep a priority. The medical world has established a broad consensus that getting six to nine hours of sleep each night (the need varies from person to person) is critical to our physical and emotional wellbeing. Our bodies need this time of recovery to facilitate proper muscle growth, weight loss, stress management, retention of memories, and more.[19]

In addition to the physical and mental benefit, the practice of sleep can itself be a spiritual discipline by which we learn to trust God. In the Genesis 1 account, each new day begins with the formula, "There was evening, and there was morning—the [first, second, etc.] day." To the Hebrew mind, each new day begins not with the dawning of the sun, but with its setting. Reflecting on this text, Eugene Peterson insightfully observes that our first responsibility each day is not to do, to make, to go and to conquer, but to rest—to enjoy a mini-sabbath. What happens while we are resting? God continues to work. And we learn to trust that he is at work, that we do not have to do it all, to fix it all, to be the world's savior. God has that covered.[20] To embrace this truth is to live a truly missional spirituality, as we are acknowledging that God is the missionary, and our mission derives from him, and we are at the same time showing the world a different way to live.

How many of us as church planters would benefit from a daily reminder of that truth? Unlike God, we are not omnipresent, so we cannot be there for everyone. Unlike God, we are not omnipotent, so we will not be able to fix everyone. Unlike God, we are not omniscient, so we will not have all the answers our people need.[21] Could it be that much of our exhaustion is due to our failure to remind ourselves of God's divinity and our humanity?

---

[19]Cameron Lee and Kurt Fredrickson, *That Their Work Will Be a Joy: Understanding and Coping with the Challenges of Pastoral Ministry* (Eugene, OR: Cascade, 2012), 116.

[20]Peterson, *Working the Angles*, 67-68.

[21]See Zach Eswine, *The Imperfect Pastor: Discovering Joy in Our Limitations Through a Daily Apprenticeship with Jesus* (Wheaton, IL: Crossway, 2015).

You can't do it all. The practice of sabbath keeping, including making time to sleep, teaches us to stop trying to be God and rather to trust him to tend to this church he directed us to start. "Rest," Dallas Willard tells us, "is an act of faith."[22]

Finally, put boundaries on the number of hours, and on the number of nights, that you will work.

Once, at a church planter assessment, I got into a heated discussion with a fellow assessor. He didn't want to pass an otherwise qualified candidate because the candidate said that, barring emergencies, he wasn't planning to work more than fifty hours per week. "A planter who wants a church of a thousand or more needs to commit to seventy to eighty hours," my friend said. "That might be true," I replied. My friend had planted a church that grew to and beyond that size; I had not. "But there is a strong likelihood that the sacrifices to that pastor's family and health will not be sustainable." Sadly, for many pastors such a workload has proved unsustainable, as it did for this friend, who suffered a fatal heart attack in his mid-fifties.

Church planting is a marathon, not a sprint. Consequently, we need to think soberly about what constitutes a healthy, sustainable pace of life, and ask our leadership teams to help us resist the temptation to work more than what is healthy. Thankfully, my leadership team has embraced this value and helps me maintain good boundaries. They will ask how many hours I'm working and suggest it should probably be less. "Are you putting down your phone at night, or still checking email? Are you taking sufficient time with your family and with friends?"

I once heard Rick Warren say that he strictly requires that his staff work no more than three nights per week, including any small groups and board meetings. I've made this my practice too and found the resulting increase in joy and productivity to be life-changing. This too is part of the practice of keeping sabbath, and how we as pastors will be formed by Christ.

Veteran pastor Pete Scazerro writes, "As someone who has been in leadership for nearly three decades, I can tell you that Sabbath is without a doubt the most important day of the week for my leadership. It is also the one day of the week I most believe—and live out—a fundamental truth of the gospel. How? I do nothing productive, and yet I am utterly loved."[23]

Diet and exercise. Shortly after turning thirty I went to my doctor for my annual physical check-up. I was reasonably active and considered myself young and healthy, so the serious expression on my doctor's face caught me off guard. After reading off my numbers for each health marker, he cut to the chase.

---

[22]Willard, *Renewing the Christian Mind*, 277.
[23]Scazzero, *Emotionally Healthy Leader*, 169.

"Here is the bottom line," my doctor said gravely. "Your diet is awful and you barely exercise. Consequently, your numbers on everything from blood pressure to cholesterol are bordering on really unhealthy levels. What's more, you've gained fifteen pounds in the last five years. I know it doesn't seem like much, but if you continue to average a three-pound weight gain every year, you will be thirty pounds overweight by age 35, forty-five pounds overweight by age 40, and dangerously obese by the time you turn 45." With each age he mentioned, his hand moved up an imaginary chart indicating what my weight climb would look like on paper. "You can realistically expect that in the second half of your life you will be at high risk for diabetes, heart disease, and will have low energy, and by the time you are a grandparent you will be painfully winded walking up a flight of stairs or standing up out of a chair."

Having grown up a skinny, unathletic kid, I had never thought about weight (other than a desire to gain more) and rarely enjoyed sports. To hear that weight and health were an issue at all was sobering. But even then, it took me nearly another decade to make any substantive change.

Many pastors, it seems, are in a similar place. The *New York Times*, drawing on a growing number of studies, reports that pastors fare worse than the general population in caring for their bodies. "Members of the clergy now suffer from obesity, hypertension and depression at rates higher than most Americans."[24] Another study out of Duke University states that pastors have a greater incidence of metabolic syndrome than the general population, and that nearly one third of pastors are experiencing burnout or depression at any given time.[25]

What's more, failure to care for our bodies is an area where we are unlikely to encounter correction. Consider this—if your church discovered you were coping with the stresses of planting by drinking too much, someone would almost certainly call this out as sin. Church leaders would be alarmed, and (hopefully) come alongside and try to offer assistance. If you persisted to abuse alcohol, you would most likely lose your job.

But what if you were coping with ministry stress by regularly overeating? Would anyone in your church even think to call this behavior out, let alone think of confronting it as an area of sin? Gluttony, once considered one of the seven deadly sins, is rarely if ever mentioned in our churches. It has become a culturally acceptable vice, if it's even recognized as a vice at all. And perhaps because overeating is a culturally acceptable sin, many pastors who would recoil at the thought

---

[24]Paul Vitello, "Taking a Break from the Lord's Work," *New York Times*, October 2, 2010.
[25]Dr. Chris Adams, lecture, Azusa Pacific University Center for Vocational Ministry, May 24, 2017.

of getting drunk or using drugs gravitate with ease toward comforting themselves by abusing food.

As pastors, we need to embrace physical health and fitness as a mandatory aspect of our spiritual lives. Indeed, many of us are not used to thinking about bodily life at all as an aspect of our spiritual lives. But what if we were to treat diet and exercise as a spiritual discipline—as one aspect of loving God with all of our heart, soul, mind, and strength?

The apostle Paul wrote to the Corinthian church, "You are not your own; you were bought at a price. Therefore, honor God with your *bodies*" (1 Cor 6:19-20). While he wrote this in the context of sexual immorality, certainly it has valid application for other uses of our bodies as well. Similarly, in Romans 12:1 we are told to offer our bodies "as a living sacrifice, holy and pleasing to God" for this is our "true and proper worship."

While we may not be used to thinking of the intentional pursuit of bodily health as a way to honor God with our bodies or as an act of worship, I would suggest that this is an indispensable spiritual discipline for the church planter. And many find that when they choose to utilize fitness as a spiritual discipline, exercise goes from drudgery to a place where they can meet God in deep and profound ways.

Part of what began to change this for me was discovering that some of my best times of prayer occurred when I was running. Something about the work of exercise synergized with the work of prayer, and I found myself craving my runs as much for my soul as for the relaxation it brought to my body. As I began to talk about my experience, I found that many other believers around me also found running, swimming, yoga, bicycling, or strength training to be deeply meditative. For the last five years I have trained four days a week with a crew of friends from my church, neighborhood, and my kids' school. They testify to this dynamic as well, and we regularly talk about the spiritual growth we experience in our workouts. Christians in earlier eras were attuned to this too, as the monks valued physical labor for the benefits it brought to both their bodies and souls.[26]

In addition to the spiritual benefits of practicing good stewardship of our health, exercise brings a physiological release of stress and releases joy-producing endorphins. Dr. Archibald Hart notes the need we have to counteract the harmful effects of adrenaline. "Adrenaline arousal can be compared to revving up a car engine, then leaving it to idle at high speeds."[27] Exercise can make you a happier pastor. This

---

[26]Gary Thomas, *Every Body Matters: Strengthening Your Body to Strengthen Your Soul* (Grand Rapids: Zondervan, 2011), chap. 10.

[27]Archibald Hart, *Adrenaline and Stress: The Exciting New Breakthrough That Helps You Overcome Stress Damage* (Dallas: Word, 1995), 27.

improved quality of life is a gift to you and, as they get to experience a happier you, to your family and your church as well.

How might we practice diet and exercise as a spiritual discipline? Consider the following suggestions.

First, find a form of exercise that you enjoy. Whether it is hiking, walking, yoga, CrossFit, running, swimming, basketball, weights, soccer, tennis, or calisthenics, you won't be able to stick with a training regimen that doesn't bring at least some pleasure.

Second, put exercise on your calendar. What is true of most spiritual disciplines is doubly true of diet and exercise: if we don't plan for it, it won't happen. When we first planted Life, a more seasoned planter was kind enough to come alongside and speak into my life. One day he gave me a word that changed my life: "Tim, you won't make as much money as most of the people in your church, but you will have more control of your schedule than they do. Take full advantage of that, without a shred of guilt. Have breakfast with your kids, go to their games and recitals, be home for dinner. You can always do more work before they get up or after they go to bed, so make a priority of time with your family."

That counsel has informed not only my family life but my approach to physical health too. If we are going to eat healthy and exercise, we have to plan for it. Bill Hybels (after a heart attack) began taking time in the afternoon to get on the treadmill. Wayne Cordeiro (after developing debilitating anxiety) began making exercise one of the appointments on his daily calendar. "How can they do this?" I wondered. Even as pastors of large, busy churches, they made a choice to schedule it into their lives.

We need to be wise enough to schedule these practices into our lives too, and preferably to begin these habits before our bodies break down and we have no choice. Plan your meals in advance, buy healthy food to have on hand, put workouts on your calendar.

Finally, make your physical health something that you consciously "do unto the Lord." I like to look at exercise through three lenses: as an act of worship, a practice of good stewardship, and a spiritual discipline by which Jesus teaches me how to be a better disciple. And he does! So much of what happens in the gym has direct crossover to the spiritual life. Through exercise I have grown much in my understanding of endurance (as I persevere though tired), community (as my training partners strengthen me to keep growing), humility (as I daily bump up against my limitations), how to be a learner (as others coach me), the nature of growth (as imperceptible changes accumulate over time), and more.[28]

---

[28]For more information on how physical exercise can strengthen our spiritual lives, check out my podcast, *Ragamuffin Barbell*, on iTunes or Stitcher.

As C. S. Lewis once wrote, "The body ought to pray as well as the soul. Body and soul are both the better for it."[29] For those in the rigorous ministry of church planting, this is wisdom we need to embrace.

Spiritual direction, therapy, or wise mentors. At a lecture on self-care for pastors, psychologist Dan Allender was asked if he recommended any bodily practices other than exercise and diet. "Yes, in addition to exercise I see a masseuse or a chiropractor once a month. I've learned that my body holds some tensions and knots that I can't get out by myself—they require someone else's help." I'm sure this is good counsel for bodily care, and I believe there is parallel counsel for soul care as well: some tensions and knots require the help of others.

In our denomination we recommend that all our pastors either be in therapy or in spiritual direction at all times. Rather than waiting until we are broken, we attempt to practice this aspect of soul care as an ongoing way of both growing in our faith and heading off problem areas before they can take root. With church planters this is even more accentuated, and we actually pay for a spiritual director for all our new planters.

What exactly is spiritual direction? To explain it to new directees, my spiritual director points to a painting in his office of two disciples sitting under a tree with Jesus. By their body language and positioning it is clear that one of the disciples is helping explain to the other disciple something that Jesus is teaching them. "I'm that friend," my director says. "What I do is listen carefully to you and to the Holy Spirit, and in doing so, to help you understand what Jesus is doing in your life at any given moment."

When I first started direction, I expected by the title that a director would be telling me what to do. That has rarely been the case. Rather, my director listens well, asks great questions, and helps me explore deeper aspects of my heart so I can see where and how God is at work. "My job," he says, "is to put my hands on your cheeks, and to gently turn your head ever so slightly, so that your gaze moves from whatever is concerning you to Jesus."[30]

The result, for me at least, has been a monthly time of gentle insights and rest where I am reminded that I am God's child—that he loves me, and is more interested in who I am becoming than in what I am accomplishing. I find that I need this monthly reminder and course-correction more than I would imagine. Also, one of the subtly life-giving aspects of this discipline is that this is one of the very few hours in my month where I am with another person yet not providing any care. Someone else is pastoring me.

---

[29]C. S. Lewis, *Letters to Malcolm: Chiefly on Prayer* (New York: Harcourt Brace & Co., 1992), 17.

[30]For more on spiritual direction, see David Benner, *Sacred Companions: The Gift of Spiritual Friendship and Direction* (Downers Grove, IL: InterVarsity Press, 2002).

Therapy is a practice that may be more familiar than spiritual direction but is one that many pastors resist. As noted above, church planting has a way of surfacing our deepest insecurities, fears, and self-doubts. "I thought I had already dealt with that," is one of the most common lines I hear from planters in their first year. Many express surprise at the strong reactions they experience as events and people trigger areas they thought were long since healed. We should pay attention to these reactions as they are indicators of the depth of inner turmoil we are undergoing. When we experience this, especially if it begins to adversely affect our families, the practice of therapy is a useful discipline.

While spiritual direction is useful for ongoing soul care, therapy can help us get at stubborn places in our hearts where healing seems elusive. A good therapist is able to peel the layers back to the point where root causes are exposed and can be brought forward for God's healing touch to take place.

Pastors sometimes resist therapy for themselves, even as they prescribe it for others under their care. We are used to doling out healing, not seeking it for ourselves. But this is an area where we need to humble ourselves and take our own medicine. We will be better pastors, spouses, parents, and friends if we are inviting God to heal us in our deepest places.

Finally, church planters need to have wise mentors. This might come in the form of a church planting coach, or simply a more seasoned pastor or leader. Of the three voices listed in this section, this is the one that is most likely to give advice specific to a planter's situation. Such advice is greatly needed, and wise is the planter who proactively seeks counsel. While books and podcasts are great, there is no substitute for a wise person who can listen to our particular situation and speak directly into it.

This, of course, is good for the church plant, but it is also good for the planter. Having a person to turn to with questions and concerns, for advice and prayer—this is deep and needed fellowship for the planter's soul.

CONCLUSION

Above are my top five practices for church planters. They are largely individual in practice, so they do not touch on crucial communal disciplines like fellowship, which will be addressed in the next chapter. Receive them in the form of grace, not law.

I leave you with one final quote from Henri Nouwen:

> It is not enough for the priests and ministers of the future to be moral people, well trained, eager to help their fellow humans, and able to respond creatively to the burning issues of their time. All of that is very valuable and important, but it is not the heart of Christian leadership. The central question is, *are the leaders of the future truly*

men and women of God, people with an ardent desire to dwell in God's presence, to listen to God's voice, to look at God's beauty, to touch God's incarnate Word and to taste fully God's infinite goodness?"[31]

DISCUSSION QUESTIONS

1. Which of the five spiritual disciplines (silence and solitude, meditation on Scripture, sabbath keeping, diet and exercise, spiritual direction or therapy) prescribed here do you find comes most naturally to you? Which is most challenging? Which practice do you feel you most need to grow in currently?

2. Are there additional disciplines, relationships, and experiences that keep you connected to the vine? What are they?

3. In light of your current practice and potential needs, put a rule of life into action. Get out your calendar, and, beginning with the disciplines that seem most important right now, schedule in times to practice these in God's presence.

4. Jesus tells us that pruning is not a punishment for lack of fruit, but the Father's way of making us even more fruitful. What adversities are you currently facing as a church planter? Ask the Father to reveal the ways he wants to use these to further develop you as a fruitful leader.

---

[31] Henri Nouwen, *In the Name of Jesus: Reflections on Christian Leadership* (New York, Crossroad Publishing, 1989), 29.

5

HOW ARE LEADERS MUTUALLY FORMED FOR GOD'S MISSION?

MISSIONAL SPIRITUALITY FOR LEADERSHIP TEAMS

LEN TANG

crucible (noun): a situation of severe trial, or in which different elements interact, leading to the creation of something new

NEW OXFORD
AMERICAN
DICTIONARY

Then I said to them, "You see the trouble we are in, how Jerusalem lies in ruins with its gates burned. Come, let us build the wall of Jerusalem, that we may no longer suffer derision." And I told them of the hand of my God that had been upon me for good, and also of the words that the king had spoken to me. And they said, "Let us rise up and build." So they strengthened their hands for the good work.

NEHEMIAH 2:17-18 ESV

I REMEMBER SITTING IN THE LIVING ROOM of John and Keiki's house, listening to their story. John was in his late forties and had previously been a pew-warmer at a parent church, never having been an active volunteer, let alone a leader, in any church. Despite his palpable sense of trepidation at getting involved in a church plant, he felt like this might be God's prompting to finally get off the bench and into the game. As he began to serve and use his gifts, then lead a home group, he discovered a passion to see other people become engaged with their faith in Christ, get off the bench, and get connected into home groups. He later joined our "Be-Team," which was the leadership team at our church plant (not because he couldn't make the A-Team but because our core values all started with the letters "Be"). Together we experienced the joys, burdens, and conflicts that come with walking alongside a budding congregation through lots of change, loss, and growth. He would go on to motivate me and other leaders to activate the congregation as he himself had become activated in faith and ministry.

THE CRUCIBLE OF PLANTING TOGETHER

Do you recall high school chemistry class when you would place a glass beaker with various chemicals over a Bunsen burner to elicit some sort of reaction? Planting a church together can feel a lot like that glass beaker—high heat, tight quarters, few resources, with a potential breakthrough (or explosion!) at stake. Sometimes leadership teams gel together beautifully, and other times certain combinations of people just don't mix, and the result is toxic. It's an intense and formative crucible for the planter and her leadership team. Leading such a team involves melding together many gifted and motivated people who may bring with them deeply divergent experiences and visions of church, or even conflicting theologies. In addition, decisions need to be made with alarming frequency ranging from the significant (e.g., naming the church, discerning the people group the team feels called to, determining a budget) to the mundane (e.g., how do we file our 501c3 paperwork? What type of coffee should we serve? Though for some, the choice of coffee matters as much as the theology!). So you have a brand-new leadership team that hasn't yet built relational trust, a high-stakes ministry to launch, and a leader who may be the point person for the first time in their ministry. Is this a surefire recipe for disaster or an opportunity for new levels of dependence on the Holy Spirit? In reality, it's probably some of both.

In the last chapter, we looked at the formation of the planter. In this chapter, we take on what it means for the whole church planting team to be mutually formed for the sake of the *missio Dei*, God's mission in the world. We return once again to the three roots of our church planting tree to frame the way forward: spiritual formation, biblical theology, and missional competencies. For church planting teams, my paraphrase of Proverbs 27:17 is "as iron sharpens iron, so one launch team member irritates another." Just as Peter and Paul clashed over how their theology was worked out in practice (Gal 2:11-14), so the relationships among launch team members are tested and tried as they work out their personal and biblical convictions in real time in a new neighborhood. Our prayer is that the intense pressure of the church planting crucible leads to the creation and expansion of a leadership team that experiences and models kingdom dynamics as never before.

Cultivating a missional spirituality (the focus of part two of this book) means that the formation of our own faith is integrally connected to our participation in God's missional calling. Rather than divorcing mission from discipleship, it is trusting that God's activity in the world is inseparable from the life that God is growing in us. In the case of Nehemiah and his call to rebuild the walls of Jerusalem, the hand of God had been on him for good, and it was out of that divine leading that the people then rose up and together rebuilt the wall that would once again protect the holy city. And together God's people "strengthened their hands" for this good work (Neh 2:18). What does it look like to discern together the hand of God so that our hands are strengthened for the good work of the gospel in our city? And can this be done in a way that is joyful and sustainable rather than fraught with burnout and division?

Sadly, many planters tell a similar story that four years into their church plant, there are few, if any, of the original members of the launch team that remain part of the church. Leaders often leave due to burnout, disagreement over differing visions, interpersonal conflict, and so on. Is this churn an inevitable reality, or a trap that can be avoided? In recent years, many church planting networks have begun using the term *launch team* rather than *core group* in order to ease the perceived sense of failure if someone who is at the core of the church ends up leaving. The term *launch team* gives people permission and freedom to move on after launch if they are not ultimately called to be part of the vision that forms.

WHEN YOUR DREAM TEAM DISAPPEARS

CHARLIE COTHERMAN

When my wife and I finally discerned together that God was calling us to plant a church, one of the first things I began to do was compile my leadership dream team. Over the next few months I shared the vision I felt God gave us, and the excitement built as an amazing team came together. I had heard that most church planting teams experience major upheaval during their first few years, but like so many others I did not think it would happen to me.

Then it did.

Eight months before our public launch, our worship leader and his wife—who was enthusiastic about heading up a children's ministry—felt God was calling them to serve at another church four hours away. Then one after another key members of our team began to suffer from bouts of severe depression and anxiety. (Only later did I fully discern the spiritual attack our team was under.)

The hardest hit was when my best friend opted out of our plant the very month we went public. He too had experienced unprecedented and crippling levels of anxiety in the months leading up to the plant. For him, relief only came as he dug deeper into the theology and practices of the Eastern Orthodox Church. After a few months he and his wife and three kids left our church for the Orthodox Church. I was crushed. Not only had we lost my friend's musical and leadership skills, but my wife lost her best friend and most reliable children's ministry helper, and my kids lost their best friends at church. Worse yet, I felt like he was rejecting me and our entire way of being the church together.

But God remained faithful. Over the next year I came to see that God was working in my disappointments and my joys. As my friend and his family thrived in their new church setting, I began to see the hand of God in their move. I also saw God work to build a team of his (not my) creation. As original leaders left, God met them in their journeys and met us in ours by bringing folks of his choosing to fill the leadership gaps. Goodbyes still hurt, but God has worked good even amid disappointment.

If I'm honest, the two launch teams that I've led have been the source of both soaring joy and heart-rending pain. Just four days before the public launch of my first church plant, our worship director told me he would be leaving the position shortly. It was a gut punch. Where had I gone wrong in the selection and formation of our leadership and staff team?

Going in to church planting expecting that both joys and pains are a normal part of the formational process may help steady us when they come and may even enable us to discern God's hand in the midst of it all.

MUTUALLY FORMATIONAL LEADERSHIP

If you're the lead planter, you and the team hopefully have a discipleship strategy—a plan for how you see people in your congregation being formed to be like Christ together and live out his mission in your community. The question is, will the leadership team get to experience this formation themselves? Or will that formation just be for those who will later become part of the church? Like a series of concentric circles, we want to encourage an approach to discipleship that begins at the center and radiates outward. Just as Jesus focused on the three disciples (Peter, James, and John), then the twelve disciples, then the crowds, so we want to help planters to both form and be formed by the launch team. Not only that, but because God is at work in the community and in the "crowd," the interaction and relationships with our team will also form us.

While today there is a relative abundance of resources for lead planters (networks, conferences, books, training, coaching, boot camps, seminary classes, etc.), there's a relative dearth of resources and attention given to church planting teams. And yet developing a missional spirituality is inherently communal, not simply individual. The leadership team becomes the learning lab to cultivate a spirituality that is indigenous to the city where the church is being planted. Again, this means that the formation of the team itself can't be separated from the mission context. It means that formation doesn't *precede* mission but happens simultaneous *with* mission. Dan Steigerwald calls us to be "experimenting with or testing a discipleship rhythm together to see what practices help the team grow, spiritually and communally, as they engage their context."[1] The key connection is that our discipleship rhythm needs to engage with our context.

As others have pointed out, our Savior is known as Jesus of Nazareth, but how much of Nazareth got into Jesus? In other words, how was the Son of God formed

---

[1]Dan Steigerwald, *Dynamic Adventure: A Guide to Starting and Shaping Missional Churches* (Centennial, CO: Christian Associates International, 2016), 4.

by the people, conversations, carpentry work, and all that he experienced in Naz-areth for the better part of three decades? And how will the context and leaders in our city form and shape us and the church's vision? Two of the key institutions in my city are Fuller Seminary and Caltech, a world-class STEM university. The deep theological and scientific questions that graduate students in both schools are raising has challenged me to go deeper in my own theology and has led us to incor-porate a Q&A time after each sermon. Their questions are shaping our ministry.

If we're not being formed by our context, are church plants exercising missional leadership? Or are we simply seeking to impose a form of ministry colonialism on our communities? A large church in our area is opening another campus, apparently without having talked with the local pastors or community leaders in the new city. Many of those long-time pastors were surprised by what felt like a takeover attempt rather than a partnership to serve a lower income part of the city. If a ministry doesn't take the time to connect with the leaders in its city, it seems less likely that its ministry would take the time to connect with the people and needs in the city and be formed by the relationships it discovers. The posture of missional leadership is to listen and to serve.

For Nehemiah, his leaders, and the people of Jerusalem, developing a missional spirituality included learning how to deal with violent opposition to the rebuilding of the wall. Their solution turned out to be that "those who carried materials did their work with one hand and held a weapon in the other" (Neh 4:17). Nehemiah's enemies were willing to kill in order to halt work on the wall, so Nehemiah's team learned that following God's call was a literal life-or-death calling, and that together they would have to protect each other, live in a state of high alert, and slow down their anticipated pace of reconstruction. What tools will your planting team need to hold in their hands to participate in the building of God's kingdom in your city?

In some contexts, the work of God is hampered not by armed enemies but by subtler but no less real challenges such as systemic racism, persistent economic inequities, or poor school districts. And yet herein lies the opportunity for lead-ership teams to be formed together for the mission by serving in ways that protect the city and proclaim the gospel. Each planting team will face opposition or idols that will require communal engagement, corporate repentance, or both.

INTEGRATING LEADERSHIP DEVELOPMENT AND SPIRITUAL FORMATION

So how do planters build leadership teams that are mutually forming one another for the sake of God's mission? What is the relationship between leadership devel-opment, spiritual formation, and missional engagement? Are these three separate, sequential things, or one thing? I would argue that developing a missional spirituality has the power to gather these seemingly disparate pieces of discipleship into one, unified whole. What does this look like? We get a glimpse of this in the church at Antioch through the call of Barnabas and Saul in Acts 13:1-3:

> Now in the church at Antioch there were prophets and teachers: Barnabas, Simeon called Niger, Lucius of Cyrene, Manaen (who had been brought up with Herod the tetrarch) and Saul. While they were worshiping the Lord and fasting, the Holy Spirit said, "Set apart for me Barnabas and Saul for the work to which I have called them." So after they had fasted and prayed, they placed their hands on them and sent them off.

In this brief passage, we can discern that the church at Antioch included a group of leaders who had identified and affirmed one another's gifts (prophets and teachers), were ethnically and socially diverse, had established some shared spiritual practices (worshiping and fasting), listened together expectantly, and engaged in a mutual discernment process (fasting and praying prior to sending out Barnabas and Saul). As a result, they were able to come to a consensus that God had indeed called these two leaders, and so they commissioned them through the laying on of hands and proceeded to send them out for God's mission in the world.

Can you imagine what it would have been like to be one of the leaders who had been part of that discernment process after Paul and Barnabas went off and planted the majority of the churches in the Mediterranean world, as recorded in the remainder of Acts? And who wouldn't want to be part of a dynamic sending team like the Antioch church?

Using Acts 13 as a model of a mature leadership team, we can identify several aspects of fruitful leadership teams that we'll explore in the remainder of this chapter: shared leadership, diverse leadership, Spirit-led leadership, formational leadership, and missional leadership.

SHARED LEADERSHIP

It's clear that the church at Antioch was functioning with a shared leadership and awareness of one another's gifts and strengths. In today's context, we generally operate under the assumption that there is an individual planter called to lead the work, and yet the very things that make the planter fruitful can work against the establishment of shared leadership. Planters' gifts and wiring are, broadly speaking, apostolic and entrepreneurial. They are self-starters who like to initiate and get things going. So far so good. But this easily turns into the tendency to initiate everything in the church plant and thereby inadvertently disempower the people around them over time.

In using the term *shared* leadership, we are making a distinction from simply delegated leadership. Delegating leadership often means that the planter is simply offloading certain predetermined tasks and responsibilities to other leaders. Shared leadership means that the planter and the other leaders are together discerning God's big-picture calling for the church. How do we get there? It begins with humility on the part of the planter.

Embracing the planter's limitations. A huge benefit of doing a deep dive into a planter's gifts and wiring (which is often discerned by attending a formal church planter assessment) is a recognition of both the planter's strengths as well as limitations so that they can intentionally seek out those who are strong where he or she is weak. There are specific gifts which God has poured out on the lead planter, which means that other gifts are *not* part of their gift mix. This knowledge of being fearfully and wonderfully made is also permission to admit, "I'm not a 'ten' at everything!"

This awareness frees the planter to embrace his or her own limitations rather than feel pressure to be omnicompetent or to cover up their weaknesses or pretend they don't exist. And as our own sense of security in the gospel and in how God has wired us deepens, we grow in genuine affection and appreciation for those with complementary gifts. While a less mature and less secure planter might perceive the giftedness of other leaders as a threat, a planter being formed by God's Spirit is able to boast in their weaknesses and rejoice that the body is much healthier due to the presence of the full range of gifts.

The costs of solo leadership. Part of our shared conviction in this book is that the stereotype of the church planter as trailblazing lone ranger, charging ahead with followers in tow, can be both unbiblical and ultimately harmful to the mission of God. The Western preoccupation with individualism certainly bleeds into ministry and leads to overfunctioning lead planters and therefore underfunctioning leadership teams and congregations. Overfunctioning occurs when planters consistently operate *outside* of their gifts, thereby robbing other members of the body of the opportunity to serve in their gifts. In addition, when planters are operating in too many areas of ministry, it causes other parts of the body to atrophy, creating a lose-lose situation. The planter becomes a ministry and mission bottleneck, not simply for the practical reason of the failure to delegate but from a broader paradigm of seeing themselves as a ministry superhero who can do it all. Jessica Schrock-Ringenberg writes:

> The nature of the current church ethos or "operating system" has singled out pastors, "heroes," individual men (and sometimes women) to carry the weight of faithfulness, success and failure for an entire people. It is literally exhausting, metaphorically

backbreaking and essentially soul taking. If the life or death of a community of faith lies upon one individual or a handful of individuals, that community is only one personal crisis away from collapse.[2]

To be fair, training others for the work of ministry does take longer (in the short term) than doing it ourselves. And so a sign of a maturing leadership team is that leaders are growing in maturity and responsibility for the overall ministry and that the planter is relinquishing roles over time.

Formation leading to self-awareness. Paul's analogy of the church as the body of Christ made up of a variety of differently gifted members still serves as a foundation for all other strengths and personality assessments, whether it be Myers-Briggs, DISC, StrengthsFinder, APEST, Enneagram, or another. These assessments have proliferated because of the growing recognition of how differently people are made and how much the organization benefits from that range of strengths. The reality of globalization and the increasing awareness of the joys of ethnic and cultural diversity have contributed to a sense that our differences are to be celebrated rather than minimized.

The leadership team of the church plant I currently serve recently had a half-day retreat where we reviewed our StrengthsFinder results together. One leader has the strength known as "woo" (winning others over) and we all affirmed how much our generally task-oriented leadership team needed her relational strength. Two leaders shared the "context" strength, which helped explain why they both appreciate knowing the background and history of an issue prior to making a decision about it. I consistently find that doing exercises where we discover with greater clarity our God-given gifts and simultaneously affirm how much we need the gifts of others brings about precisely the kind of joyful interdependence that God desires. Notice how in 1 Corinthians 12:12-14 Paul weaves together diversity of gifts alongside other kinds of diversity in the body: "Just as a body, though one, has many parts, but all its many parts form one body, so it is with Christ. For we were all baptized by one Spirit so as to form one body—whether Jews or Gentiles, slave or free—and we were all given the one Spirit to drink. Even so the body is not made up of one part but of many."

Self-awareness leading to relinquishment. A planter's self-awareness drives the necessity of relinquishing control. As a planter is formed by God with humility to acknowledge and embrace his limitations and weaknesses, it opens the door for genuinely shared leadership. But this is easier said than done!

---

[2]Jessica Schrock-Ringenberg, "Motivation, Passion and Longevity in Church Leadership," 5Q Central, March 6, 2018, www.5qcentral.com/knowthyself/.

The point is that while planters may theoretically desire shared leadership, the *actual* sharing of the leadership and vision is both difficult and painful. The planter is typically the one who feels the most pressure to deliver results to donors or sponsor churches, so letting go of authority and responsibility to let leaders and teams thrive requires a Goldilocks touch—not giving too much freedom but not giving too little either. It requires the work of God's Spirit in us to cultivate immense amounts of spiritual, psychological, and relational maturity and agility. So it's most likely that *as* a planter is leading the church plant, she truly comes face to face with her limitations, and then must decide whether to cover them up or acknowledge them to God, herself, and her community.

This is a profound moment of dying to self—dying to one's self-image as a competent (and maybe even extraordinary) leader and dying to the real or perceived expectations of the launch team, network/denomination, and financial supporters. These moments of reckoning form crucial inflection points in the formation of both the planter and the leadership team. They may come in a leadership meeting when a planter resists the urge to have the answers, or in a one-on-one meeting when a planter isn't sure what to do and asks, "What do you believe we should do?" Such conversations may become eureka moments for our leaders who suddenly grasp their own significance in God's mission. Again, our own formation and the mission of the team are inextricably connected. To paraphrase Jesus, you must lose your leadership illusions in order for your leadership to be saved.

JR Woodward describes a "polycentric" (or many-centered) approach to leadership teams that moves "from solo leadership to team leadership—people with mutual authority leading together and submitting to one another, thus serving as an example for the entire community." He goes on:

> I began to realize that there was something about the ministry structure, the very one that I had helped to set up, that gave me an ever-greater temptation to shift my heart for God and his kingdom to *my* image and *my* kingdom. And I'm convinced that being the solo senior leader was a large part of my problem. . . . As you consider your leadership approach, we want to ask, What is your ultimate goal? Do you see the church as an industrial complex or as a movement?[3]

In practice, most planting teams will still have and need a lead planter. Team-based leadership does not necessarily mean leading by consensus or that the lead planter abdicates her responsibility or authority. But it does mean that the lead planter's role is to practice an empowering form of leadership that recognizes leaders with

---

[3]JR Woodward, *The Church as Movement: Starting and Sustaining Missional-Incarnational Communities* (Downers Grove, IL: InterVarsity Press, 2016), 55-56.

complementary gifts, raises them up, and values shared leadership for the sake of God's mission. Without the significant sharing of leadership, multiplying leaders and churches cannot occur. Christopher James writes,

> Planting churches with a community of leaders also testifies that the missionary nature of the church lies primarily in its corporate call *as a community* to witness to Christ. *Missional* is a more fitting adjective for churches than for individual Christians because the practice of Christian witness belongs most fundamentally to the People of God collectively and takes place primarily through local Christian communities. Individual Christian witness is derivative.[4]

Furthermore, it is not only shared leadership in and of itself that empowers a team toward missional fruitfulness, but the specific makeup of that team. I'm grateful for the work of Alan Hirsch, who has lifted up Ephesians 4:11-13 not merely as a description of equipping gifts but as a template for the makeup of leadership teams that leads to a healthy, mature, and missional body.[5] Whether the apostle Paul intended for this model to be prescriptive is certainly up for healthy debate, but the idea that specific and diverse functions should be present on a leadership team seems self-evident. Hirsch uses the acronym APEST to describe the five leadership gifts identified in Ephesians 4: apostles, prophets, evangelists, shepherds, and teachers. Hirsch has persuasively argued that the Western church was built on a Christendom model that emphasized and elevated the shepherd/teacher functions to the exclusion of the apostles/prophets/evangelists.

By and large, churches led by shepherd/teachers make up the vast majority of churches. These churches tend to be strong in biblical teaching and in caring for one another but are not generally equipped to engage the culture with the gospel. As a result, Hirsch and others have playfully and provocatively posed the question, "Where have all the APEs gone?" In other words, as we move swiftly toward a post-Christian culture, how do we exercise affirmative action on the part of entrepreneurially gifted apostles, truth-oriented prophets, and gospel-preaching evangelists? Let's keep our eyes out to tap the APEs on the shoulder and tell them how needed their gifts are for the sake of God's mission.

While a full discussion of the APEST model and its implications is beyond the scope of this chapter, suffice it to say that the giftedness of those who are on the launch team will clearly affect the DNA of the church plant. So a dilemma that every planter faces is the tension between valuing any warm body willing to serve and

---

[4]Christopher James, *Church Planting in Post-Christian Soil: Theology and Practice* (New York: Oxford University Press, 2018), 151, emphasis his.

[5]Alan Hirsch, *5Q: Reactivating the Original Intelligence and Capacity of the Body of Christ* (100 Movements, 2017).

participate, and the need to prayerfully select and be mutually formed by a group of leaders who bring a diversity of gifts that will in fact clash with one another by design. Apostles want to charge ahead while shepherds want to slow down and make sure the sheep are fed and cared for. Prophets are always pointing out the church's failures to live into the gospel while teachers believe that explaining the Scriptures will iron out any deficiencies. Sharing leadership with those quite different than ourselves is difficult work but is precisely part of engendering a beautiful and radiant bride of Christ, the church.

DIVERSE LEADERSHIP

Diversity of gifts among the leadership team represents one significant aspect of maturity and health but of course isn't the only form of diversity that our context may require. Simple demographics show how racially diverse the United States already is and will become. Census Bureau projections show that by 2020, more than half of the nation's children will be part of a minority group, and furthermore the nation as a whole will be made up of a majority of minorities by 2044.[6] How exciting to see the nations continue to come to the United States. What a remarkable opportunity this is for planting both ethnic and multicultural churches!

Current conversations around diversity focus almost exclusively on the most obvious and visible forms of diversity—gender and race. We can immediately see who is "on the platform." And this visible diversity matters and is sending signals all the time. But there are multiple axes of diversity. And so another act of humility for the planter and leadership team is recognizing how their social location may limit their viewpoint and perspective on a community and its needs.

In the Acts 13 passage, the people listed in the church at Antioch include Barnabas, Simeon who was called Niger, Lucius of Cyrene, Manaen (a lifelong friend of Herod the tetrarch), and Saul. At first glance it seems like just a list of names. But digging deeper reveals a diverse mosaic. We know from Acts 11:19-26 that this church began when Christians fled from Jerusalem to Antioch to escape persecution. It was made up of Jewish believers from Cyprus and Cyrene who then shared the gospel with the Greek-speaking Gentiles in Antioch. And there were prophets who came down from Jerusalem to Antioch (Acts 11:27) and spoke of an upcoming famine.

It makes sense that the leaders of a diverse church included people of different gifts, races, geographic backgrounds, and even different levels of political power. Barnabas was a Levite from Cyprus (Acts 4:36). Simeon called Niger (which means

---

[6]United States Census, "New Census Bureau Report Analyzes U.S. Population Projections," March 3, 2015, www .census.gov/newsroom/press-releases/2015/cb15-tps16.html.

black) was most likely a black African Christian. Lucius of Cyrene was from North Africa. Manaen grew up in Jerusalem as a lifelong friend (the word used refers to a "foster brother" or "intimate friend") of Herod the tetrarch (who had John the Baptist beheaded and who interrogated Jesus).[7] Clearly Manaen and Herod took very different paths regarding their response to Jesus! But based on their close relationship, it's likely that Manaen grew up with education, privilege, and power through his access to Herod. This is very different than many of Jesus' disciples, who were fishermen! In fact, oftentimes there may be greater differences between people of different socioeconomic levels than between people of different ethnicities in the same socioeconomic class.

Charlie Cotherman, one of this book's contributors, is planting a church in rural Pennsylvania. While we typically think of rural settings as lacking diversity, his context possesses significant vocational and socioeconomic diversity, which means there are varying levels of social capital and local power. In his church plant there are blue-collar and white-collar workers. One team member early on was a leader of a local union, while another was a former superintendent of the local school district. Both made huge contributions in part because of their relational networks and understanding of local politics.

Mark DeYmaz has pointed out that churches that are homogenous may have a more limited impact in their community because their perspective and reach is limited to one or two cultures, whereas highly diverse churches (particularly in urban centers like Los Angeles) may have greater evangelistic and missional impact because the makeup of the congregation touches multiple sectors of the city.[8] At a recent church planter event hosted by Fuller Seminary on multicultural church planting, I met a Palestinian Christian named Sam and an African American named Tyrell who are co-planting a church in Southern California. In addition to their own multiracial partnership, their core team is forming with people they already know from highly diverse backgrounds because Sam and Tyrell themselves grew up in a multicultural environment. For them, the paradigm of planting out of diversity is normative, and I am excited for the impact and witness of a church like this for such a time as this.

Herein lies the opportunity—will the leadership team function as a kaleidoscope through which we see our city and calling in ways that reflect the kingdom of God? Or will the similarities of the leaders' outlooks create tunnel vision that reinforces one another's myopia? The desired makeup of our leadership team is a

---

[7]John Stott, *The Message of Acts,* The Bible Speaks Today (Downers Grove, IL: InterVarsity Press, 1990), 216.
[8]Mark DeYmaz, "Disruption: Repurposing the Church to Redeem the Community," lecture, Exponential Conference West, Los Angeles, October 4, 2017.

direct reflection of the people to whom we feel called. So planters can stretch their imagination and pray specifically that God would draw the kind and diversity of leaders needed to fulfill their calling in a particular community. Our leadership team must surely include the very people we are seeking to reach.

SPIRIT-DRIVEN LEADERSHIP

In the book of Acts, it seems more accurate to say that the early church's leadership was characterized by discernment of the Spirit's work much more than human vision, which is often highlighted today as a must-have quality of church planters. The Holy Spirit is actively initiating, leading, and guiding the disciples toward every aspect of the expansion of the early church.

Often in leadership circles, Proverbs 29:18 is lifted up as a leadership imperative using the translation, "Where there is no vision, the people perish" (KJV). But a more accurate translation is "Where there is no *revelation*, people cast off restraint" (NIV). The distinction between vision (human initiation) and revelation (divine initiation) is one of the major themes of Scripture and of this book. While church planters generally have a bias toward action (myself included), Luke's clear emphasis in Acts is the portrayal of the Spirit as the primary actor: "The Holy Spirit said, 'Set apart for me Barnabas and Saul for the work to which I have called them'" (Acts 13:2).

What does it look like for planters to be attentive to the Spirit's leading? For one it means identifying, welcoming, and affirming the voices of leaders who are sensitive to God's Spirit, as revealed in the brief history of the church at Antioch. Not long after the persecution that spawned the church in Antioch, "a great number of people believed and turned to the Lord" (Acts 11:21). This resulted in the Jerusalem church sending Barnabas, who is described as "full of the Holy Spirit and faith" (Acts 11:24). What a great description of leaders for the church! Then prophets from Jerusalem came to Antioch and Agabus "through the Spirit predicted that a severe famine would spread over the entire Roman world" and the believers sprang into action by taking an offering for the Judean church (Acts 11:28). The believers seemed to cultivate an openness to the Spirit speaking and leading through spiritually gifted leaders—even ones from other churches. After a time of prayer at one of our church's leadership meetings, a young woman shared, "As we were praying, I had a picture of a hot air balloon being filled up." Our leaders received that image as confirmation that God's Spirit was blowing life into the ministry area we had been talking and praying about. Over and over we can lift up and validate the voices of those who are listening to the Spirit for the next step rather than moving into the primarily or exclusively strategic mode that planters are wont to do.

And we can be sensitive to the Spirit's leading us in mission through the concept of the person of peace (or, as chapter three refers to them, a person of influence). Modeled after Jesus' instructions to the seventy-two disciples in Luke 10:5-7, the person of peace is someone who is open to God and who welcomes and receives you as followers of Jesus and introduces you to new circles of unbelievers. In the Gospels we see Jesus encountering the woman at the well (Jn 4) as a person of peace who introduces Jesus to many in her city of Sychar. And throughout Acts, God identifies many persons of peace, including Cornelius (Acts 10), Lydia (Acts 16:13-15), and the Philippian jailer (Acts 16:22-38). Each person demonstrates a God-given receptivity and an ability to gather others in their sphere of influence to experience the gospel. Having our spiritual antennae up to discern persons of peace is a way we follow the Spirit's lead into our neighborhoods and community rather than merely charge ahead blindly with marketing strategies.

Our church plant has a science and faith ministry at Caltech, a nearby STEM-focused university. At a cafe on campus, an atheist professor overheard some Christian grad students discussing theology and asked them what they were talking about. They told the professor about the book they were studying and then shared about the science and faith forums we help host on campus, and he was intrigued. He felt these were important conversations and offered to help in any way. A couple months later, he participated as one of the presenters and after the event, I handed him his honorarium check but he gave it right back, saying, "I love what you are doing here and want to donate my honorarium back to your organization. I will be back at your next event as a participant." Since then, he has helped us contact other university faculty to speak. Clearly, this professor is a person of peace!

The final example of Spirit-driven leadership at Antioch is that together they sensed the call on Barnabas and Saul for the new work the Spirit was calling them to. Clearly, they had been formed to listen and obey. It is a powerful model for church planters to make time in our own lives and to make space in our leadership gatherings not only to decide but to discern, not only to cast vision but to listen for revelation.

FORMATIONAL LEADERSHIP

Even from the brief description of Acts 13, it's clear that the leaders at Antioch had some corporate practices in place: they gathered, worshiped, fasted, prayed, listened, engaged in mutual discernment, laid on hands in prayer, and commissioned people for ministry. How did these practices emerge? Of course, for those who were Jewish by background, gathering for worship of the God of Israel and prayer would be as natural as breathing. But what about mutual discernment or commissioning? Could these be discipleship practices that developed as the early disciples watched Jesus send out the Twelve and the seventy-two? Their experience of Pentecost and the life of the early church in Acts 2 surely must also have deeply shaped their leadership and formation.

The point is that there was a process by which the church at Antioch grew as disciples of Jesus and as leaders of the church. And those practices were shaped by their sense of what God was already doing in the world. As they followed the leading of the Spirit throughout the Mediterranean world, they began to proclaim the gospel to the Ethiopian eunuch, to the murderous Saul, to Cornelius the Roman centurion. Along the way, they sensed the great need for evangelism and follow up. They sensed that they were being called to send out their best and brightest to join God's mission in the world. And we can imagine that practices like discerning the calling of God together and laying on of hands became urgent practices for participating in the work of God's kingdom. These leaders were developing a missional spirituality.

> Throughout the history of the church, author and historian Alan Roxburgh notes, we find local communities shaped by practices of life or disciplines that cause them to stand out and cause others to take heed. These communities learned to live as a "contrast society" shaped by such practices as hospitality, radical forgiveness, the breaking down of social and racial barriers, and self-sacrificial love. As we live inside God's story, these habits of life empower us to give the world a taste of this Kingdom of God that is coming. . . . Teams need to experiment with their chosen rhythms and disciplines and amend or change aspects of them along the way so that they're achieving their goal of shaping you as a people.[9]

How will your team experiment with rhythms so that your life together as a church can be life-giving, prophetic, countercultural, and impactful to your community? How will God's Spirit lead you and form you to be sent into your community as a "contrast society"? Formational leadership is the process by which a community of people is mutually shaped for mission.

MISSIONAL LEADERSHIP

Last but not least, the leadership team at Antioch displayed missional leadership. By listening to the Spirit, placing their hands on Barnabas and Saul, and commissioning them for ministry, the Antioch team sent them off to embark on the first of what eventually became four missionary journeys that reshaped the Mediterranean world for Christ. A natural consequence of the *missio Dei* is that the church understands

---

[9]Steigerwald, *Dynamic Adventure*, 88.

TEAMS THAT REFLECT THE MISSION

LEN TANG

I am currently planting Missio Community Church in Pasadena, California. Seeking the right makeup for our church plant's leadership team has been an ongoing challenge and balancing act. Yet, at each point in time, God has provided the right people as we have sought to live our calling to be a multicultural congregation on mission in our neighborhoods and campuses. In our early days as a home group, we were about half Asian and half Caucasian. So we tried to make sure that those asked to facilitate the home group included both groups and encouraged leaders to share some of their cultural narratives.

In terms of mission, reaching the Caltech community was always a key part of our calling. But early on, we had no Caltech people actually attending. Finally, at one of our science/faith outreach events, I invited a Caltech grad student who ended up on our worship team and leadership team. Through her, another seeker grad student got connected to our church. Now we have about a dozen people from the Caltech community and are seeking to add another Caltech student to our leadership team who can help us deepen our understanding of and outreach to Caltech graduate students. We also have several students from Fuller Seminary and several months ago began a home group consisting of both Fuller and Caltech students, co-led by one of each. Another axis of diversity is age, and since most of our leaders are in their late twenties and early thirties, we are now reaching out to older adults in our congregation to provide wisdom, experience, and stability.

itself to be a sending agency. All too often the local church sees itself only as a gathering point rather than a launching point. Here in Acts 13 we see the direct intervention of the Holy Spirit in sending out these two gifted leaders rather than holding on to them. It never seems to occur to the other leaders that they are losing Barnabas and Saul but merely that they are obeying by sending them.

Imagine how Christian history might have unfolded without the missionary work and missionary journeys of Paul and his companions: the miraculous provision of God would not be recorded in Scripture for every generation to marvel at; the churches throughout Galatia, Asia, Macedonia, Achaia, and Rome would never have been founded; Paul's nine letters to the churches he helped plant would never have been written (leaving the New Testament a third shorter); the gospel may not have been proclaimed to the Gentiles; and Christian faith itself might still be viewed as a sect within Judaism. Of course, we trust God's sovereignty enough that had it not been the church at Antioch that engaged in the *missio Dei*, ultimately God would have raised up other heralds and planters to proclaim and extend the gospel to the ends of the earth. But the point is that the spirituality engendered by the Holy Spirit at Antioch through worship, fasting, and prayer resulted in the calling and commissioning of the greatest missionaries the world has ever seen. Through this act of discernment and obedience, they defined themselves as a church that existed not for itself but for the sake of God's mission in the world. They manifested a *missional* spirituality.

Missional leadership must always keep God's mission of the renewal of all humankind front and center. Churchill is credited with defining a fanatic as someone who can't change his mind and won't change the subject. Missional leaders must be fanatical about God's mission, and repetition is a key tool of the fanatic. It means having a relentless focus on the mission of God in the world rather than defaulting back to the Christendom model that we were cautioned about in this book's preface.

The Exponential Conference is described as "the largest annual gathering of church planting leaders on the planet."[10] Their vision is to increase the percentage of US churches that ever reproduce from less than 4 percent (currently) to more than 10 percent. They are lifting up the value of multipliers who "focus on biblical disciple making and an intentionality to deploy rather than accumulate."[11] In other words, having a tenth of American churches think in terms of multiplying themselves would create a tipping point that would change the landscape of Christianity by mobilizing Christians, releasing leaders, and planting churches in our country. In order to do so, they are challenging church leaders and church planters to stop thinking of growth by accumulation or even by planting individual church plants but to instead be characterized by a movement of raising up other leaders who will be sent out to plant church-planting churches. Such a perspective would be consistent with the missional mindset of the Antioch church. It's not that the Antioch church was fully formed before it sent out Barnabas and Saul. Instead, a missional posture is to respond immediately to the Holy Spirit's prompting by sending out leaders as soon as they are called, rather than wait for some illusory numerical attendance goal to engage in reproduction by sending.

Rather, many plants are "planting while pregnant," meaning that from their inception (or conception to keep the pregnancy theme running), a church plant identifies a planter to serve on the church planting team who is already in training to lead the next church plant. The advantages are clear: the planter-in-training is experiencing and observing every step of the church planting process and as you can imagine, is extremely teachable and motivated because she or he knows that they

---

[10]Exponential, home page, accessed April 16, 2018, www.exponential.org.
[11]Todd Wilson, *Multipliers: Leading Beyond Addition* (Exponential Resources, 2017), 15.

will shortly be living this out. This just-in-time training breaks the sequential thinking around church planting and shows a way of simultaneously discipling and sending. At the church I lead, God graciously brought a church planting resident to us just nine months after our public launch, and we are currently preparing to help his church launch later this year.

Who, then, among your leadership team might God be calling and commissioning? If God's Spirit led your church as he did the church at Antioch, would you and your team be prepared to send out your two best leaders? Again, such a missional challenge clearly draws us back into core issues like the death of ego and self and the formation of a robust spirituality that is able to decrease in order that God's mission might increase.

To sum up, in the context of a diverse, increasingly post-Christian country, a leadership team that is genuinely shared, diverse along many axes, and missional in its core DNA cannot but help to produce a healthy church. Over time, as your team serves together on mission and is further invested in and connected to its city and its missional context, it develops patterns and practices of missional living that emanate outward and catalyze the missional spirituality of the whole church plant (which will be covered in the next chapter). This is not meant to be a formula but rather markers of health that inform the kinds of leaders and mix of leaders that we are asking God to draw together.

PRACTICAL NEXT STEPS

Most of this chapter has focused on the *who*—the kind of people to form a leadership team. But *how* do we go about forming a core group? The remainder of the chapter does not offer a specific model for developing a leadership team but rather seeks to establish some developmental markers and milestones along the way. Many of the specifics will depend on the type of church planting model you are using, and chapter ten will focus more on the steps for forming a team. While acknowledging that every context will require spiritual and communal discernment, here are some next steps to consider in forming a team for God's mission.

Focus on leaders and the lost. In the early stages of a church plant, it's best to invest the bulk of your time in two areas: (1) building relationships with unbelievers in your community, and (2) discipling and equipping the emerging leaders on your launch team. By doing so, you are both learning about the way unbelievers think and relate so as to form authentic connections with them and their cities, as well as strengthening the leadership core by relationally investing in those with leadership gifts who demonstrate interest and maturity. Ideally, you can then practice the with-me principle by inviting leaders to come with you to the meetings and conversations you are having with unbelievers so that you are showing and not just telling leaders how to live on mission. The whole leadership team is then being mutually formed by what you are learning about what God is doing in your city. Debriefing the gathering with your leader(s) provides yet another teachable moment.

Practice the little-big principle. Who should be brought onto the leadership team? A planter's default answer might be "any warm body," but a better approach is to apply the little-big principle that Jesus articulates in Luke 16:10: "Whoever can be trusted with very little can also be trusted with much, and whoever is dishonest with very little will also be dishonest with much." As you give little tasks to volunteers, those you observe to participate faithfully and open handedly (as opposed to those who request or demand to be put in a leadership position) are demonstrating greater readiness to be entrusted with big responsibilities. Over time, these are signs (which of course still need to be prayed through and discerned) that this leader is ready to help oversee others.

Use flexible team structures. Established churches typically have well-defined and long-term leadership teams (such as an elder board, executive staff, session, etc.). But church plants are dynamic organisms, so the makeup and format of the leadership team may have a short shelf life—which is normal and even healthy. Certain leaders may be on a leadership team for a season and then move back into a specific ministry team that is a better fit. Newer leaders may be vetted and invited on to the leadership team. Flexibility enables church plants to respond to growth and momentum in nimble ways.

Normalize conflict. The significant responsibilities and fast pace may lead to leadership conflicts over vision, methodology, or interpersonal style. When we step back and look at the pressures facing a church planting team, and observe hundreds of other church planting teams, we realize we need to normalize conflict rather than treat it as an aberration or even failure among God's people. Even Peter and Paul faced conflict (Gal 2:11-14), and Barnabas and Paul (whose missional partnership we celebrated earlier in the chapter) actually parted ways over a disagreement about whether or not to include John Mark (Acts 15:36-39). If you're in the trenches, you're going to get your hands dirty. If we see conflict as par for the course, we're less likely to overreact to it. Recalling the crucible image from the start of the chapter, it's inevitable that gifted people with strong vision and passion, and who are relatively new to each other, will disagree on the mission or methods of the church plant. Planters are tempted to think of themselves as pastoral failures for not averting a conflict or navigating the aftermath. But if we can see conflict as a normal and even necessary part of building a leadership community and forming resilient disciples, then conflict can be productive even while it's hard.

Develop a leadership covenant. How can a leadership team develop the fortitude to withstand such conflicts? Discerning and developing a leadership covenant can be a useful tool (see two examples below). This is an agreement that guides the way the team interacts. A leadership covenant takes the church's overall core values and distills them into practical guidelines for how leadership team members relate to one another, to the broader church, and to the unbelieving community.

CONCLUSION

Planting a church together is most definitely a crucible in which the elements of calling and context interact, leading to the creation of something new. Will that new thing arrive stillborn or healthy? Will it be barren or have many children? When the planter and leaders are together being shaped by your context; when your discipleship, outreach, leadership, events, and preaching are all being formed and

---

LEADERSHIP COVENANT EXAMPLES

LEADERSHIP COVENANT, FIRST CHURCH IN PHILADELPHIA, PENNSYLVANIA

As a leader of First Church, I recognize that others will be influenced and impacted by my attitudes, lifestyle, and character. I will embody and reflect the values and principles of First Church and will follow the leadership of First Church. I understand that my personal freedoms may be limited because of my responsibility to others under my leadership to whom I am an example. In accepting a leader role I agree to live according to biblical values and standards to the best of my ability including the following:

I will strive for personal integrity

. . . by supporting the core beliefs and values of First Church.

. . . by maintaining sexual abstinence in singleness and fidelity in marriage.

. . . by not drinking alcohol to excess.

. . . by committing to honesty in my personal and professional conduct.

. . . by not causing others to stumble. (I understand that as a leader my personal freedoms are trumped by my responsibility to be an example for others. Leadership is ultimately about serving.)

I will protect the unity of our church

. . . by supporting the staff and senior leadership of our church.

. . . by refusing to gossip, complain, or participate in conversations where others gossip or complain.

I will support the mission of First Church

   . . . by praying for and inviting others.

   . . . by warmly welcoming guests.

   . . . by living my life in a way that honors God and points others to him.

I will support the ministry of First Church

   . . . by attending regularly.

   . . . by giving financially.

   . . . by serving the church and community.

Conflict Resolution Covenant from Cedar Creek Church

We, the leaders and staff of Cedar Creek Church, desire to model a godly, biblical way of resolving conflict and preserving the unity of Christ's Church and so commit to the following covenant. In the power of the Holy Spirit, we strive to create a healthy congregation that is able to resolve conflict when (not if) it happens. We are guided particularly by Matthew 18 and Matthew 5 which when taken together call us to resolve conflict and seek reconciliation whether we are the one who has sinned or are the one sinned against:

> Matthew 18:15-17 *"If your brother or sister sins, go and point out their fault, just between the two of you. If they listen to you, you have won them over. But if they will not listen, take one or two others along, so that 'every matter may be established by the testimony of two or three witnesses.' If they still refuse to listen, tell it to the church; and if they refuse to listen even to the church, treat them as you would a pagan or a tax collector."*

> Matthew 5:23-24 *"Therefore, if you are offering your gift at the altar and there remember that your brother or sister has something against you, leave your gift there in front of the altar. First go and be reconciled to that person; then come and offer your gift."*

In light of these passages, we commit to:

> Keep short accounts: If I have a concern or conflict with another person, I will prayerfully go directly to them to resolve it. If another person comes to me with a concern or conflict about someone else, I will reference Matthew 18 and our church's desire to be healthy and biblical, and exhort them to go directly to that person.

> Offer mediation: If a person comes to me but feels unable to go directly to another person, I will either offer to be present as a third party or help them identify an appropriate third party such as an elder or small group leader.

> Be persistent: If my first attempt to resolve conflict with a person is not fruitful, I will pray about it and bring another leader with me.

> Refuse to be used: If a person repeatedly comes to me about a conflict with another person but is unwilling to seek resolution, I will lovingly but clearly decline to listen to their concerns about that person.

informed by the interactions with your community and core; when your leaders are shaping one another and gaining a heart to reach out to the neighborhood; then you know you are developing a missional spirituality. We'll turn next to the inevitable impact such a dynamic will have on the whole congregation—and the churches yet to be planted out of that congregation.

DISCUSSION QUESTIONS

1. Would people on the leadership team describe their experience as life-giving or resulting in burnout?

2. What tool(s) might help leaders identify their gifts and strengths individually and corporately?

3. How has conflict formed or deformed your church planting team?

4. What are ways that the planter and the team inadvertently conspire to cause the planter to become the ministry bottleneck?

5. What forms of diversity on your leadership team would best enable your church plant to faithfully embody the gospel in your context?

6

HOW DO WE LEAD
A COMMUNITY INTO
FLOURISHING?

MISSIONAL SPIRITUALITY FOR
CHURCH PLANTS

SCOTT W. SUNQUIST

*With all humility
and gentleness, with
patience, bearing
with one another in
love, making every
effort to maintain the
unity of the Spirit in
the bond of peace.*

EPHESIANS 4:2-3

I FELT HONORED TO BE INVITED TO SUNDAY DINNER at our pastor's home with my new wife. It was a fairly large church, and since we were only twenty-two years old and had not accomplished that much in the church, it was a privilege to be in the home of a spiritual leader we had come to respect. His sermons were biblical, memorable, and, well, they were one reason the church kept growing. Frankly the sermons (and the great group of younger people) were the reason we had chosen this church after we got married. During dinner the (very shy) pastor said little. He seemed preoccupied. His wife, a gifted woman of hospitality and emotional engagement, listened to us, asked us questions, and seemed to function as a parent for young marrieds away from home.

The pastor quietly got up and said he was going to take a nap. He was gone.

The pastor's wife apologized on his behalf, but she remarked that he is very shy and being with lots of people (like thousands every Sunday morning!) really wore him out. It caused me to wonder about his health, leadership style, and how the church was or was not a healthy community for the pastor. I repeat, he was a great pastor of a very large and growing church. But his relationships were sparse, inconsistent, and distant. Is this the destiny of all church planters: eventually we come under extreme pressure and become alienated from wholesome and healing relationships? And that is when we are "successful"?

We have already looked at the spiritual life of the church planter and leadership team. We might look at these concerns as the deeply personal life in God where we are vulnerable, exposed, and where we receive healing and power for ministry. But we are not lone rangers, nor are we meant to be alone in ministry. So often ministry models like the one above, or the ones many pastors and popular Christian books implicitly support, look more like the lone cowboy riding off into the sunset than a model of shared leadership and deep relationship with God and others. This temptation may be especially strong for church planters who often find themselves feeling relatively alone in the early days of a plant. Indeed, how many church planters leave a larger established church full of kids' programming and friends at similar stages in life only to find themselves launching a church with almost none of those relational support networks? In our estimate this scenario is a fairly common part of church planting. So many church planters know who they are sent *by* (the missional, sending God), who they are sent *to* (a local context or people), but have a harder time figuring out who they are sent *with*. Who is joining them as they seek to be part of the *missio Dei*? How will these ministry partners and friends grow together in their personal relationships and in their relationships with God? How will they develop a missional spirituality together that will not only sustain them in the difficult times and protect them from the allure of a machismo or lone-ranger church planting model, while also preparing them to be sent as an entire community?

With these concerns and questions in mind, we now want to look at what it means to plant churches that are healthy communities of spiritual growth and vitality. At the beginning, we need to admit that this may be the biggest struggle in planting a church: developing a *genuine community* that dispenses grace, reaches the lost, welcomes the wounded, and empowers for ministry. In a world that is supercharged by the private and individualistic, building communities of servanthood is countercultural. Our argument here is that it is also inviting and winsome to develop communities of mission and growth. Such communities lead to the flourishing of individuals and communities. In a world of isolation, rampant depression, and loneliness, a healthy community is like an attractive oasis in the desert. In this chapter we look at how to develop from the very foundation a healthy relational life in a church plant.

COMMUNITY OF GRACE, GROWTH, AND GOING

One of the key elements in the health and life of a church plant is the vitality of the relationships in the core leadership. The church will reflect the personality and spirituality of the planter, but even more so the church will reflect the life of the community of leaders. Though it is not always recognized by observers or even by all church planters, every church that is planted is planted by a team, not an individual. And all these teams, as we have seen, will be put under great pressure (church planting is a crucible, remember) together. This core leadership team will be an icon or model for the rest of the church. Their Christian character and level of trust will be the pattern of character and trust for the whole church. This is why it is wise, as we noted in the previous chapter, for this team to work closely together, telling their stories and learning to support one another before inviting others in to a future church. In short, the church must be led by *character and relationships*, not *coercion and rules*. Character is formed in a community through a deepening spirituality, which is dependent on honesty and accountability.

Here is another way to frame the importance of communal spiritual growth among the leadership team. When we are planting a church, we are planting a community of *grace, growth,* and *going.* We receive *grace* from God and offer it to each other. It is a wonderful thing to become involved in a grace-filled community where you are accepted for who you are and supported and loved, even when you are not so lovely. We also gather to *grow* in God's grace, which means we will grow in knowledge, self-control, humility, and wisdom. We will be different as a result of our grace-filled community life. This is something that happens as a community where we help one another with knowledge of God's Word and God's ways. We also learn to confess our sins, which accelerates our growth into Jesus Christ. Finally, and woven together with the other two, we are planting communities that are on the *go.* This means that our grace-filled and growing community is attentive to where the missional God is calling and sending us into mission locally and across the world. The three—grace, growth, and going—are the basic elements of our communal spirituality. And, as we saw in chapter two, these elements (also framed as communion, community, and co-mission) will help to answer the question of what God's kingdom will look like in a local community.

Think of the napping pastor from the beginning of this chapter: he will model for the other leaders, and for those who will eventually join the church, what it means to grow as a Christian, either as a loner or as part of the community. If the pastor is a loner, private in his spiritual life, this will communicate to others something deeply broken about our life in Christ. The life in Christ is, in fact, a life of love and grace; love and grace always require others. Times alone, as we saw in chapter four, are intentional times of silence and retreat, not unintended isolation and loneliness. Love (except for the narcissist) requires an *other.* In fact, virtually all the commands from the New Testament involve relationships. Very few commands are for only private concerns.

Think about this: What is love? It is about serving other people. A person cannot love alone. In addition, love is increased with greater knowledge and understanding of others. Love requires discipline and a deepening knowledge. For example, I can love my wife far more perfectly than a member of the church who has only attended for three weeks. The church grows as a community of "one anothers" as they get to know each other more intimately over time.

Here are some "one anothers" from Scripture that show a deepening community life in the church. We encourage you to reflect on these with your church plant leaders or in another small group in your church:

> Now that I, your Lord and Teacher, have washed your feet, you also should *wash one another's feet*. (Jn 13:14)

> Now may the God who gives perseverance and encouragement grant you to *be of the same mind with one another* according to Christ Jesus. (Rom 15:5 ESV)

> *Accept one another*, then, just as Christ accepted you, in order to bring praise to God. (Rom 15:7)

> I myself am convinced, my brothers and sisters, that you yourselves are full of goodness, filled with knowledge and competent to *instruct one another*. (Rom 15:14)

> And may the Lord cause you to increase and *abound in love for one another, and for all people*, just as we also do for you. (1 Thess 3:12 ESV)[1]

These passages remind us of our responsibility for each other in service to Jesus Christ. Not all communities (and certainly not most religions) have such mutuality and love at their core. One quick example will help.

Our family lived for eight years in Singapore, where I was pastor of a young church that was also planting churches. During a period of three years working with what were actually three separate congregations being planted in three areas of the city (actually, three areas of the country!), I did over fifty weddings. The average age of the congregation was twenty-two, so many people were getting married. Over 90 percent of our congregation were first-generation Christians, so the family members who attended the weddings were generally Buddhist, Taoist, or some type of Chinese religionist (an official designation on the census). Thus, the wedding congregation did not know how to act in a Christian worship service. Think of doing a Christian wedding in a Buddhist temple.

Christian worship is communal. Buddhist devotion is private, or possibly includes family, but it is not communal. Because the wedding congregation was

---

[1]For more "one anothers," see Jn 13:34; Rom 12:10, 16; 14:13, 19; 16:16; 1 Cor 11:33; Gal 5:13; 6:2; Eph 4:2, 32; 5:19, 21; Phil 2:3; Col 3:9, 13, 16.

mostly not Christian, we had to give very specific directions about what could or could not be done during a wedding. Buddhists worship when and where they like and are unaware of others around them. They might leave an offering at one altar, get a bite to eat, go meditate on an image of the Buddha, or make a phone call. It struck me during each of these weddings what a wonderful thing the church is! Our newlywed couple is entering into a community. Their new Christian friends (the church) prepare the wedding reception and at times a wedding meal. New friends support them and invite them into their homes. New friends become an extended family supporting their marriage and, if God should so bless, the raising of their children. New friends stand with them in times of joy, suffering, and transition. The Buddhist or Taoist goes to the temple alone or with family members. There is no community like we experience in a Christian wedding or even at a Christian worship service.

Again, this type of commitment and service is countercultural. In a Buddhist context it is countercultural to be part of a religion that is so communal, where so many non–family members gather and care for each other. In the West, the church is countercultural because our society, filled with advertising, internet pop-up ads, movies, social media, and indeed most all media, focuses on you the individual who can and should make your own decisions for your own good. We are privatized, individualized, and, frankly, alone. In contrast, the church is part of our good that God provides. In this case, the good is a community of grace, growth, and going. But this community does not just happen. It involves intentionality and commitment to cultivate genuine community. How does this happen?

IT'S A FAMILY AFFAIR

First it must be said that we begin with the family, because that is where God begins. From creation to the call of Abraham and throughout the narratives of the Old Testament, family and genealogies take center stage. God works through families. It may be that the breakdown of the family is the greatest cause for the decline of Christianity in the West.[2] Studies have repeatedly shown that the rapid exit of youth from our churches is directly related to the relevance (or lack thereof) of the faith to young people as expressed in the family and community. When parents integrate their personal faith within the family and when, as a family, they are involved in a Christian community, children generally grow up to affirm the faith and the vital importance of the church for their lives and their faith.

---

[2]Kenneth Woodward, *Getting Religion: Faith, Culture, and Politics from the Age of Eisenhower to the Era of Obama* (New York: Convergent, 2016), 399-414.

Many studies show that people between the ages of eighteen and forty-five who now self-identify as "nones" are not becoming atheists. This group is growing rapidly and the majority (78 percent) say they were raised attending a church.[3] They still believe something, and are often unhappy and disengaged believers, but their belief has become a type of personal therapy rather than a robust and integrated belief. The integration of faith starts with the family. The lack of integration of faith, or the disconnect between profession of faith and lifestyle, is the single greatest cause for children disconnecting from the church when they grow up. Parents who say they trust God and believe in Jesus but cheat on their taxes, yell at or divorce their spouse, show greed, have addictive behaviors—such parents lead children away from the faith.

When the faith is integrated well in the family, children often grow up to be spiritual leaders. Parents who pray, know their Bibles, care for the poor, struggle with wealth and possessions, and live out their own Christian struggles in the family—these parents make disciples. And, as we all know, stronger marriages build stronger and more resilient children.

Church planting teams need to first strengthen their own marriages and families, whether they are married, married with children, or single. It is out of healthy family life that healthy churches can develop. In addition, these churches will then become places where marriages have positive models, when there are so few today. Children thrive when they have others around them to support them. In fact, the Sticky Faith research project at Fuller Seminary has made it clear that children thrive and keep their faith if they have five committed adults around them, supporting them and praying for them.[4] A healthy church where adults connect with children is good for young people and helps build strong families.

The same is true of marriages. When there are other adults around a struggling couple, the marriage has much more hope. We recognize that divorce does occur, and grace and forgiveness must be the context of what I am saying here. However, we never hear someone say, "My divorce was great. I want to get married and divorced again." The church community should invite broken families, as it invites broken individuals, to provide support, accountability, guidance, and stability. The

---

[3]The Pew Research Center has done some of the best and most nuanced research regarding nones, those who do not identify with any one religion or religious belief. See Michael Lipka, "A Closer Look at America's Rapidly Growing Religious 'Nones,'" Pew Research Center, May 13, 2015, www.pewresearch.org/fact-tank/2015/05/13/a-closer-look-at-americas-rapidly-growing-religious-nones/; and Michael Lipka, "Why America's 'Nones' Left Religion Behind," Pew Research Center, August 24, 2016, www.pewresearch.org/fact-tank/2016/08/24/why-americas-nones-left-religion-behind/.

[4]Kara E. Powell and Chap Clark, *Sticky Faith: Everyday Ideas to Build Lasting Faith in Your Kids* (Grand Rapids: Zondervan, 2011), 93-122.

family was God's idea and we should see it as our responsibility to help build families that are both resilient and joyful.

Another part of this spirituality of the family is that when we have strong families in the church, we have the possibility of strong extended families. There will be homes where the lonely, the homeless, the grieving, and the widow can come and be part of a family. Every holiday and every church event is an opportunity to invite in single adults or others who are away from home or family. Every family with an apartment or house can look to invite in international students, immigrants, and others who need to be part of a family. Family is not a private club as much it is a welcoming home.

Obviously, strong marriages, families, and cultures rooted in extending familial hospitality to others will benefit church plants and established churches alike. But in the early stages of a church plant, the strain on marriages and families can be especially intense. In those first months and years when children's programing and pastoral support committees are still lacking or underdeveloped, when many church planters are working bivocationally to make ends meet, it is extremely important that planters and launch teams keep families and marriages in mind (especially their own!) as they worship, pray, plan, and gather. The church is the family of God, built from, and building up, strong families. The stress of planting a church is so great, and the failure rate is so high, that it is essential to build a church on strong families.[5]

As noted above, strong families begin with strong marriages. If a church planter or pastor is married, the health of the church will be deeply impacted by the health of the pastor's marriage, as well as the marital health of other key leaders. It is no wonder that the enemy so frequently seems to focus some of his strongest attacks on church leaders in this area. All of this means that in the stress and busyness of a new church, planters need to be especially attuned to their marriages. It is never worth losing a marriage to build a church. By valuing his or her own marriage—and by demonstrating that he or she values the marriages of other leaders and volunteers above their service in the church—a church planter builds an esteem for marital health into the fabric of a community from the beginning.

The family stresses of a church planter also extend beyond the marriage. As more than one church planter with kids has discovered, creating a positive environment where children and teens can be spiritually formed in a church plant can

---

[5]It is very hard to get good statistics on the failure rate of church plants. The Southern Baptists and some other denominations do a much better job now supporting and preparing church planters, so the success rate is close to 80 percent over an eight-year period. See Kevin Ezell, "Measuring Church Planting Success," accessed February 21, 2019, www.bpnews.net/44452/measuring-church-planting-success. However, many networks with more zeal than patience set up church planters for failure. In this tension, marriages and families suffer.

be challenging to say the least. In some cases this is because a church plant simply does not have the funds to hire a children's pastor or the volunteer base to staff a nursery or children's program. Also, in their early stages many church plants attract a higher number of twentysomethings and single adults. For the church planter with young children it may be a while before there are other children who can serve as friends and can create a critical mass to form a children's ministry. The challenge can be even more pronounced for church planters who are parenting teens. In these scenarios it is especially important that the entire church community prayerfully discern how they might create space and intergenerational relationships in which children and teens can flourish.

LITTLE CHURCHES IN THE BIG CHURCH

I remember many decades ago visiting my grandmother in her church in the small eastern Kansas town of Oswego. The Presbyterian Church of Oswego had seen more glorious days; it probably boomed immediately after the Second World War, then people started leaving the small midwestern towns and the stately churches began to feel cavernous and museum-like. However, even in its heyday it was not a very large church—maybe a few hundred in attendance. When we attended in the 1960s, my grandmother, the former editor of the town newspaper, knew everyone and everyone knew her. She was cared for in her declining years by a congregation that knew she was one of them in Jesus Christ. It is both a great joy and a little scary to attend a church where everyone knows you.

When a church is starting out, or if a church is very small, it is easier to develop the kind of community that can carry out the "one another" commands. However, most congregations are too large for everyone to care for and pray for everyone else. Even from Jesus' example, little churches of Jesus' disciples have been the basic structure of the church. For Jesus, it was his twelve disciples and his three closest friends. It shouldn't be that different for us.

It is worth thinking a little bit further about Jesus' church planting movement and his formation of disciples as his top priority. Throughout the Gospels Jesus' primary concern was to form a small community of twelve. On numerous occasions he steps away from a large, popular movement. In the first chapter of Mark the tension is already evident. Jesus is tempted, calls his first disciples, teaches, heals people late into the evening, and then early in the morning goes out for solitude and prayer. People come after him. "Everyone is looking for you!" he hears. Rather than playing to the crowd, he ducks out the back door. "Let us go somewhere else—to the nearby villages—so I can preach there also" (Mk 1:35-38).

After his good friend John the Baptist was killed, Jesus withdrew in a boat to a deserted place. The crowds pursued him and would not leave even when it was past dinner time. He had to feed them (five thousand men plus women and children). Again, rather than building on this popular movement, he sent away his disciples, and Jesus went up the mountain to pray (Mt 14).

Many times—possibly most of the time—his teaching and healing were done with and for the benefit of his twelve closest associates. We almost get the idea that the crowds were not the real purpose or audience for Jesus' ministry. In Matthew 16, Jesus interacts with the religious leaders and calls them part of an "evil and adulterous generation." Then he turns to the Twelve, warns them about the religious leaders, and then asks this intimate group the key question: "But who do you say that I am?" (Mt 16:15). Jesus' true identity, his intimate connection with people, comes not to the crowds, not to the five thousand hungry souls, not even to a group of religious leaders, but to a small group of twelve. But more than that, his even greater revelation of himself comes to only three: Peter, James, and John are led up a mountain to experience one of the greatest most powerful moments of self-revelation. Jesus is transfigured and he is seen communing with Elijah and Moses. Something of such intimate and cosmic proportions was shared only with his three closest disciples.

I do not think it is a stretch to apply such levels of intimacy and spiritual growth to our church plant. In leading a new church, we need to have a few intimate friends with a very high level of trust. These are no-matter-what friends. They will speak to you directly about your strengths and where you are failing. They are not people pleasers, but truth tellers. They do not worship you, but they respect you. They will not shrink from holding you accountable because they are willing to risk friendship for holiness, intimacy for truth.

Then there will be a larger, more diverse group of ten to twelve to whom you impart both teaching and responsibility and from whom you receive advice and correction. This may be your leadership team. With this team there is a high level of commitment, care, and confession. The powerful thing about having a small group of leaders working in deep partnership is that you don't have to prove anything to the larger congregation because you already know that you are imperfect, you know you have made mistakes, and you are already forgiven. You can be genuine, humble, and strong in your leadership when you lead out of a good healthy team of ten or twelve.

Little churches in the big church start with the leadership team, but that is only the beginning. As the church grows and develops, as it plants new churches and starts new initiatives, the leaders must always recognize that the basic ecology of the church is built on cell groups. We use different names for these smaller groups because they function in many different ways to bring about health and wholeness for the congregation. In general, everyone in the church should find a group or two where there is spiritual health, accountability, and opportunity to serve others. It is not healthy for anyone to participate in a cell group only for what they receive. There must always be an understanding that even the most infirm, aged, poorly educated, or emotionally wounded enters the group to grow and serve others. This is what it means to live out a "one another" lifestyle. Here are some examples of little churches that might develop in the big church.[6]

Affinity groups. There is no reason to resist people coming together because they are all thinking about what it means to be a public-school teacher and faithful disciple of Christ. There should be room in the local church for teachers to come together and pray and study the Bible together. Christian lawyers have a need to get together. Young mothers, or young parents, or college students should be able to get together to share similar struggles and concerns, and to think about these issues biblically (together). However, people should not meet *only* with affinity groups because if they do so, they are only reinforcing what sets them apart from other people.

Crosscultural and crossgenerational groups. Churches that are developing in urban areas must have as part of their calling to bring together diverse groups. Diversity is more than culture (but it is culture), for it also includes gender, economic class, and age. Small groups in the church can be the place where reconciliation occurs naturally. Rather than doing studies or sponsoring classes on reconciliation or race, live out a life together through small groups.

Neighborhood groups. Another way of developing small-group life is in neighborhoods. Small groups can develop in areas of the city or town with an understanding that they are sent communities serving their local communities. Neighbors can be invited in, and in this way the church grows naturally and geographically. This is one of the most natural ways that a church can express its missional existence.

Youth. Most of us think of youth groups as evening meetings with recreation, food, and a devotion. This all-too-common model may actually contribute to the high rate of attrition of American Christian youth from churches. Youth are not objects to be controlled through moral activities but integral members of the community. Youth need their time together, but they also need wholesome experiences

---

[6]For a *larger* discussion of smaller communities in the big community, see Scott W. Sunquist, *Understanding Christian Mission: Participation in Suffering and Glory* (Grand Rapids: Baker Academic, 2013), 286-95. See also Sunquist, *Why Church?* (Downers Grove, IL: IVP Academic, 2019), chap. 8.

of Christian life with adults, and even with children. They need to be fully connected with the church family, even as they have their own space and time to connect with peers. A church that integrates and listens well to its youth will soon find less loneliness and alienation. The church will also find that other youth will want to be part of such a community. A good way of remembering this is the way we think of other areas of the church, the body of Christ: particular and corporate. Youth have their own special needs today (navigating technology, sexuality, racism, etc.) but they also should be treated as integral and important members of the body.

I learned this when our own boys were entering high school. When our oldest son was entering ninth grade, I asked him if he wanted to invite five other friends (our van only seated seven) to have breakfast at 6:30 a.m. on Wednesdays, tell jokes, and study the Bible. He said yes, and so we did. Almost every Wednesday during the school year, between seven and twelve of us (some started driving themselves when they turned sixteen) met at a local restaurant near the school for breakfast, jokes, and Bible. We called it the "Breakfast Club." It lasted six years and it helped lead some to faith and reinforced the faith of others. Not all attended our church, but it was a small group for youth that connected with the larger Christian family.

Service or mission groups. Small groups in the church can also meet to carry out the mission of the church. Not all mission or outreach should come from the leadership. Small groups meeting on their own should be encouraged to pray, study Scripture, and reach out locally, serving in shelters and soup kitchens, for instance. Some groups may study how to reach unreached people in Asia or in the West and then help to lead the church in global outreach (see "actions groups" below).

It is true that some of the formation or sanctification of church members occurs from and during Sunday morning worship. But most of the transformation takes place in smaller groups, where people discuss and apply the Scripture, confess their sins, receive support and encouragement, and then come back again and again to support "one another." When we live out the faith in community, we find the truth of the teachings and the life of the theology we study. Small groups encourage embodying the teachings of Jesus. Like Jesus' community of twelve, small groups or little churches are places where genuine community develops, where lives are spiritually formed, and where individuals and communities are prepared to be sent to "Jerusalem, Judea, Samaria, and the ends of the earth." As in families, these smaller communities provide a level of intimacy, honesty, trust, and knowledge that feeds our growth in grace and mission.[7]

---

[7]For a brief history of the significance of small groups, see Sunquist, *Understanding Christian Mission*, 293-94.

CHURCH AS COMMUNITY NOT LIKE US

As we were shopping for a house in Pasadena, our agent drove us through various neighborhoods and we quickly discovered that we could not afford a house anywhere—of any size. Then the agent surprised us by saying, "I am going to drive through some neighborhoods, and you tell me, when you look at the homes *and the people*, if you feel like this is a place where you could live and be happy." Wow. He wanted to give us a choice to live with people like us. It is called segregation.

Well, he did not realize whom he was showing around. Nancy and I had previously lived in a predominantly black area and (in Asia) a predominantly Chinese, Indian, and Malay neighborhood, and I was going to be the dean of a school of *intercultural* studies. We love cultural diversity. Rather than wanting to stay with our own people, we have grown to love living with people from diverse economic and cultural backgrounds (with different foods!). We believe God loves cultural diversity too, because he has given us a few glimpses of heaven and it is a very multicultural place (Rev 7:9-10).

A church is to be a "called out" (*ekklēsia* from *ek* and *kaleō*) people from a local context. Thus, the church should reflect the local community, not an imposed or artificial community, but a real community in a particular place. This means, of course, that if a local community is diverse, the church, beginning with its leadership, should also be diverse. But it also means that the church should include and welcome all types of people: old and young, well-educated and less educated, immigrants and long-term residents, large families and single people, wealthy and unemployed, and those with different abilities. This is what always struck me about going to church when I was young. The people who were our friends from church were not the people we would choose to be our friends. You don't get to pick your parents or family, and you don't get to pick your church family. They come to you and you accept them and learn to serve one another (even the strange ones).

If a church is going to be diverse (including gender diversity) it must begin with diverse leadership. For instance, all the leaders from the start cannot be white guys from the same softball team. From the beginning, a diverse community of leaders must forge a divine alliance of being for "one another" for the sake of the community. You should pray for diverse talents, economic backgrounds, ethnic identity, vocations, and you need both men and women, young and old. As this diverse leadership team learns to serve and love each other, they will be the model for the type of church you are planting. In addition, a diverse leadership team will attract a more diverse congregation.

We attended a church once that had a mixed-race couple or two in the congregation. The praise band was led by an African American woman with Anglo, Korean

American, and African American musicians and vocalists. Within two years, a number of interracial couples began to attend and some joined. In addition, we found that some African immigrants and Egyptians felt comfortable attending the church. What I learned from this is that the diverse leaders from the start (multiracial couples and multicultural musicians) made people from ethnic minorities feel comfortable in the church. Visitors from other ethnic groups did not feel like they stood out. This was an urban congregation, but I think the same is true with other groups.

When there is a ministry to the deaf, for instance, other families with deaf members feel welcome. Any type of diversity, not only ethnic or racial, will both challenge people to love beyond their own group and build stronger community.

I believe that one of the great tests of spiritual growth is our ability to love and serve those who are different. In this chapter, we are thinking about formation in community. Christian formation is always challenging because we are becoming more like Christ, who loves all people and nations, regardless of their sinfulness or giftedness. When we close ourselves up into our own homogenous community, we are not living into our calling as disciples of Christ. Intentional community with those who are different from ourselves is a signpost to others that God is alive. "Look at those people! How they love one another."

This type of formation means that we need to be attentive to the different subcultures and groupings of people in our neighborhood or parish. Again, this does not happen naturally; it requires intentionality and commitment. The church must seek out the different populations in their parish or local area and then invite in groups that are diverse economically, racially, culturally, educationally, and so on. One of the theses of this book—and a commitment shared by all the contributors—is that the church must resist the divisions of the broader culture and always seek diversity. This is part of our spirituality, not just part of our ecclesiology.

DISCIPLINES? LET'S JUST CALL THEM COMMUNITY RHYTHMS

Either up close or from a distance, I have watched ten or fifteen of my students graduate and then go out to plant churches. Most of the students have had a very difficult time. It is hard work to pull together more people than just your closest friends. I assume from the beginning of a church plant that we want to reach more people, not fewer people. And I assume that we want greater transformation and not less. Put another way, there is no special sanctity in remaining small, and there is no missional heroism in looking just like the culture around us. This is not to say that bigger is better nor that the more dramatic and edgy the better. I just think that Jesus' concern to reach all the nations is a really big task, and his salvation is so wonderful, that I want to find ways to reach more and more people with this good news.

So here is what I have noticed. The two themes of reaching more people and praying and working for greater transformation are related to a third theme: community rhythm. Think of them as three strands of a cord. One strand is pretty weak, but two may be stronger. Three strands, though, are very strong and much to be preferred. The third strand of community rhythm is what makes personal transformation possible and therefore makes the community attractive. People are attracted to a church that is bringing about transformation of individuals and of a community, and that is also bringing about some kingdom changes in society. I will call this type of community church X. The type of church that stays in the doldrums I will call church Y. These characteristics of growth and transformation are very attractive qualities and they especially attract the people that Jesus attracted in his itinerant ministry: the poor, hurting, sick, and oppressed. Although there are a number of issues that explain the differences between these churches, let me focus on what I see is the key: communal disciplines.

Communal disciplines. I have observed that the churches that grow have certain disciplines in place as a community. On the other hand, the type Y churches, those that grow to thirty or fifty, or maybe seventy-five, and then after another ten years remain static (bringing in new members and losing others), lack basic communal disciplines. In these churches, the leadership does not provide the structure for these disciplines. In general, there are very low expectations of the congregation, and the leaders do not inspire sacrifice or excellence (what the Bible calls holiness). As a community, basic disciplines or rhythms of growth are missing.

Church X's leadership community is involved in practices that bring about greater conformity to the life of Christ. From the early church, through the Middle Ages, the Reformation period, and during seasons of great revival and awakening, spiritual disciplines are evident. In fact, in many periods what we call theology was really writings about how to be more spiritual. It was assumed that the reason we study the Bible and write about theology is to become more like Jesus Christ. One of the great theological works of the late Middle Ages, which has been important even up until this morning (when I read two pages!), is *The Imitation of Christ* by Thomas á Kempis. This work is read by Roman Catholics, Reformed, Baptists, Lutherans, and Pentecostals. It is also read by mothers, farmers, and college students. Filled with Scripture, the basic thesis of this work is expressed in the first sentence, which is a quotation from Scripture: "Whoever follows me will never walk in darkness" (Jn 8:12).

The Christian life is a communal life of responsibility and accountability as, we learn to be more like Jesus in all we think, feel, and do. As leaders in Church X develop these spiritual patterns together, their lives, and the lives of their families are transformed. Such lives are noticed by others. We call the results of these disciplines Christian virtues or even the fruits of the Spirit. And being around people who are becoming more like Jesus is attractive. Don't we want to be around people who are gentle, kind, forgiving, and willing to serve others? And this is the connection between personal transformation and church growth. True growth in numbers of new Christians comes from true growth in transformed lives. We want both types of growth because they are really of one nature.

In contrast, church Y may be growing in numbers, but chances are there will be few new births because the church has little to attract others. When communal disciplines are not in place, when there is not a culture of accountability and mutual support, transformation will be difficult. Maybe you've experienced churches where the expectations are low, and the leaders show little in the way of godly virtues. If church X is identified with discussions about formation and spiritual disciplines, church Y is evident by the absence of these same discussions. Such a church is unremarkable, where church X is remarkable by the testimonies of lives changed.

What am I talking about here? What is a communal discipline? In short, these are communal practices that are expected of all people and which are part of the community's life together. Like a basketball team doing lay-up drills together or a choir practicing scales together, communal disciplines prepare the church to serve better. Spirituality, personal and communal, is not just for me or for ourselves; it is for others. Every healthy church cultivates some communal disciplines, some intentionally, some spontaneously. I attended a church when I was in college where a young couple with small children were frustrated getting to know other people. About three or four hundred people would attend each of the two services, smile, make small talk, and go home. So the couple politely complained to the pastor, who responded, "What do you suggest would help?"

The father was prepared for this and answered: "How about a hotdog fellowship event? It's easy. Just boil water, put out paper plates, buns, hot dogs, chips, and condiments. People can just drop a couple dollars in a bucket and eat as much as they want. They would stay around and talk."

Not to be outdone, the pastor said, "That's a great idea. I'll buy the hot dogs the first week, and you two cook and get some people to help clean up." This little community discipline brought people together to talk, share, pray, cry, laugh, and invite in people from the community. It lasted about five years and was transformative.

A communal discipline can be spontaneous, but it needs discipline to really help the people grow in grace and in going. Below I briefly describe some communal disciplines that connect the concern for community, growth, and outreach. We suggest talking about the few communal disciplines that will be characteristic of your church *before* planting the church. Then, as the church grows, others can be added when appropriate. Again, spirituality is for the sake of others.

Prayer and healing services. People are broken and in need of healing. Times should be set aside to focus on praying for those who are broken because of illness, loss, or despair. Such services, if they become part of a regular pattern (weekly or monthly), will reach the very people Jesus came to serve. "It is not the healthy who need a doctor, but the sick. I have not come to call the righteous, but sinners" (Mk 2:17). Jesus went about healing, casting out demons, preaching and teaching. A separate healing service creates space for a church to model this pattern of Jesus' ministry.

Little churches that study and serve. We have spoken already about small groups or little churches in the big church. Rather than thinking of these as fellowship groups, we can also think of them as action groups—those who gather to study Scripture, to pray to help each other grow in Christ, but also to focus on a particular action on behalf of the larger church. They study particular issues, problems, or groups and then suggest ways to move forward. For instance, these groups might study immigration, homelessness, poverty, unemployment and help find solutions locally. Or they might study about how to reach out to youth and begin new patterns of youth ministry, or maybe they learn about the unreached people groups in their region and begin to reach out to some of them.

Communal fasting. Jesus assumed we would fast every week (Mt 6:16). The early church practiced weekly fasting (usually two days a week), as well as fasting during Lent. There is no reason that a new church cannot establish basic patterns of fasting, with teaching about why we fast and how to use the time of fasting for spiritual growth, prayer, and communion.

Common meals and hospitality. Some churches, from the very beginning, provide breakfast before or after church, or they have a communal meal every Sunday evening or Wednesday evening as part of churchwide fellowship gathering. Meals are very important in the Gospel accounts of Jesus' life and ministry. Meals do not have to be complex to become a healthy church discipline. Soup, bread, and some raw vegetables are enough to bring people together to share something of their lives. Such simple meals are places to invite outsiders who may be lonely or homeless.

Bible reading. Another communal practice that can unite the church or groups in the church is communal reading of the Bible. There are many ways this can be done. Some churches have individuals or small groups sign up to read through the Bible in a year. If everyone is reading the same passage, then each week the readings can be discussed and reinforced in small groups or even through the worship services. Another Bible reading discipline can be the public reading of Scripture where people come and just listen. I have seen this done in a downtown church at noon during the work week. Many people would come just to hear the Bible. It could also be done before the worship service as preparation for worship. Finally, memorizing passages (Psalms, parables, Sermon on the Mount, etc.) as a community can be transformative. It could be important for the church planting team to memorize important passages that are core to the Gospel—passages often used in evangelism.

Quarterly events for the community. This is a great discipline that can become a character trait of your church. "Oh, yes, that's the church that throws a party for children each May!" An enjoyable, entertaining, and wholesome block party celebrating children or different cultures can be a great gift for your community. Such events could also be moveable feasts that travel around the city or neighborhoods.

"Sell Stuff, Serve Others" days. America is a pioneer in the practice of building structures to store stuff we want to keep but don't use. Most of us have way too much stuff. Holding an annual "Sell Stuff, Serve Others" day is a good pattern to connect with others in the community and to help the community to think about others. The money can be used to sponsor children through Compassion or World Vision or to help support a local food pantry or women's shelter.

Of course, there are many other disciplines or rhythms that a church can develop as you discern what needs and opportunities the Holy Spirit is highlighting in your community, but whatever is decided must be received and entered into with joy and expectation. We are not talking about restricting people with more and more demands, we are looking for liberation and joy in such practices. These are practices that form us and practices that reach out to others. Formation is for mission.

LEADING A COMMUNITY FOR THE LARGER COMMUNITY

Leadership starts with personal formation (see chapter four above). And our own formation both influences and is influenced by the leadership community that guides the young church. In other words, as the leaders of the church plant have robust and healthy community relationships, others will follow. By this point in this chapter and this book, the interconnectivity of our individual spiritual formation and the spiritual formation of our community with the overall health of a church plant and its capacity to join in the *missio Dei* should come as no surprise. Healthy, fruit-bearing trees are composed of healthy parts (roots, trunk, branches, etc.).

Similarly, healthy, fruit-bearing churches are marked by spiritual and relational health in the pastoral leadership, the leadership team, and the wider community. Unlike a tree, however, for our churches to be healthy in their various parts, we must be intentional about these relationships, even pleasantly legalistic. This is so important because the health of our community at all levels prepares us for participation in the *missio Dei*. Our formation is not for ourselves, but for others. Our wholeness as a community becomes a gift *for* the larger community, the parish.

Church as a gift for the community: My story. Part of an evangelism class I taught in seminary involved listening to testimonies from students and outside guests. One student, Marcos, came from a broken family—actually, *broken* is too tame a word. His father left the family, and his mother, after many drug problems, also abandoned Marcos. Grandma ended up with Marcos and she was not a happy surrogate mother. In fact, she would often lock the door and not let Marcos in the house at night, even when he was as young as nine years old.

One of Marcos's friends noticed that he was not always clean and often wore dirty clothes to school. When he found out what was happening, Marcos's friend gave him some new clothes and invited him over for dinner. Marcos thought he was just getting a good meal, but he was actually getting a new family. His school friend, Sam, was a pastor's child. The pastor found out about Marcos's family situation and invited him to spend a few nights with them and then contacted the local welfare services. Eventually the pastor's family raised Marcos. He went to college and then went on to seminary, which is where I met him and heard his story.

As you might imagine, the health and wholeness of the pastor's family became a blessing to the neighborhood. Not only Marcos but other children and people from the neighborhood knew that this was a home that was a blessing to the children and families in the region.

Our local churches should be like this. The formation that takes place through small groups and families, as well as among the leaders (see chapter five), becomes the platform and vitality for mission. Healthy formation in a local church helps it become a foretaste of the kingdom. What is the kingdom of God like? "Come to our church and you will get a foretaste" should be part of our answer.

When communal disciplines are in place, visitors realize they are entering something strange and wonderful. There are patterns of growth that are inviting and challenging. People are being changed, and the change comes about as a community serves others. Just imagine a visitor coming to your new church or missional community and hearing this: "Welcome to our church! Do you have plans for dinner? Five of us are meeting at the church for prayer and then going down to Main Street to invite a few homeless people to have dinner with us at Subway. We would love to have you join us. Our treat the first week!" The kingdom of God, after all, is like a great banquet (Lk 14:15-24)!

The flourishing church as yeast for the community. Finally, the vitality of a local church's community is not for itself. We as followers of Christ are a sent people, a people who, like Abram in Genesis 12, are blessed to be a blessing. A loving community is both a mark of the church and a missional instrument to reach the local community. Church history is instructive here. In the great Puritan revivals in New England, local communities were changed as a result of large groups of people coming to faith and becoming involved in local churches. Observers at the time would remark that in the evenings there would be lights on in houses where people would gather to study the Bible together and sing hymns. Walking along the streets, visitors could hear people singing hymns in the evening. In some towns, local taverns had to close because people attended worship gatherings in the evening. Yes, it is possible that the local economy will be affected by vital Christian communities having an impact on their cities.

This type of community impact is both intentional and accidental. It should be intentional in that churches being planted are praying from the beginning about how they can serve the local community where they worship. The leadership team prays for the local schools, the poor, the local prisons, the elderly, the homeless, and their neighbors. Active, engaged, vital prayer for the local community is essential from the very beginning of a church plant. Walking the streets, groups of church members pray for the homes and institutions they observe and wait for God to open doors for service, proclamation, and love.

But I believe that just as much impact will come from accidental community fellowship. This is how it happens: Everybody is broken and lonely. In the small groups in our church we slowly begin to open up to share our hurts, pain, loneliness, and scars. When we do so, we find that, as a small community, Jesus ministers to our emptiness and our pain. We also find that God is using us as individuals (broken people being healed) within the community to help encourage, strengthen, and advise one another. It brings great joy to see this happening. Of course, we make mistakes, but in time we look forward to coming together to hear how prayers are being answered and how God might use each of us through this group.

Then, after a few months or a year, someone in the small group tells the group about a colleague at work who lost a child, or who lost her job, or who is new to the area and has no friends. They pray for her and invite her to the small group dinner the next month. She is well received and likes the group, even though she is not so sure about all the "Jesus stuff." However, she returns and brings a neighbor she just met who was recently divorced. The small group prays explicitly for each of these new people. They are loved and they begin to pray on their own.

And so it continues. In a society where there is greater and greater alienation and loneliness, genuine community centered in Jesus Christ is very attractive. Our churches, from the very first gathering to pray about a new church plant, must nurture communal flourishing, care, and learning. Such a community expresses the life of Jesus for others to see. This is the key to our life in Christ, but it is also the key to the renewal of local communities and society as a whole. And so the local church acts as yeast for our local communities.

We turn now to look at the local community that God has called us to serve. As our local church develops into a spiritual and worshiping community, at the same time we find ways to connect with our local communities to become the presence of Christ for others. Such a church becomes value added for its part of the city or its rural town. Loving "one another" overflows from the newly planted local church into the neighbors' houses and local institutions. This is the basic pattern of a church community—a church *in* and *for* a local community.

DISCUSSION QUESTIONS

1. What are some small groups or little churches that you sense God is leading you to form in your context?

2. Affinity groups within the church can have mixed results. How can you intentionally build affinity groups so that they are geared to participate in the *missio Dei*?

3. What are some spiritual rhythms that your community is currently practicing? Are there any new rhythms that you think your community might benefit from practicing together?

4. How might your community better care for children and incorporate them into your community's spiritual formation?

PART 3

HOW DO WE EMBODY THE GOSPEL IN OUR CONTEXT AND CULTURE?

MISSIONAL COMPETENCIES

MARSHALL MCLUHAN FAMOUSLY SAID that "the medium is the message," meaning that the presence and the posture of the messenger tells us a lot about the message itself. So what does it mean that God's good news came to us in the person of Jesus of Nazareth? The incarnation tells us that, to paraphrase the old Hallmark card slogan, God cared enough to send the very best. He didn't send flyers or drones; he came in person, in a real human body. What are the implications for how we embody the gospel in our neighborhoods and cities?

Jesus' statement, "As the Father has sent me, I am sending you" (Jn 20:21), is one of the most significant texts regarding missional theology. It tells us that Jesus is sending us as his disciples into the world in the same way that the Father sent him— namely, to come in person, to come as a community of disciples, to serve and not be served, to move toward people and cultures, to cross boundaries to reach those far from God (sinners, tax collectors, Samaritan women, Roman centurions, etc.). As Yale missiologist Lamin Sanneh reminded the church nearly thirty years ago, all of this is rooted in one epic contextualization—the incarnation. Jesus translates God to us and thereby sets the precedent for the church's contextualization that follows. Unlike many faith traditions that rely on cultural diffusion to spread their message by linking it to a specific culture or language, the history of the church from its earliest days has been one of translation, the contextualization of the good news for a specific people at a specific place and time. Of course, as the history of global colonization has demonstrated, Christians have not always embraced the centrality of this translation principle, but even when it was neglected, the basic Christian stories of the incarnation, Pentecost, and the Jerusalem Council refused to be silenced.

Part three highlights the way this translation (or contextualization) principle impacts our work as church planters in practical ways. It seeks to help us contextualize the gospel by giving us missional competencies to reach an increasingly post-Christian culture. Chapter seven shows us that when the sending God calls us to particular people in particular cities, his Spirit has already gone ahead of us, and we are to embody the gospel in ways that respect the context. Chapter eight shows how our own leadership must be suited for and adapted to the people group we are called to reach and concludes with stories of how three planters have done just that. And chapter nine demonstrates how the church brings, speaks, and spreads the good news of Jesus in our communities.

7

TO WHOM HAS GOD SENT ME?

CONTEXTUALIZING THE GOSPEL

**JOHNNY RAMIREZ-JOHNSON
AND LEN TANG**

You are well aware that it is against our law for a Jew to associate with or visit a Gentile. But God has shown me that I should not call anyone impure or unclean. So when I was sent for, I came without raising any objection.

ACTS 10:28-29

FELIPE ASSIS IS A BRAZILIAN AMERICAN who replanted Crossbridge Church in Miami. He was called to a community that was rapidly becoming younger and more ethnically diverse. He describes his work of contextualization as

> applying the Gospel to particular people in ways that take into consideration how they live and what they value. It requires promoting the changes that are necessary, not the ones that aren't necessary. For example, missionaries of the past are often accused of going in and bringing American culture with the Gospel. You don't want to do that. You want the people you are contextualizing for to become more of who they are. If they are Hispanic, you want them to become more Hispanic, not less. You don't want to make them more like you. You want them to receive the treasure of the Gospel in a way that it makes sense in their culture. . . . Even though I was bicultural, even though I was coming from South America to Miami, you still have to learn the culture. That's the main thing that I tell pastors and church re-planters that are coming in: "Look, take your time. Don't rush through things. Be a learner of the people and of the culture. Live in the neighborhood."[1]

Felipe's story captures many of the themes from this chapter on missional competencies: the need for planters to be students of the cities and people groups they're called to, the perspective of living as intercultural

An insider is a person who has won the trust of the community and learned how to build relationships in the area. Becoming an insider involves a willingness to be a learner, to be instructed and informed by knowledgeable individuals who can swing open the doors to a particular subculture.

JOHN FUDER

---

[1] Redeemer City to City, "A Church for a Changing Miami: An Interview with Felipe Assis," interview, part 1, February 15, 2018, www.medium.com/redeemer-city-to-city/a-church-for-a-changing-miami-an-interview-with-felipe-assis-part-1-5bf13db78468; and part 3, February 19, 2018, www.medium.com/redeemer-city-to-city/a-church-for-a-changing-miami-an-interview-with-felipe-assis-part-3-85401643a091.

missionaries to our own cities, and the imperative to intentionally bring the gospel to people in ways that honor and respect their cultures rather than imposing our own cultural expressions. It's hard to love someone without knowing them, and contextualization is the process of knowing real people and communities so well that we can translate and embody the good news of Jesus Christ in ways that people can receive and embrace. German theologian Helmut Thielicke wrote that "the gospel must be preached afresh and told in new ways to every generation, since every generation has its own unique questions. This is why the gospel must be constantly forwarded to a new address, because the recipient is repeatedly changing his place of residence."[2]

What is the "new address" to which the unchanging truth of Jesus Christ must be forwarded in your context and culture? If you've grown up in North America, you may feel like you already know and understand the culture. But just as a fish could not describe water because it swims in it 24/7, sometimes even we as church planters are blind to the embedded cultural values, assumptions, and idols that are right in front of us. So just as we are called to do good exegesis of the biblical text, so we are called to do good exegesis of our communities for the sake of the gospel. How do we read our context? In this chapter we will look at a trinitarian understanding of contextualization in which (1) God initiates mission, (2) the Holy Spirit changes how we see our people group, and (3) the incarnation of Jesus is our model for ministry. Then in the fourth section we'll get practical by describing how to use the social sciences as lenses to see what God is already doing in your neighborhood and city.

GOD INITIATES MISSION

Church planters are by nature good at starting things. They take initiative and regularly begin new ministries from scratch. But before we planters spring into action, we need to revisit the nature of our sending God who takes the initiative to contextualize the gospel. Contextualization is typically understood as the one-way process of adapting the message of the gospel to a specific people group—a technique to be learned and mastered that sometimes leads us to see people and communities as objects to be studied and parsed. But in light of this book's emphasis on the deep synergy between our own formation and our call to mission, contextualization at its heart is about God's Spirit forming in *us* a new heart and a new lens to see and understand those to whom we are called. It is not merely a shift in how we do ministry but in how we fundamentally perceive ourselves and our relationship to others.

---

[2]Quoted in Peter Kuzmic, "How to Teach the Truth of the Gospel," in *Proclaim Christ Until He Comes*, ed. J. D. Douglas and Lausanne Committee (Minneapolis: Worldwide Publications, 1986), 198.

It involves tearing down the walls that make us feel comfortable with our insider status with God, as opposed to those on the outside who are far from God and who are ignorant of the "right" message and beliefs. Cultivating a perspective that allows us to see all people as brothers and sisters is surprisingly difficult because as believers we have been trained to see all unchurched people as needing us and our message. But the reality is that God is shaping *us* through our relationship with them just as we are part of bringing God's message of the gospel to them. Understanding God's missionary heart and how God sees our neighbors will lead us to new ways of seeing them as well as to fresh opportunities for our own hearts to be enlarged.

As we saw in chapter one, the *missio Dei* makes it clear that church planters and their congregations are not the originators of mission. God is the original missionary; we simply respond to what God is already doing in those to whom we are sent. So the question "to whom has God sent me?" is closely connected to *who* is doing the sending. Or better yet, we must also ask who is going ahead of me, before me, and beside me? God has already gone ahead of us. The fact that we as church planters are sent by God to "the other" or to "them" means that God already has that person or people group on his heart and mind. Those who are other to us are never other to God. They may not yet be known to us, but they have been known by God since the beginning of creation. Contextualization, then, is the process for the church to see the other as God sees the other—as family!

David Bosch, whose missiological contributions were highlighted in chapter one, writes that mission "was thus put in the context of the doctrine of the Trinity, not of ecclesiology or soteriology. The classical doctrine on the *missio Dei* as God the Father sending the Son, and God the Father and the Son sending the Spirit was expanded to include yet another 'movement': Father, Son, and Holy Spirit sending the church into the world."[3] In this sense, all Christians are missionaries— "sent ones."

Church planting, then, is the adventure of accepting the invitation to join the triune God in the boundary-crossing mission he has already begun. The planter is merely a follower of Jesus who is working alongside the Holy Spirit. God is the one who contextualizes the ministry and we follow God's lead. The primary concern of contextualization is not how far *I* am willing to go in contextualizing the gospel message, but how far *God* goes in contextualizing the gospel. We the church, we the evangelists, we the church planters, take ourselves far too seriously. We never owned the mission.

---

[3]David J. Bosch, *Transforming Mission: Paradigm Shifts in Theology of Mission*, 20th anniversary ed. (Maryknoll, NY: Orbis, 1991, 2011), 381.

This means that the church's activity is subordinate to God's activity, and so we should distinguish between the terms *mission* (singular) and *missions* (plural). *Mission* refers to the *missio Dei*, that is, God's self-revelation as the one who loves the world and who is involved in and with the world. The *missio Dei* announces the good news that God is a God-for-people. *Missions* (the *missiones ecclesiae*: the missionary ventures of the church) refers to particular forms, related to specific times, places, or needs, of the church's participation in the *missio Dei*.[4]

Consequently, the various missions of the church are nothing more than extensions of the mission of God. We are called into a partnership where God has already encountered the sender as well as those to whom she or he is being sent.

Because God cares about his mission more than we do and because the gospel is an upside-down, countercultural message, contextualization can be difficult, disorienting, or even threatening. Many things that believers may consider core aspects of the gospel or core practices of the church may in truth be our own cultural, intellectual, or spiritual idols that need to be dismantled.

A first-century example may help. When Jesus healed the Gerasene man who had been demon-possessed and told him to go declare how much God had done for him (Lk 8:39), was Jesus telling him to teach the Baptist gospel, or the Catholic faith, or the Assemblies of God dogma? This man had no knowledge other than that the man named Jesus saved him and offered him acceptance back into society! That was his message. Was that enough for him? Yes, indeed!

Jesus recruited a Gentile and sent him out as an evangelist even before the truths of the gospel were clear to him (or even to the disciples) at that point. Given how little he knew, might the well-intentioned Gerasene man have gone out and started a synagogue to worship Jesus, since that may have been the cultural appropriation of worship that was familiar to him? The synagogue, like the church, was a sociocultural manifestation of God's message, just as the words of Jesus were a sociocultural (Gerasene-Gentile) manifestation of the message of the gospel! The point is that the work of Jesus in people's lives is not limited to our conceptions of orthodoxy, but to God's much wider view of what the good news is.

To use a contemporary example, many of the "nones" define churches (or any religious institution) by what they do, not by what they profess to believe.[5] According to Pew Research, "a majority of the unaffiliated agrees that churches are too focused on rules (67%), too concerned with money and power (70%), and too involved with

---

[4]Bosch, *Transforming Mission*, 10.

[5]Cary Funk and Greg Smith, "'Nones' on the Rise: One-in-Five Adults Have No Religious Affiliation," Pew Forum on Religion & Public Life, October 9, 2012, 62, assets.pewresearch.org/wp-content/uploads/sites/11/2012/10/NonesOnTheRise-full.pdf.

politics (67%)."[6] Thus, from the perspective of the nones, asking them to believe in Jesus is tantamount to violating their cultural views in order to satisfy evangelical cultural norms. So to contextualize the gospel for nones, the church needs to understand their cultural values and communicate using those values, just as Jesus did when he communicated the gospel through farming analogies that would have resonated with his first-century Jewish audience.

The story of Peter and Cornelius from Acts 10 is one of the most significant biblical stories of contextualization. Peter had a very difficult time accepting God's ministry of contextualization. He was of course deeply ingrained in the worldview that all converts to Jesus must also become converts to Judaism. And as someone who believed that God never changes, it would be nearly impossible for him to call a nonpracticing Gentile clean. Let us now delve into how God's Spirit changes both Peter and Cornelius.

THE HOLY SPIRIT CHANGES HOW WE SEE OUR MISSION FIELD

As we might expect in light of the *missio Dei*, Acts of the Apostles would be better titled "Acts of the Holy Spirit in and through the Disciples." The coming of the Holy Spirit at Pentecost was the beginning of the disciples' mission.[7] Thus the mission of the church planter is to participate in another wave of the acts of the Holy Spirit, a continuation of what God is already doing in the world and in the neighborhood where we are called to serve as church planters. This is a radically different perspective than seeing ourselves as called to do the work of God, as if God left and expected us to do the remainder of the work. No! It has never been the work and mission of the church; it will always remain the work of God and the ministry of the Spirit of Christ (1 Pet 1:10-12). This outlook, held by Bishop Niringiye and the apostle Peter before him, changes everything about how we see our ministry, our calling, and the people to whom we are called to serve.

At the time of the Acts 10 narrative, which took place about a decade after the resurrection of Jesus, Peter believed that his mission was simply to find Jews or Jewish converts willing to follow the risen Savior. At best his vision ignored the mission to the Gentiles. But the Holy Spirit began to change both Cornelius's view of the risen Savior as well as Peter's view of Gentiles as unclean outsiders.

The story begins one afternoon when Cornelius stepped away from his command of the legionnaires and withdrew to his private prayer space. In response to his familiar routine, he received an unfamiliar answer to his prayers—an

---

[6]Funk and Smith, "'Nones' on the Rise," 23.
[7]David Zac Niringiye, *The Church: God's Pilgrim People* (Downers Grove, IL: IVP Academic, 2015), 129.

angelic visitation! Cornelius "clearly saw an angel of God" who told him that God had taken notice of his devotion and desire for him. The angel then told Cornelius to fetch Peter.[8] Notice that this angel had the audacity to act without consulting Peter or any of the other believers! Had the angel consulted with anyone other than God, the order would have been to stay away from Cornelius, or at least to instruct Cornelius to first become a Jew. Instead, the angel embraced Cornelius as a centurion, as a Roman, as a non-Jew. All this took place independent of the church. The angel instructed the centurion to seek out a believer because the believers were not going to look for him! Today's church planter should expect no less. God is already acting in contexts other than the one that keeps your denominational church safe and sound. God is at work in many households like Cornelius'—at work apart from the institutional church, that is.

The first contextualization principle is that the role of the church is always to keep up with the work of the Holy Spirit. The church often feels uncomfortable with the prior steps and initiative the Holy Spirit has taken. The church would like to hold back the Spirit of Christ and say, "Holy Spirit, you are going too fast, too far, and taking too many risks!" Because in the minds of many believers, Cornelius might have won the least-likely-to-be-converted award. He was a Roman leader, an enforcer of the conquering empire's laws, and the epitome of one furthest from the Jews. And yet Cornelius's petitions extended all the way to the God of heaven and earth and God answered them: "That is the point: there is no one and no place beyond God's reach."[9] Jesus is the Son of the supreme God who recompenses all who attentively call on him. As a church planter my role is to meditate on the ways of the Holy Spirit, and to repent of the ways that my church and its creeds exclude countless people groups, deeming them unreachable by God.

The Jewish view of Gentiles as alienated from God is comparable to typical evangelical assessments of people of other faiths (such as Muslims and Hindus), as well as many others who are apparently disqualified by their particular behaviors if not by their religious beliefs. For instance, does my 1.5-generation Korean congregation inadvertently exclude other Asians? Do I think that God could never reach the homeless people that surround our urban setting? Can we imagine that the Holy Spirit is at work among these people groups? Or do we evangelicals think that they are outcasts to God's mercy and love? Bishop Niringiye has reminded us all that "no one is beyond the reach of the sovereign God! God may be at work in them in ways we are not able to see because we have excluded them in our minds."[10]

---

[8]Niringiye, *The Church*, 138.
[9]Niringiye, *The Church*, 139.
[10]Niringiye, *The Church*, 139.

To Cornelius's credit, he is described as "a devout man who feared God with all his household; he gave alms generously to the people and prayed constantly to God" (Acts 10:2 NRSV). But still more remarkable is that when he was instructed by the angel to send for Peter, Cornelius—the one accustomed to giving orders—responded in obedience and immediately sent for Peter the Jew. So we as planters must acknowledge that God is already at work and in direct communication with the people group I am called to serve. I am not the first one arriving there! In fact, when Peter did arrive, Cornelius "was expecting them and had called together his relatives and close friends" (Acts 10:24). Cornelius and his whole household gathered in eager anticipation of a spiritual revival.

Back in the 1980s, I (Johnny) was participating in a church plant in a barrio of San José, Costa Rica. I visited a household and was welcomed by Don Pedro, who was seemingly expecting my knock on the door. His eagerness seemed to crescendo as I explained to him the simplicity of the gospel message. He had been carrying a very heavy burden, seeking to atone for his own sins and wracked with deep feelings of guilt. I remember the look on Don Pedro's face as he responded, "I was told to expect you; I am glad you arrived!" He had already been convicted by the Holy Spirit and had received a word from God to expect a messenger who would open up the Bible.

When Peter does arrive at Cornelius's home, it is a wonderful example of Spirit-inspired awkwardness! Peter acknowledges right up front that his presence is a direct violation of Jewish law: "You are well aware that it is against our law for a Jew to associate with or visit a Gentile" (Acts 10:28). Imagine a visitor is sent to you by God, and he announces his displeasure at being inside your home! But in that moment, God is revealing to Peter the wonders of his boundless love: "God has shown me that I should not call anyone impure or unclean" (Acts 10:28). In so doing, the Spirit is now declaring that people who had been perceived as off limits for centuries are now included in God's mission. Peter then concludes, "*I now realize how true it is* that God does not show favoritism but accepts from every nation the one who fears him and does what is right" (Acts 10:34-35). As others have pointed out, this passage is not merely about the conversion of Cornelius, but about the conversion of Peter from religious myopia as well!

The story continues with Peter announcing the good news of the gospel to the whole household. And while Peter "was still speaking these words, the Holy Spirit came on all who heard the message" (Acts 10:44). All the circumcised Jewish "believers who had come with Peter were astonished that the gift of the Holy Spirit had been poured out even on Gentiles" (Acts 10:45). It was obvious to them that the Holy Spirit had been poured on this whole Gentile household because "they heard them speaking in tongues and praising God" (Acts 10:46).

Through this outpouring, the Holy Spirit incontrovertibly demonstrated that through the gospel God had accepted the Gentiles. To this Peter declared, "Surely no one can stand in the way of their being baptized with water. They have received the Holy Spirit just as we have" (Acts 10:47). What follows is the climax of the human side of the story. Peter and the other believers who came with him had not been in control at any point of this story. They were being pushed and pulled by the Spirit, compelled to act against their natural ethnic, racial, and religious instincts. But after Peter witnessed the threefold vision to call all people clean, the repeated orders to visit Cornelius, the religious fervor of the Gentile household, Cornelius's hospitality toward them, and the outpouring of the Holy Spirit on the Gentiles, then—finally—the most controversial words of the book of Acts were spoken, as Peter "ordered that they be baptized in the name of Jesus Christ" (Acts 10:48).

This baptism changed Christianity for good. The Jerusalem Council's initial reluctance but ultimate affirmation of accepting Gentiles into the church in Acts 15 is the natural conclusion to the dramatic change introduced by the Holy Spirit. This contextualization was not human-initiated, nor should any other contextualization of the gospel be. The Jerusalem Council's principle of contextualization prevails to this day—"it seemed good to the Holy Spirit and to us" (Acts 15:28).

When we step back, we can see how God's Spirit was slowly but surely leading the early church through a series of incremental steps to turn outsiders into insiders: (1) At Pentecost, Gentiles who did not speak Hebrew heard the apostles in their own tongue via the empowerment of the Holy Spirit (Acts 2:1-13). (2) Following an ethnic dispute over food distribution among widows, Hellenist Jewish believers were accepted into leadership positions (Acts 6:1-7). (3) As we just saw, Gentiles like Cornelius were favorable toward Jews received the same Holy Spirit power as the Jewish followers of Jesus (Act 10). (4) Gentiles with no connection to Judaism were the next group to be accepted into the Christian church, as with the conversion of the Greeks at Antioch (Acts 11:20-21).

The Holy Spirit used every available means—angels, visions, and even strife—to drag the apostles into embracing Gentiles as equal believers in Jesus and leaders in the church. The Jerusalem Council created a new space for Gentiles as full members of the church. Thus we come to the second contextualization principle: God invites the church planting team as partners in accommodating the gospel to the context of the new people group. I realize that the word *accommodating* may sound too radical or too compromising or too heretical—to name just a few of the critiques we hear whenever the gospel crosses another barrier, be it an ethnic, racial, religious, or people-group barrier. Indeed, the New Testament church as recorded in Acts and the Epistles was traumatized, conflicted, and resistant to the contextualization of the gospel to the Gentile ways.

Just as Paul was called as the apostle to the Gentiles and Peter to the Jews in Jerusalem, God calls each church planting team to a particular people group. The people group we are called to reach, by definition, will be the other, a group that has for some reason been rejected by us institutional Christians (we are not disparaging the church; we love the church). Today, many denominations have laws, policies, doctrinal positions, and cultural views that are human burdens that have been added to the gospel as accepted by the Jerusalem Council! As you reflect on your own style of worship and ministry, are you promoting something that resembles "a yoke that neither we nor our ancestors have been able to bear" (Acts 15:10)?

One of my (Johnny's) students, Steve, was called to plant a church in Arizona but wondered why so many plants had failed within a particular gated community. Steve discovered that all the prior church plants were based on a traditional model of establishing a brick-and-mortar "church as we know it"—meaning a building with a sanctuary that holds a worship service that consisted of singing, preaching, communion, and liturgy, along with classroom space for children's ministries.

But through a process of dialog with the residents and the Homeowners Association (HOA), his perspective on the gates that separated the community from the rest of the city shifted. Rather than see the gates as a barrier that doomed the five previous church plants, his conversations with residents led to new ways of framing them as a positive attribute for the community members. All reframing of meaning takes energy, time, and even grieving the loss of prior dreams and visions. Steve and I continued to dialogue about how to approach this community.

After further interviews with members of the community, he discovered a high degree of interest in establishing a community center. So Steve started his church by opening one! The new community center/church plant offers a daycare, aerobic classes, support groups, and non-Sunday morning worship—all as part of a vision of service and worship of God.

As a result, the church plant is manifesting itself from within the sociocultural parameters of the HOA and its members' needs! Steve was able to see the community members as his partners in God's ministry who had needs.

INCARNATION AS OUR MODEL FOR MINISTRY

How do we ensure that the way we are doing outreach, worship, preaching, and ministry in our community is appropriate to our context? In part by living among the people as Jesus himself did. The incarnation meant that not only was Jesus born as normal human baby, but also that he spent thirty years growing up and living as a Nazarene before inaugurating his public ministry. The Creator God of the universe took time to inhabit his body and his city, so wouldn't we also? As Eugene Peterson's well-known rendering of John 1:14 puts it, "the Word became flesh and blood and moved into the neighborhood" (*The Message*).

While Jesus' incarnation was a radical act of identifying with people in the specific context of first-century Palestine, and more generally with humanity as a whole, it was also more than simply an expression of solidarity. As missiologist Andrew F. Walls notes, the incarnation was also *translation*: "When God in Christ became man, Divinity was translated into humanity, as though humanity were a receptor language. Here was a clear statement of what would otherwise be veiled in obscurity or uncertainty, the statement, 'This is what God is like.'" Walls goes on to note that like this translation was geared to meet the needs and cultural framework of a specific place and time, "when Divinity was translated into humanity he did not become generalized humanity. He became *a person* in a particular place and time."[11] Jesus was God with his feet literally on the ground in a particular place. He was God contextualized—God translated into our language.

Within a generation the church was able to apply the principles of translation inherent in the incarnation as it participated in the *missio Dei* and planted churches in various Jewish and Gentile contexts. Even the original Gospel writers translated the words of Jesus from Aramaic to Greek when they wrote the Gospels. In so doing they followed in the way of the incarnate *Logos* and initiated a method of mission oriented around *translation* rather than cultural *diffusion*. As missiologist Lamin Sanneh notes, the difference was significant. Whereas the missionary method of diffusion, as exemplified in religions like Judaism and Islam, made culture the carrier of the message, Christianity, especially Christianity after the Jerusalem Council (Acts 15), had within it an inherent emphasis on incarnation and translation that allowed "the religion to arrive with the requirement of cultural deference to the originating culture."[12] Of course, a cursory glance at history shows that the church did not always choose to align itself on the culturally respectful side of the translation/diffusion divide. A promising start in Acts 15 was soon overshadowed by Christendom, replete with crusades and colonialism. Even in a post-colonial age, the Western church is still tempted by modes of evangelism and ecclesiology oriented more toward diffusion through cultural imperialism rather than a commitment to the translation principle. Still, anywhere the incarnation is preached, the

---

[11] Andrew F. Walls, *The Missionary Movement in Christian History: Studies in the Transmission of Faith* (Maryknoll, NY: Orbis, 1996), 27.

[12] Lamin Sanneh, *Translating the Message: The Missionary Impact on Culture* (Maryknoll, NY: Orbis, 2009), 33.

power of translation remains present, and even if dormant for a season will eventually break out anew.

All this is extremely significant for our work as church planters. The work of translating the message of the kingdom of God to a local context didn't end with Jesus. Neither did the work of incarnation, if incarnation is understood more broadly as inhabiting a specific place for kingdom purposes. When we inhabit our specific contexts, we can learn how best to translate the good news of the kingdom of God in a way that reaches the hearts of our friends and neighbors in our community. Sometimes this may entail literal translation, but much more often it could mean that we learn to translate the message in a way that speaks to the social, cultural, and relational languages that shape the lives and worldview of folks in our context.

Whether or not we as church planters will be able to effectively apply the translation principle inherent in the incarnation depends on the posture we take toward our community. Do we assume that we have all the answers (read: perfectly crafted strategies) or do we begin with an attitude of humility that seeks to listen and learn before speaking? The way a missionary enters a community says volumes about their ministry even before they utter a word, so it's crucial that we assume the posture of a listening learner from the very start. As Felipe Assis said in the interview we quoted at the beginning of this chapter, "Be a learner of the people and of the culture. Live in the neighborhood."

While few would debate the value of taking time to listen and learn in the case of crosscultural mission, for church planters in North America assuming the stance of a learner is often less emphasized and sometimes even a bit more difficult. When we approach the cities and rural towns of North America, we may assume we already know them because we have grown up there and breathed the same air and cultural influences as our neighbors. But the culture is shifting rapidly, and we are now missionaries to the West. Every good missionary pursues crosscultural training and possibly language training, and so should we as church planters.

What does it look like to see our cities through an incarnational lens? How do we embed ourselves in the city's culture and values for the sake of the gospel? When there are already seemingly innumerable Bible translations in languages like English, what does translating Jesus' message of the kingdom to the heart language of my specific context look like? As church planters we seldom know these answers ahead of time. Usually we learn them by listening for the voice of the Holy Spirit and by living life with open eyes and ears in our specific communities. This means we follow the lead of Jesus, who in his incarnational presence sought to minister to the physical, social, and spiritual needs of his community through healing, teaching, and proclaiming the kingdom of God. It means we enter into a community as a resident rather than a foreigner, as a stakeholder rather than a taker, and as one who invests rather than exploits. Engaging the culture is the process of stepping into the rhythms of people's lives in your community in such a way that you understand *what* people do for work and for play and *why* they do it. It is becoming involved in a culture and community so that you understand it from the inside out. It's eating at the same restaurants, going to the same schools, and walking the same sidewalks as people in your town.

In short, incarnational contextualization is learning to become cultural insiders, as Dan Steigerwald calls them. It is becoming embedded enough with the neighborhood's rhythms that we know its forms of celebration and recreation. "Embedding is about submerging deeply into context and establishing a stable, long-term presence together. Team members, individually and collectively, engage in a missionary lifestyle. . . . Over time the team becomes cultural insiders who are not only conversant on issues that concern the city but are also responsive to the city's good news, brokenness, and pain."[13]

A classic biblical text on speaking the language of your community is Paul's exegesis of Athens in Acts 17. Paul immediately saw that the city was full of idols and was "greatly distressed" by it (Acts 17:16). He then engaged with several local philosophers and accepted their invitation to the Areopagus, the place of public intellectual debate. Then in his sermon, he acknowledged their religious nature and even their altar to an unknown god. This shows that Paul could discern the work of God even among the pantheon of false gods! He quoted one of their own poets, affirming some aspects of their worldview while challenging others. He closes by heralding the day when Jesus the risen Lord will judge the world in righteousness. Paul's message was clearly informed and shaped by the place, intellectual climate, poetry, and rhetorical forms of Athens. The more we know our community, the more we can present the glory of our Lord in ways they can see, hear, and feel.

For instance, if you're planting in Texas, you probably ought to know about the local high school football team and attend the games on Friday nights. Or if you're in Seattle, becoming an insider typically means becoming a coffee connoisseur. Granted, these are stereotypes, but they convey the sense that our expression of the gospel is grounded in a place and not simply photocopied from another planter in another city. Worse yet, sometimes our expression of ministry can actually violate

---

[13]Dan Steigerwald, *Dynamic Adventure: A Guide to Starting and Shaping Missional Churches* (Centennial, CO: Christian Associates International, 2016), 30.

the cultural values of a community. One church plant participated in a local beach clean-up day where they picked up trash and plastic bottles. But the church hosted a booth where they handed out more plastic water bottles with their church logo emblazoned on the labels. That's a mixed message!

So far in this book, we have said very little about models of church planting, largely because the decision about which model to use has a lot to do with context. For example, it would probably not be contextually appropriate to plant a Hillsong-type church in rural America. And it likely wouldn't be contextually appropriate to reach a retirement community with skinny jeans and a full band.

In the church I (Len) am planting, one community we're reaching is made up of brilliant Caltech students who are trained to ask probing questions. So, as I mentioned in chapter five, we eventually decided that including Q&A after each sermon would be a way to honor their inquisitive nature. Responding to questions that come by text or raised hands has now become a regular fixture in our worship service.

What are some tools we can use to see our communities as God intends them to be?

SOCIAL-SCIENCE TOOLS AS CORRECTIVE LENSES

Social-science tools function as corrective lenses for church planters and their ministry teams. In learning new ways of seeing the other and the other's context, the planter's eyesight is being corrected to see the church to be planted as God sees it and as God has already revealed to those the Spirit of Christ has already called—such as my former student and his HOA experience in Arizona. God had envisioned a church that this student could not initially see. It took him wearing the social-science corrective lenses to see God's plan as revealed to the HOA members. Are you excited for what God will reveal to you?

As we'll look at in detail in the next chapter, Paul most famously summarized the heart of contextualization in 1 Corinthians 9:20-23. Paul adapted not merely the language of the gospel but his very self by becoming "like one under the law," or "like one not having the law," or even becoming "weak." Paul was willing to "become all things to all people," "for the sake of the gospel" so that he might "share in its blessings."

Social sciences help in the work of contextualization by enabling us to (1) identify the various roles people groups have; (2) become as them for the purpose of sharing in blessings of the gospel; and most importantly, (3) see the world as God sees the world.

As we begin, picture the digital animations that start with satellite images of the whole earth from space and then keep zooming in past continents and countries with greater and greater detail until you can see individual neighborhoods and homes. That's what we'll do here. We'll describe a funnel in which we begin with a

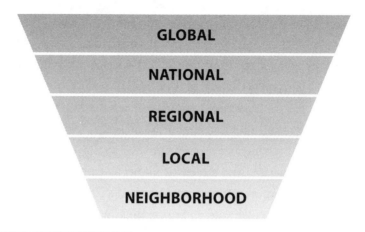

Figure 3. Contextualization funnel

wide, global perspective and move down to consider the particular community that you're called to serve (see figure 3).

Imagine all seven billion people in the world at the top of a huge funnel, and the people in your neighborhood at the bottom of the funnel. Who are we called to reach? Well, as we descend the funnel, our ministry to those people becomes more and more geographically specific and more focused on a particular people group. The goal is to bring the gospel with clarity and power to the people God has prepared for us to reach, not to market the church to the maximum number of people. Let's consider how each and every level of the funnel influences and forms our ministry to our neighborhoods. Counterintuitively, sometimes our ministry can and should be shaped by factors higher in the funnel and not just lower, as we'll see. Let's walk through each section of the funnel and consider how the gospel relates to people at each level.

Global level. While we may initially think that contextualization would dictate that we share very little in common with people on the other side of the globe, the reality is that globalization increasingly affects us all and creates common concerns. While acknowledging that hundreds of millions of people still live at subsistence levels, much of the world is now deeply interconnected through travel and technology. We are now neighbors with many around the world because we are competing in a global market, influenced by international students at our universities, connected worldwide through social media, and are all affected by global phenomena such as climate change. So what does this have to do with church planting? It means that our ministry, prayers, preaching, and concern for people is increasingly multinational, multiethnic, and global. Global realities now affect ministry in local communities because of globalization and immigration. For instance, there is a church plant in Spokane, Washington, that ministers to immigrants by meeting them at airports, standing alongside them during their assimilation process, and advocating for immigration reform. The people in our communities are instantly aware of global concerns, and these issues may be precisely what God's Spirit uses to form and shape our church plant, particularly in large urban areas.

National level. Even though the United States has over 325 million people, many current events and political discourse affect the daily lives of people in our community more than ever before. In particular, the 2016 presidential election revealed more clearly than ever the deep fault lines along race and economics in our country and brought issues of race—an issue many evangelicals have been reluctant to confront—to the forefront of the country and the church. On social media and in national media coverage, it's hard to go a day without highly divisive political issues being raised.

It is becoming increasingly difficult to ignore politics in ministry, not because the gospel is partisan, but because these issues deeply and directly affect so many in our communities. For instance, the national coverage of the shooting of many African Americans in our country has sparked a deep and urgent need for conversation and action around social justice. Just as the gospel was radical in the first century for reconciling Jews and Gentiles who sat next to each other in worship, so now it is increasingly difficult for God's people to remain on the sidelines.

For me (Len) personally, the high profile of racial unrest in our country has caused me to reflect on and repent of how poorly my own ministry and the church more broadly has done at addressing, convening, and leading conversations on racial reconciliation. Despite many calls for a national dialogue on race, in my community I'm not seeing anyone doing that. Why not God's people? And so my sense of calling as we began to plant our church was to seek out African Americans for partnership and learning. We now have a sister church in our city that is primarily African American, and we are starting several cultural-curiosity groups that help gather both believers and unbelievers to tell their own cultural narratives in light of the gospel. So the national issue of racial reconciliation is inevitably intersecting with local expressions of racial justice in our church and community.

While issues of racial inequality and systemic racism head the list of divisive issues in our society, race is by no means the only cause of division in America today. Political divisions at the national level even extend to our geographical and cultural situatedness. Again the 2016 election is telling. Of the divisions signified by the 2016 presidential campaign, few were as distinct as the rural-urban divide. As church planters, part of our ability to understand our national context is to investigate and appreciate the local culture to which God has sent us—be it rural, urban, or something in between—and then look for ways to engage with humility and a listening posture with those who do not share our geographical background and by extension our political persuasion. Indeed, in the context of national healing, no institution is better poised to cross boundaries—be they the symbolic distance of race or the literal distance of miles between country and city—than the church.

Regional level. The ministry dynamics in many cities are often determined more by their regional culture than by the specific city. For instance, the greater Houston area is large and diverse but has been deeply shaped by the oil industry and by the tremendously diverse ethnic groups that converged in Houston for jobs in that industry. Or here in Southern California, many of the stereotypes are true—it's very sunny, people are very busy, and there is a ton of traffic. Much of Southern California is defined by the car culture—long commutes to work, the stress of traffic, the difficulty of finding parking. This one dynamic has profound implications, leading to a deep sense of individualism and isolation that is deeply woven into the fabric of the culture. For instance, the practice of hospitality and having others into your home is rare because residents are conditioned to segment their work, home, and church lives. In fact, the car culture makes LA different than some other metropolitan cities that are connected by subways or public transit and the ways that those common experiences connect people. What are the regional realities in your context that shape how people travel, find entertainment, engage the arts, and so on?

Another consideration is whether your region is marked by a general sense of hopefulness or hopelessness. This is often fairly easy to chart by observing population statistics. Are people moving into or out of your region? Though it would not hold true all the time, in general it seems that places marked by increases in population (e.g., the Sun Belt) have a higher sense of hope for the future than places like Appalachia or the Rust Belt, which are losing population. As church planters it is important that we understand the general level of hope in our region and contextualize the gospel to meet different temptations and cultural pitfalls of our specific region, all the while realizing that individuals in different geographical locales might experience an entirely different sense of what is to be expected or even what is possible.

Local level. As we move down the contextualization funnel, we get to the local level—the social, relational, and spiritual dynamics of our particular city. Later in the chapter, we'll look at the various "city gates" that can unlock influence in our city.

Even though I (Len) grew up in Pasadena, California, I did not know it or see it missiologically because I was raised in a nominally Christian home. It was only when I went to seminary and later planted a church outside of Portland, Oregon, that I began to gain church-planter eyes, meaning that I now see a community in terms of its missional opportunities and possibilities. For instance, whenever I walk into a building with an open floor plan, I think to myself, "Someone should plant a church here!" When I returned to Pasadena in 2014, I began to rediscover some things about my city and even about myself. Pasadena is home to Caltech, a STEM university filled with brilliant aspiring scientists. Being around Caltech students reminded me of my own somewhat forgotten background as the son of two scientists. I had studied electrical engineering and computer science (EECS) at Berkeley, and being around these scientists reawakened my inner geek! As I began to get to know Caltech undergrads and grad students, I discovered a growing burden for them to know the gospel and experience freedom from the enormous academic pressure to perform. Now our church has many Caltech students and I am on campus at least weekly.

As we engage in our community, we find that our hearts grow and our ministries become more appropriate. This means that one of the things we need to avoid as church planters is what Donnie Griggs refers to as a "copy + paste" methodology which assumes that if something works well in one context it will work well in my local context as well. As Griggs notes, "The irony of all of this is that usually the guys who are being copied are themselves great missionaries to their culture. Tim Keller, the lead pastor of Redeemer Presbyterian in New York City, immediately comes to mind. Everywhere I go around the world, I can see people pretending to be Tim Keller and assuming their context is just like his."[14] If you've spent much time in church planting circles or pastoral conferences, you know that Griggs is right, and his point extends much further than simply incorporating a pastor's homiletical style or method of leadership. Even seemingly mundane things like mailers get copied and pasted from one culture to another. In some contexts, such as a college town or metropolitan area marked by transient populations, mailers might be a helpful (or at least only mildly annoying) means of promoting a church plant or worshiping community. In smaller places, however, mailers may actually be counterproductive, being received as a lack of neighborliness.[15] In a rural or small-town context you don't want people to say, "Oh, you're the church that sent mailers out to all those folks like me who already have a church."

Neighborhood level. A growing number of church planters are focused not just at the level of the city but are being particularly attentive to the neighborhood or

[14]Donnie Griggs, *Small Town Jesus: Taking the Gospel Mission Seriously in Seemingly Unimportant Places* (Damascus, MD: Evertruth, 2016), 108-9.
[15]Brad Roth, *God's Country: Faith, Hope, and the Future of the Rural Church* (Harrisonburg, VA: Harold, 2017), 104-5.

parish level, sensing the relational patterns that make one neighborhood distinct from even the neighborhoods immediately adjacent to it.

Specifically, a church planter is seeking places to simply hang out in the community—especially since they often lack office space and begin with an empty calendar. So it's helpful to zero in on the "third places" that function as centers or anchors of community life that bring social vitality. Ray Oldenburg defines the characteristics of a true "third place" as somewhere that is free or inexpensive, highly accessible to many people (ideally within walking distance of home), involves regulars who gather there often, and is welcoming and comfortable.[16] What are the third places in your community? For some it is a local Starbucks, for others it may be a local park or school. Third places help us build relationships and understand the city's rhythms.

As we get to know our context at the neighborhood level, the specific relational patterns become important to discern. As Michael Frost points out, our ability to build authentic communities that can live out the *missio Dei* together depends on the three elements of proximity (how physically close we are living to others), frequency (how often we can encounter one another face to face), and spontaneity (the possibility of nonscheduled encounters with others, requiring a degree of margin in our lives).[17] If our church planting teams can begin to live lives with gospel intentionality that engage our neighbors through proximity, frequency, and spontaneity, then we know we are living incarnationally.

As we consider the global, national, regional, local, and neighborhood levels of the contextualization funnel, we find places of need that fit with our gifts and passions, and God as the divine matchmaker shows us the places where we begin to embody the gospel.

Demographics. Demographic study of the city is a must. Such a survey is available through the national government databases such as the US Census Bureau or the Department of Commerce.[18] Demographics categories include racial, ethnic, language, political affiliations, cultural affiliations, mobility, people group routines, and displacement. Studying demographic surveys is a fundamental step for every church planting plan. You may also use websites such as Percept (perceptgroup .com) or MissionInsite (missioninsite.com) that overlay spiritual preferences on top of demographic data. Demographic research may confirm or challenge one's

---

[16]Ray Oldenburg, *The Great Good Place: Cafes, Coffee Shops, Bookstores, Bars, Hair Salons, and Other Hangouts at the Heart of a Community* (New York: Marlowe & Company, 1989).

[17]Michael Frost, *Exiles: Living Missionally in a Post-Christian Culture* (Grand Rapids: Baker, 2006), 54-64.

[18]For the US, see www.census.gov. Other countries may have similar web-based resources; if not, public libraries, local schools, universities, or chambers of commerce might have access to census data for your city.

preconceived notions or observations, but they give us a bird's-eye view that may spur us to see the community with greater clarity and compassion.

Additionally, national, regional, and city surveys are the geographical tools for sociologists to analyze people groups. Like other academic disciplines, geography has a well-developed set of perspectives: lenses like place, space, and scale, as well as geographical domains of synthesis, which consider how the space of the city—its geographical location and related resources, including the relationship between the environment and society—works.

Windshield surveys. A windshield survey (so named because these things can be discerned by driving around and looking through one's windshield) is a method for assessing the location of the people group we are aiming to evangelize.[19] This methodology assumes that there are specific geographical locations where the people we are seeking to reach live, work, and play. It also assumes that there is free access to navigate by car, public transport, or walking among the people group we have been called by the Holy Spirit to reach. Things to notice in a windshield survey include natural boundaries (such as highways, rivers, and mountains); population centers; industry, trade, commerce, and farming; economic levels (and disparities) of the residents; ethnic groups and size; dominant religious institutions in the area (including the number of those classified as evangelical), and areas where they are no religious facilities.[20]

Cultural influences. Some communities are less connected by their geography and more connected by their cultural influences—the music, arts, films, and technology that shape their everyday lives. Becoming culturally fluent means being able to answer questions like, What music do people listen to? Which social media apps do they use? What podcasts do they listen to? What are their sources of news and information? What books or magazines do they read (assuming they read recreationally)? Knowing the cultural influences means you are familiar with how people think, which informs our preaching in particular. Tim Keller has been famous for knowing New Yorkers' intellectual and cultural influences so well that his preaching could anticipate and answer their objections more astutely.

City gates. Another lens through which to view a community is to identify and seek to walk through its "city gates." In biblical times, cities were typically surrounded by walls for protection from invasion. As a result, access in and out of the city was limited to specific gates. For instance, Jerusalem was surrounded by eight gates, including the Sheep Gate mentioned in John 5:2. But in addition to physical access, a city's gates often functioned like a public square where business deals were

---

[19]Charles Brock, *Indigenous Church Planting: A Practical Journey* (Neosho, MO: Church Growth International, 1994), 111-12.
[20]Brock, *Indigenous Church Planting,* 111-12.

sealed, announcements were made, and courts were sometimes convened. For instance, in Ruth 4:1-11, Boaz sits at the city gate with other elders in order to claim the legal right to marry Ruth. Today there are generally not physical gates to enter into a city. But what are the institutional and relational gates to your city that may allow your planting team access in order to serve and influence a city with the gospel? Seeking the welfare of your city may often involve investing time to understand and then enter through one or more of these city gates.

In a sense, city gates are an acknowledgment of God's common grace in which many stakeholders are seeking the welfare of the city, whether or not they are Christians. Partnering with such people and institutions makes sense on several levels. First, it affirms that because of the *missio Dei*, Christ is already at work in the culture and that our role is to come alongside what God is already doing. Second, it frees us from the Christendom mindset that we must recreate a sanitized, Christian version of everything in the culture (which would be a lot of work anyway). Third, it allows us to learn from, affirm, and partner with the good work already being done by others. We can then take the humble posture of joining God and not feeling that we must somehow control or have a corner on doing good in the city.

There may be many forms of city gates in your community, and the Spirit of God may be opening specific gates that you are intended to walk through. Four categories of city gates that most cities have include education, recreation, government, and business. Let's walk through each city gate one at a time.

Education. Schools and other educational initiatives may be the most natural partners for gospel ministry because both churches and schools share a deep commitment to children and families and a desire to help kids grow to their full God-given potential, as well as providing a physical gathering point for the community to build relationships.

The most straightforward form of partnership is volunteering at and investing in the schools attended by the families on the church planting team. But there are many other ways church plants can seek the welfare of their community's schools. Many principals are eager to partner with an organization that provides a ready source of trustworthy volunteers who will love on the teachers and children in their school. This could involve meeting with school principals or PTA chairs to identify needs, volunteering in classrooms, giving away school supplies at the start of the year, serving at work projects to beautify schools, having appreciation events for teachers, helping with after school programming, and more.

For instance, in the church plant that I (Len) led in Oregon, we began a partnership with an elementary school across from our building. I met with the principal who turned out to be a Christian and we began with a one-day service project. It later led to our church sending volunteers to restart an after-school homework club that had been shut down the prior year due to budget cuts. Our volunteers came once a week to provide snacks and small group tutoring with low-performing kids.

Being involved in education can also extend to community colleges and even local universities. Involvement at a university can bring amazing opportunities to minister not only to college students but to the growing number of international students.

Schools aren't the only forms of education. There are lots of other kinds of wrap-around services that churches can provide to invest in kids' learning, build relationships, and create opportunities for the gospel. These include homework clubs, local Boys & Girls Clubs, music studios, mentoring at-risk kids, and so on.

Recreation. With the dramatic rise in organized youth sports, recreation is often a key city gate to connect with families in a city. Youth leagues, travel teams, and rec clubs abound for nearly every major sport.

The most straightforward way to connect is to volunteer as a coach, particularly if you have kids already on a team. Training your team to intentionally build relationships on the sidelines or in the bleachers, carpooling with teammates to practices and games, and hosting end-of-season parties are ways to invest in kids and their families. One church planter in a sports-crazy town in Oregon was a former NCAA athlete, had four athletic kids, and coached lots of team sports. Because of their deep involvement in the youth sports culture, families from that church were a permanent fixture on the sidelines of every major sport, and they became the first church that people checked out.

When I (Len) planted in Oregon, the local YMCA was a clear city gate and I was able to join the board of the YMCA, which led to great partnerships with civic and business leaders and even the ability to host public Bible studies there.

Government. Municipal governments exist to better their cities, and again church planters can link arms with city officials in providing common grace to their cities. State assembly persons or even US representatives host town halls or gatherings to discuss the region's primary concerns. Cities are often promoting activities, such as art walks, that your church can participate in.

If you can get to know the mayor, attend city council meetings, volunteer on a city committee (Parks & Rec, Arts Commission, etc.), you truly become a citizen, knowing the people's concerns, participating in the civic good, and helping the church become true stakeholders in the community. In particular, you can often get a window into a city's future through meetings with city planners whose job it is to do things like give growth projections and issue new housing and apartment permits.

Commerce. The city's business community often has a strong pulse on a city's gaps and needs. The local Chamber of Commerce meetings are the most common entry point into the business community, and they typically will host monthly networking events, ribbon-cutting ceremonies at all new businesses (including churches!), and local mixers for business people. If you have business people in your church plant, encourage them to become involved in the Chamber.

These four city gates—education, recreation, civic life, and commerce—are by no means the only entry points for gospel impact on a city. For many communities, the arts and nonprofits are significant points of connection that overlap with the visions of church planters. But these four are ones that will likely appear in every community in some form and provide an established infrastructure for serving, volunteering, and building community. Each avenue can provide ways for church plants to invest in a community and not simply try to recruit from a community. Which city gates your church plant ends up focusing on will typically flow out of the planter's mission and vision for the city and the specific relational networks (or persons of peace) that God's Spirit brings. As the planter meets with persons of peace and walks through the doors that God opens, conversations and relationships deepen. We begin to interview and befriend community stakeholders.

Out of these conversations a composite portrait of the community begins to come together. And some of these needs will cause the planter to lean forward in their chair and their heart rate to rise. Pay attention to these cues! Based on the wiring and gifting of the planter, certain relationships and needs will emerge. God's Spirit may begin to raise up partners who are open to you as a planter and to your sense of mission to and for the city. Remember, you are being formed by what God is already doing in the city, just as God is using you to participate in his kingdom coming and his will being done in your city.

Relational networks. Of course, the ultimate purpose of gaining high-level understanding of the city through the social sciences is to facilitate relational impact that then leads to city transformation for the sake of the gospel. Relational knowledge moves planters toward specific connections, interviews, and relationships within the city. Certain professionals in a city typically have a deep knowledge of the people and their motivations for choosing or staying in that city, and planters can prayerfully initiate contact with these professionals as a means to deeply understand the city. For instance, realtors are constantly interacting with people moving into (and out of) the city and so have an excellent sense of the hopes and concerns of residents and understand the socioeconomic and geographical distribution of the city.

For instance, I (Len) met with my realtor to ask her about the city of Pasadena and who was moving in. After I asked her many questions about Pasadena, she began to ask me questions about the church plant and she became interested. She explained that she and several others in her real estate office were "floaters" who had attended church at one time but were not meaningfully connected to any church. She was someone willing to introduce me to others who were spiritually seeking.

Earlier we mentioned education as one of the city gates, and so meeting with an elementary school principal for fifteen to thirty minutes in the neighborhoods that you're serving would give you lots of knowledge about the main issues facing families, including achievement gaps that could be addressed. Similarly, a local YMCA Director would be an excellent source of information about the recreational needs and desires of local residents.

Under the guidance of the Holy Spirit, using the tools of social science can lead to a growing understanding of and love for the people of your city, suburb, town, or rural village. As you learn how the good news intersects with the people you're called to, the shape of the church's ministry then becomes a key that God uses to unlock the hearts and minds of people across the street and across the town. This begins to inform each aspect of the life of the church, from the third places where you hang out to the style of evangelistic conversation, and from the form your home groups take to the preaching on Sunday mornings. Faithful contextualization shapes the leaders and congregation even as the leaders and congregation are shaping the ministry.

DISCUSSION QUESTIONS

1. What people group or neighborhood might you need to see anew, as God sees them?

2. Just as the Holy Spirit challenged Peter and the early church to revise their doctrine and practices, how is the Holy Spirit challenging your preconceptions as you engage in your mission field?

3. In what ways is Peter "converted" by the Holy Spirit in Acts 10? How is the Holy Spirit helping you see that you "should not call anyone impure or unclean" (Acts 10:28)?

4. What social science tools have you used to help you understand and love your city?

5. What city gates might you and your planting team have a natural connection to?

8

HOW DO I BECOME ALL THINGS TO THIS PEOPLE?

CONTEXTUALIZING THE CHURCH PLANTER'S LEADERSHIP

TIM MOREY

"So when are we going to start having church?"

"What do you mean?" my church planter friend stammered. "We have been 'having church' for three months!"

He can laugh about it now, but at the time the question was both crushing and perplexing. John and his fellow launch-team members had moved into the neighborhood months ago, begun meeting their neighbors, and reaching out and ministering to needs in a variety of practical, sensitive ways. Given that the launch team was composed of well-educated, suburban, almost entirely Anglo-American young adults, they were worried that their new neighbors (mostly low-income, poorly educated, and African American) might not accept them. John and his friends definitely stood out, but after initially arousing some suspicion, the church planting team was well received—even appreciated—in their efforts around the neighborhood.

When the time seemed right, they began letting their new neighbors know that they would be starting a church and invited them to attend their first Sunday service. Most of the traditional black churches were not well attended, especially by younger adults, so John and his team had been thinking about utilizing a different, fresh approach that might connect with unreached portions of this community. They settled on a model that had worked well for John in his ministry to university undergrads. It was casual and contemplative, candlelit, with some meaningful silences and readings from the Bible and the church fathers woven throughout. The "sermon" (they didn't like calling it that) was more of an informal dialogue, with no pulpit, John sitting on a stool, and lots of interaction.

On the day of their first worship service, a good handful of neighbors they had built trust with attended. The service came together well, and John and his team breathed a sigh of relief as they gave each other high-fives. Many of the visiting neighbors expressed appreciation, and a few of them continued to attend in the weeks to come. Until, that is, the day one of their regulars asked that question John would never forget: *So when are we going to start having church?*

John was stunned. For him and his fellow launch-team members, the worship services were profound and meaningful. For the residents of the neighborhood, on the other hand, they were interesting and sometimes edifying, but they were also confusing. Where was the preacher? Where was the celebratory music? Why was everyone dressed casually? Why was everything so quiet? To the residents, these gatherings didn't count as church!

What went wrong? Was theirs a bad model? No, the model itself was fine—it was just better suited for a community of church-weary urban hipsters than it was for a low-income African American neighborhood with a strong memory of traditional black church. Was the planter the wrong person for this neighborhood or not suited for inner-city ministry? Possibly, though in this case (after this church plant closed), John went on to successfully lead a multiethnic congregation in a different city, utilizing a much different approach, with members of the neighborhood helping give the church its shape.

No, the issue was one of contextualization. This leader failed to contextualize their leadership for the community they were seeking to reach.

THE RIGHT MODEL?

The question I hear most frequently from new and prospective church planters is, what is the best model for planting? My answer: It depends. Not every model, even if it is a good model, is the right fit for every community. Nor is every model, even if it is a good model, the right fit for every church planter. To find the "best" model we need to understand both the community we want to reach and the pastor or planting team who will be utilizing it. Good contextualization will need to account for both the mission field and the missionary.

Missiologists Michael Frost and Alan Hirsch define contextualization as "the dynamic process by which the constant message of the gospel interacts with specific, relative human situations."[1] More colloquially, missionaries might say that

---

[1] Michael Frost and Alan Hirsch, *The Shaping of Things to Come: Innovation and Mission for the 21st-Century Church* (Grand Rapids: Baker, 2003), 83.

contextualization has occurred when "the gospel offends for the right reasons and not the wrong ones."[2] In other words, while the content remains the same from one locale to the next, the container might need to change for the message to be heard in a way that makes sense to the hearers.

While we typically and properly associate contextualization with how we communicate the biblical message, we also need to consider whether our leadership has been contextualized. We need to ask not only if my hearers will be able to receive the message in a way that makes sense to them, but also, will they be able to receive *me as messenger* in a way that makes sense to them?

Lesslie Newbigin writes, "We must start with the basic fact that there is no such thing as a pure gospel if by that is meant something which is not embodied in a culture. . . . Every interpretation of the gospel is embodied in some cultural form."[3] This is not only true for the message, but also for the model and methods we employ in leading a congregation. There is no such thing as a pure leadership form disembodied (or dissociated) from culture.

I've seen, and perpetrated, my share of contextual missteps, and maybe you have too. Sometimes these missteps have to do with employing a model that doesn't fit the ministry context, like the above-mentioned urban-Anglo-hipster-style church in the African American neighborhood. At other times, though, the planter is employing a model that is fine for the neighborhood, but doesn't fit their particular gifting, personality, or temperament.

Think, for example, of the church planter who may have correctly discerned that a Sunday-centric, Rick Warren-esque ministry will be an effective model for the new suburban development in which they are planting. But what if they don't have the requisite up-front presence and preaching gifts to pull off this model? Or conversely, I've seen planters whose strongest gifts are in preaching to larger groups, but inadvertently neutralize these gifts because they are committed to a house church model with a completely different teaching style. Each model can be very effective, but each requires the planter and their team to have different strengths.

It is a bit like the History Channel show called *Man, Moment, Machine*. The premise of the show is that major events that we might associate with a particular historical figure are typically not just the result of that dynamic person's influence alone. When we look closer, we see that the event's occurrence was really the convergence of the right person appearing at the right moment in history, combined with technologies that arose at that time. Martin Luther's significance, for example,

---

[2]Frost and Hirsch, *Shaping of Things to Come*, 83.
[3]Lesslie Newbigin, *The Gospel in a Pluralist Society* (Grand Rapids: Eerdmans, 1989), 144.

was not just due to his particular genius. His impact also had to do with him coming on the scene at a moment where there was popular appetite for reform and when the new technology of the printing press enabled the rapid dissemination of his ideas. Remove any one of these three factors and you might not have the Reformation as we know it.

Good contextualization involves the convergence of several factors as well. It means the right person or team goes to a place for which they are well suited and employ a model which is well suited to that place and to the gifting they bring. All these factors play into how the leader may need to contextualize her leadership.

When it comes to contextualizing one's leadership, there are two questions every planter needs to ask. First, *who has God made me to be?* And second, in light of the reality of who I am, *how do I need to adapt my leadership to my ministry context?*

To explore these questions, we are going to look to two biblical figures as models. For the first question we will look at Moses, the deliverer of Israel. His story will serve as a guide for us in considering the contours of who God has made us to be and how that impacts our particular call to ministry. For the second question, we will look at the apostle Paul. Paul's life and teaching will guide us in understanding how we can take a deep self-understanding, and while being faithful to how God has made us, meaningfully adapt our leadership to fit a given ministry context. Finally, these two questions will be fleshed out in case studies from church planters in several very different settings speaking about how they have each learned to contextualize their leadership.

WHO HAS GOD MADE ME TO BE?

In the same way that one cannot begin to adapt the gospel message for a given context without having sufficient clarity on what the gospel message is, a person cannot begin to adapt their leadership for a given context until they have clarity on who they are. The Quaker educator Parker Palmer writes, "The deepest vocation question is not, 'What ought I to do with my life?' It is the more elementary and demanding, 'Who am I? What is my nature?'"[4]

In reflecting on my own life and those of other pastors, it seems that we do not always think deeply about our calling beyond our initial call to ministry. We do not always go beyond the recognition that we are to be a pastor and take the next step of asking, what *kind* of pastor am I supposed to be? What are the particular gifts God has given me that will help me serve best in certain capacities, and not as well

---

[4]Parker Palmer, *Let Your Life Speak: Listening for the Voice of Vocation* (San Francisco: Jossey-Bass, 1999), 15.

in others? True, most of us won't struggle much to discern whether we are better suited to be a middle school pastor or an executive pastor (do I get more joy from playing chubby bunny or from working on the staff's annual reviews?). But have we given serious, prayerful thought to the question, what has my unique mixture of gifts, passions, and backstory prepared me to do?[5]

I find that the call of Moses provides a good primer for thinking through one's calling. We will look at four aspects of his story.

Sovereign foundations. "Then his sister asked Pharaoh's daughter, 'Shall I go and get one of the Hebrew women to nurse the baby for you?'" (Ex 2:7).

Moses' story begins, not with his actions, but with God's. Even before he is adopted by Pharaoh's daughter, the author of Exodus is letting us in on the divine whispers that something out of the ordinary is going on.

The opening lines of Moses' story contain whispers of God's movement, foreshadows of how God would use him. The text describes Moses as being a "fine" child (Ex 2:2). The Hebrew here is *tov*, the same word God uses at creation to describe what he has made: "and he saw that it was *tov*." As the author of Hebrews puts it, Moses' parents immediately recognized that "he was no ordinary child" (Heb 11:23), so they attempted to hide him and keep him alive.

When it seemed they could do so no longer, Moses' mother placed him in a papyrus basket, coated it with tar and pitch, and put him in the reeds along the Nile river. The word used for the basket, *tebah*, is used only here and one other place in the Scriptures—for Noah's ark, also sealed with pitch. Moses is then set among the reeds, which some scholars take as a foreshadow of his later leading the Israelites through the parted Sea of Reeds.

It would seem that the author is drawing the reader's mind back to the themes of creation and redemption. God's work of bringing deliverance to the Israelite slaves is bigger than just them—it is part of the greater work he is doing in the world.

Most famously, we find that the three-month old Moses is set afloat in the Nile with his parents' desperate hope that he might be rescued from Pharaoh's genocidal quest. Not only is Moses rescued, but he is found by Pharaoh's daughter, and raised as her son in the royal palace. "Shall I get one of the Hebrew women to nurse the baby for you?" his clever sister asks. And just like that, we learn that Moses will be bicultural—the son of Hebrew slaves and the son of a royal princess.

These details are not incidental—they are core to his future calling.

Could we imagine a better situation for the future deliverer of Israel? He grows up, on the one hand, as a prince of Egypt, educated as a king's grandson, utterly

---

[5]We recommend making use of a church planting assessment center if possible (some are available online as well). Another useful tool in digging deeper into one's call is David T. Olson, *Discovering Your Leadership Style: The Power of Chemistry, Strategy, and Spirituality* (Downers Grove, IL: InterVarsity Press, 2014).

familiar with the halls of power, with an insider's understanding of government, economy, and the use and misuse of power. At the same time, Moses grows up hearing from his Levite parents the story of Abraham, Isaac, and Jacob; that God has promised to bless the Israelites and make them a blessing. We can only imagine all the ways that this dual understanding, this biculturality, would equip Moses for the life to which God would call him.

What is going on here? The author of Exodus is telling us that God is at work. Before Moses could grow up to be the deliverer of Israel, God had set him apart. His foundations were sovereignly laid with this purpose in mind.

Typically, we find that our calling reflects aspects of our own sovereign foundations. God, it seems, has prepared us in certain ways, often outside our control, which have shaped us for the work for which he has called us. What formative experiences have shaped my passions? What are my natural giftings and temperaments? Are there circumstances and events, joyful or painful, that God has used in shaping who I am? Taking a careful and prayerful look at one's past and noting the foundations God has sovereignly laid is an important aspect of learning who we are.

When I was leading our denomination's assessment center, we would sometimes have a planter who felt called to minister in the inner city, despite having no experiences in their upbringing or ministry background that would indicate they were well-suited for this. Almost always, our collective discernment would be that this was probably not the best context for them to minister. So we would affirm the planter's holy longings to minister to the poor or pursue racial justice but help them consider if there might be a better way for them to live out these longings.

While of course there is the occasional exception, typically we find that God has prepared a person not just for planting in general, but for planting in a particular place among a particular group of people. What, we ask, are my sovereign foundations telling me about who I am as a planter?

What I can't not do. "Looking this way and that and seeing no one, he killed the Egyptian and hid him in the sand" (Ex 2:12); "But Moses got up and came to their rescue and watered their flock" (Ex 2:17). Who was Moses, at the core of his being? In a word, Moses was a liberator.

The contours of our calling will be greatly determined by what we see—by what arouses our passions, what stirs a "holy discontent" in our hearts.[6] Why do we see what we see? Not all of us will see and be moved by the same things, and that is fine. I might feel compelled to start a church because I look at our city and see that the young adult population is dramatically unchurched. You might look at our same city

---

[6]This phrase originates from Bill Hybels, *Holy Discontent: Fueling the Fire That Ignites Personal Vision* (Grand Rapids: Zondervan, 2007).

and start a church because you see the churches are segregated along racial lines, and someone needs to start a church that reflects God's heart for racial reconciliation. Someone else might start a church because they look at our city and see a great need to minister to the working poor.

No one of us alone is going to be able to see and be moved to action by every need and injustice. But God sees it all, and he will press on our hearts those things that he has sovereignly prepared us to see. In any case, if we are pressing into God's heart for our city, we can expect that God will press on us something that he sees, and that we will be moved to action by what moves him.

Moses, looking at the plight of the Israelites, could see injustice and he had to act. But unfortunately, his first attempt at being a liberator was a failure of epic proportions. Seeing one his fellow Hebrews being beaten, he steps in to right the injustice but murders the perpetrator and is forced to flee for his life (Ex 2:12-15).

But even Moses' failure reveals a profound truth. Note what happens when Moses first arrives in Midian. Moses is sitting by a well, presumably wallowing in defeat, when a group of young women come to draw water. A band of shepherds come and bully the women away from the well. But Moses, again seeing the injustice, "got up and came to their rescue and watered their flock" (Ex 2:17).

This is no small feat! Moses is alone, defeated, and, it would seem, resigned to having failed as Israel's deliverer. Yet in the midst of this, he single-handedly takes on a gang of thugs when he sees them taking advantage of these young women!

Being a liberator is who Moses is. He can't not do it. (I know that's bad grammar but it's good theology.)

I have yet to meet a church planter who doesn't have failures as a significant part of his or her story. My own story is littered with them. Leadership missteps which led to painful departures, grand visions I confidently placed before the church which didn't pan out, elevating a person into leadership who I thought would grow into the role but who simply wasn't ready. Every wrong step comes at a cost—to my ego and to the confidence of those who follow my lead.

Yet, contrary to how it feels in the moment, failure can be a gift. Almost inevitably it leads to reevaluation of one's call. Did I hear God correctly? Am I in the right place? Should I be doing something different?

I've come to the conclusion that such reevaluation, though painful, is healthy, and perhaps even necessary, in our development as church planters. In fact, the typical church planter's journey is littered with failures, setbacks, and disappointments—it's almost expected.[7]

---

[7]For more on failure and calling, see my forthcoming book *The Spiritually Formed Church Planter* (Downers Grove, IL: InterVarsity Press). See also J. R. Briggs, *Fail: Finding Hope and Grace in the Midst of Ministry Failure* (Downers Grove, IL: InterVarsity Press, 2014).

As planters, we do well to ask, what is it I can't not do? What are those things which are so hardwired into who I am that I do them without even thinking about them? Or conversely, what are those things which are so important to me that I couldn't serve a church that didn't value these things?

As a church planter, I spend a good portion of my work week at Starbucks. On a handful of occasions, as I've watched the crew serving coffee drinkers, I've wondered what it would look like if I were to work there. As I tried to picture it, I found I would still pastor, lead, and teach. I would always be pulling aside one of the baristas asking, "How are you doing after the breakup?" or "Did that thing work out with your mom?" or "Would it be okay if I prayed for you about that?" I would always be rallying the crew around some common goal ("Let's do a toy drive this Christmas!"). And I'd always be teaching something, hosting seminars on making a better latte or learning to work with deeper joy or becoming a more supportive community for one another (I would drive the crew nuts). Reality is, I can't *not* do these things. Whatever my job is, whether it is ministry-related or not, these urges to pastor, lead, and teach would always find a way to bubble to the surface.

Frederick Buechner puts it like this, "The place God calls you to is the place where your deep gladness and the world's deep hunger meet."[8] Often that place is revealed in the things we can't not do. Or as Mark Labberton has said, "Call is primarily about who we are and what we do all the time."[9]

Hearing God's voice. "When the LORD saw that he had gone over to look, God called to him from within the bush, 'Moses! Moses!'" (Ex 3:4).

After the incident at the well, the girls' father recognizes good marriage material in Moses, and Moses becomes the husband of Zipporah and employee of Jethro, his new father-in-law. For the many years which followed, Moses tends his father-in-law's sheep. His life has taken a major turn from his life's early direction as a deliverer, and if his conversation with God is any indication (Ex 3:11–4:16), Moses has convinced himself of every reason he should never have tried to be a deliverer in the first place. He asks the same questions many of us ask as well: Who am I, a nobody, to take on this role? Can I represent God well to the people? What if they don't take me seriously? What if my gifts aren't adequate to the task?

In the years that I led our denomination's assessment center, I would occasionally hear questions like these, but just as often I would hear bravado. The candidates were primarily young, idealistic, and to date their ministry scorecards showed more wins than losses. But in the years I have coached church planters, I've heard

---

[8]Frederick Buechner, *Wishful Thinking: A Seeker's ABC* (San Francisco: HarperCollins, 1993), 119.
[9]Mark Labberton, *Called: The Crisis and Promise of Following Jesus Today* (Downers Grove, IL: InterVarsity Press, 2014), 135.

questions like these a lot. Once church planters have been working in the field and begin accumulating the bumps and bruises to prove it, doubts and insecurities begin to emerge (or reemerge): Do I have what it takes? Am I the right person for this? Perhaps I should be doing something else?

The confidence and strength to continue once ministry gets hard requires assurance of call. Therefore, it is essential as church planters seeking to know who we are that we intentionally seek out the Father's voice. We need to know deep in our bones that we have not dreamed up this mission on our own—that we are seeing ourselves as the Father sees us and are living out a mission for which he has designed and sent us.

There are many excellent books on hearing God's voice, and I don't have space here to recap the excellent wisdom they provide.[10] But there are two aspects of hearing God that I am struck by in Moses' story.

First, God speaks only after he knows he has Moses' attention. "*When the Lord saw* that he had gone over to look, God called to him from within the bush, 'Moses! Moses!'" (Ex 3:4). The impression I get is that God had been wanting for some time to speak, but this was the first time Moses had ears to hear it (cf. Mk 4:9). How many times, I wonder, had Moses walked across this patch of sacred ground completely unaware that the God of the universe was waiting to speak a word to him that would completely change the direction of his life?

We all want a "burning bush"—a moment of God speaking with such force, clarity, and specificity that our call is beyond question. But we find that both in our lives and in the Scriptures such experiences are rare. The norm tends to be a slower, more patient knowing, or as Zach Eswine defines calling, "an inward desire that ebbed and flowed but didn't fade."[11]

The voice of God more often comes to us as a confirmation of what he has been stirring all along—the culmination of our sovereign foundations, that accumulation of experiences that reveal to us our gifts, passions, and those things we can't not do. And within that, we begin to sense the voice of the Spirit saying, "Yes. This, my child, is what you are meant to do." But such insight only comes as we steadily give our attention to God and what he is doing.

Second, look for affirmations of call in community. Moses encounters God alone, but his call is soon confirmed by others. His encounter with God is followed by three

---

[10]A few that have meant the most to me: Dallas Willard, *Hearing God: Developing a Conversational Relationship with God* (Downers Grove, IL: InterVarsity Press, 1984); F. B. Meyer, *Secret of Guidance* (CreateSpace, 2014); John Ortberg, *All the Places to Go . . . How Will You Know?* (Carol Stream, IL: Tyndale House, 2015).

[11]Zach Eswine, *The Imperfect Pastor: Discovering Joy in Our Limitations Through a Daily Apprenticeship with Jesus* (Wheaton, IL: Crossway, 2015), 213.

other encounters, which in different ways affirm Moses' call. The first encounter is with his father-in-law, Jethro, "the priest of Midian," who when told of Moses' desire to return to Egypt blesses him (Ex 4:18). The second is with Moses' brother Aaron. We learn that God had spoken to Aaron as well—not the particulars of Moses' call, which Moses would have to explain, but which Aaron was prepared by God to receive (Ex 4:27-28). The third is with those that Moses and Aaron will be ministering to—the Israelites. The Israelite elders receive the brothers' message as being from God and respond with belief and worship (Ex 4:29-31).

If the calling we sense is indeed from God, then we can expect those around us to affirm that call as well. The Holy Spirit does not just indwell us as individuals but collectively as the body of Christ (1 Cor 3:16). We can rightly expect that others will pick up on the way a call continues the patterns God has been laying in our lives through our foundations and our passions. Wise spiritual friends and mentors will have experienced God's work through us and be able to say along with the Spirit's voice within us, "Yes, this is what you are meant to do."

While I was writing this chapter, I got an email from a church planter that we assessed some years back. At his assessment I remember him wrestling with whether he should become a church planter or go the academic route and teach. There is something almost sacred about the environment created in a good assessment process. Assessors fervently pray over each candidate and do their best to listen well to that person's story and to the Spirit's leading in that person's life. In the midst of this environment, words are sometimes spoken that are deeply formative. Such was the case here, as a wise assessor spoke a life-changing word into this young man's life. "You can be both," he said. "God has made you to be both." The young man went on to plant a church, and at the same time has actively engaged his academic gifts through study and writing. He wrote today to say he was starting his doctorate. "Thank you," he said. "That word was so life-giving; somehow I hadn't considered a solution that involved both until the assessor said it." Sometimes we are so close to our own gifts that we can't see them unless another in the body points them out.

What is in your hand? "Moses answered, 'What if they do not believe me or listen to me and say, "The LORD did not appear to you"?' Then the LORD said to him, 'What is that in your hand?'" (Ex 4:1-2).

God has told Moses that he is to go and deliver his people from Egypt. Moses has responded with a string of fears and doubts about his inadequacy for the job: "What if the people I am supposed to lead don't believe that you sent me? What if they don't listen to me?"

God's response is surprising: "What is that in your hand?" God directs Moses' attention to his shepherd's staff—the simple tool he uses each day in tending his flock. God directs him to throw it on the ground, and it becomes a snake. This, God tells him, is indicative of the signs he will perform to show that God is with Moses.

And indeed, for Moses the staff becomes almost a character in the story, used to perform miracles in Pharaoh's court, at the Red Sea, and with the Israelites in the desert. It even receives a name—what was a simple piece of wood becomes "the staff of God" (Ex 4:20).[12]

To Moses' great surprise, the simple tools he brought to the mission were sufficient to topple an empire. For us too, if God has called, he will use whatever raw material we bring to accomplish his purposes through us. In God's hand, our very ordinary gifts and talents become extraordinary.

When we undertake a God-sized venture like planting a church, it is a natural reaction to look at the tools—the gifts, talents, and resources—that we bring to the task, and to seriously wonder whether they are adequate. While we want to give serious consideration to whether we are truly suited for the task, and invite other honest and wise individuals (an assessment process, trusted mentors, those who have experienced our ministry) to speak into our suitability as well, the story of Moses reminds us that if God has indeed called, he makes us adequate to the call. What is already in our hand will do.

Twice I came inches away from dropping out of seminary because I was certain I didn't measure up. The first time it was because of preaching. I knew I had insight into the text but couldn't imagine my naturally mellow delivery style inducing anything other than boredom in my hearers. The second time was because I was not a flashy, dynamic leader like those classmates with whom I compared myself. *Who would ever follow me?* I wondered. In the end, though, I couldn't bring myself to quit. The call was too strong, and I couldn't walk away. My prayer became, "God, I'll serve you as a pastor, even if I suck. But I'll enjoy this a lot more if you would please make me better at it."

So, am I an amazing communicator? Am I a dynamic leader? Honestly, no. But I find that as I have trusted God to use those gifts, and as I've been diligent to continue developing those gifts through the years, I find that God has indeed used me in his work of building a healthy, fruitful, church-planting church. And what's more, he has been faithful to lead me into ministry ventures that are suited to the particular shape of my teaching and leadership gifts, and he led people to me who find my gifts more than adequate.

Again, we do need certain gifts in order to plant a church and must wisely discern with the community of saints whether we are called to this particular work. We

---

[12]Thank you to Rev. Dan Palomino for pointing this out to me.

remember too that we are not expected to embody all the gifts but to be part of a team who collectively are gifted for the task. But my point is this: God is in the business of doing extraordinary things through ordinary people. If he has truly called us, then what is in our hand will be enough.

All four of these elements contribute to our understanding of who God has made us to be, and that understanding better equips us to ask our second question.

HOW DO I NEED TO ADAPT MY LEADERSHIP TO MY MINISTRY CONTEXT?

Once we begin to understand who God made us to be—who we are and who we are not—we will be able to begin thinking properly about how we might best adapt our leadership to our mission field. This adaptation will always need to happen within the broad confines of who we are if it is to comport with our calling. But adaptation will need to happen, as we carefully discern the character, culture, and context of those we serve.

It is at this point that contextualization can be misunderstood as an attempt to take the offense out of the gospel, or to sugarcoat biblical truth and market the church in a way that makes the gospel more palatable. Good contextualization does none of these things. The cross is offensive and the way of Jesus is difficult. We cannot (and should not) change that. On the contrary, our goal is to adapt our message or leadership so that the way of Jesus can be properly understood and lived by our hearers. If we do not, we risk unnecessarily offending for reasons other than the cross!

The apostle Paul serves as a model for how to faithfully contextualize one's leadership. In particular, we will look at 1 Corinthians 9, where he explains his philosophy of ministry in this area, with some examples from Acts 17, where we see him put this philosophy into practice.[13]

Embracing the costs. "Don't we have the right? . . . But we did not use this right" (1 Cor 9:4, 12).

Contextualizing one's leadership means incurring personal costs. Paul identifies three very costly sacrifices he willingly made to bring the gospel to the Corinthians and others: the right to marry, the right to receive pay for his work, and the right to his cultural preferences, as represented in "food and drink" (1 Cor 9:3-6). And Paul specifies these are not merely perks he might request, but rights to which he is entitled yet chooses to forgo! "But we did not use this right," Paul says. "On the contrary, we put up with anything rather than hinder the gospel of Christ" (1 Cor 9:12).

---

[13]For more on what Paul's philosophy of contextualization looked like in practice, with implications for today, see Tim Morey, *Embodying Our Faith: Becoming a Living, Sharing, Practicing Church* (Downers Grove, IL: InterVarsity Press, 2009), chap. 3.

When we pause to reflect on the weight of what Paul has given up, we are right to stagger a bit. Ministry is hard. For many of us, the strength we draw on to persist in such hard work is derived in large part from the comforts we enjoy outside of ministry. The smile and touch of a spouse's companionship, for those who are blessed to have that, is a welcome contrast to others who may have caused us pain in our mission field. To finish one's ministry for the day and simply rest is a tremendous gift. Yet Paul, as so many bivocational ministers, finishes the day's ministry only to go on to additional work needed to pay the bills. Even the comfort we derive from the pleasure of enjoying the much-loved foods and drinks with which we grew up—a pleasure which might seem small when compared with marriage and receiving pay—should not be minimized. Those tastes and smells that we associate with the fellowship of family are incredibly powerful in their ability to bring us comfort. To forego these things is a costly sacrifice.

But Paul's eyes are not on these comforts, significant as they are. Instead of clinging to comforts, Paul embraces the cost itself as his privilege, and also to the blessings yet to come. "What then is my reward?" Paul asks. "Just this: that in preaching the gospel I may offer it free of charge, and so not make use of my rights as a preacher of the gospel" (1 Cor 9:18). And again, "I do all this for the sake of the gospel, that I may share in its blessings" (1 Cor 9:23).

Whether God calls us to give up rights as significant as these or to make sacrifices that are more modest, the planter who wants to effectively contextualize her leadership must be ready to embrace the costs required to bring the gospel unhindered to a given community.

Identifying with your community. "Though I am free and belong to no one, I have made myself a slave to everyone, to win as many as possible" (1 Cor 9:19).

Embracing the cost is not an end in itself but a means to Paul's goal of bringing the gospel to his hearers in a way that they can understand. Having laid aside comforts which may create a barrier to effective ministry, Paul is free to adapt his leadership to better identify with those to whom he ministers:

> To the Jews I became like a Jew, to win the Jews. To those under the law I became like one under the law (though I myself am not under the law), so as to win those under the law. To those not having the law I became like one not having the law (though I am not free from God's law but am under Christ's law), so as to win those not having the law. To the weak I became weak, to win the weak. I have become all things to all people so that by all possible means I might save some. (1 Cor 9:20-22)

Whether Jews or Greeks, law-observant or lawless, strong or weak, Paul is ready not just to understand but to identify with those he serves.

We see this embodied in the story of Hudson Taylor, the nineteenth-century missionary to China. In the beginning of his ministry he adopted what was then a typical missionary strategy—to bring the Chinese into the missionary compound, dress them like the English, educate them in English, and thus "civilize" them so that they could receive the gospel. But over time, his love for the Chinese caused him to identify with them more deeply. Rather than insisting they adapt, he adapted. He went to them. He dressed like the Chinese, ate their food, learned their language, and cut his hair in the Chinese style—a shaved head with a long, thin pigtail. And for him too, this came at a cost. Back home it was front-page news that Hudson Taylor had gone native, and he could only watch helplessly as his financial support evaporated.[14]

It may be further worth noting that Paul holds no illusions that his sacrifices ought to automatically bear tremendous fruit. "I have become all things to all people [adapted his leadership, at a cost], so that by all possible means I might save *some*." The adapting leader cannot approach ministry expecting that their efforts will result in tremendous fruit. It may, but it also may not.

Again, we think of the early missionaries to China who labored their whole lives without seeing a single convert. Today, centuries later, that gospel seed has grown into one of the most stunning people movements in history. As Paul says elsewhere, we are responsible to sow and to water, but only God can bring the fruit (1 Cor 3:6-7). We must be content with that, not insistent that God reward our sacrifice by giving what we deem to be sufficient success.

Remaining grounded. "Do you not know that in a race all the runners run, but only one gets the prize? Run in such a way as to get the prize" (1 Cor 9:24).

Contextualizing our leadership is not without its dangers. If we fail to adapt enough, our message or methods may not be understandable to those we seek to reach. If, on the other hand, we over-adapt, we might compromise the gospel message. Neither is an acceptable outcome for the Christian leader. Lesslie Newbigin articulates this tension well:

> On the one side there is the danger that one finds no point of contact for the message as the missionary preaches it, to the people of the local culture the message appears irrelevant and meaningless. On the other side is the danger that the point of contact determines entirely the way that the message is received, and the result is syncretism. Every missionary path has to find the way between these two dangers: irrelevance and syncretism. And if one is more afraid of one danger than the other, one will certainly fall into the opposite.[15]

---

[14]Howard Taylor and Mrs. Howard Taylor, *Hudson Taylor's Spiritual Secret* (Chicago: Moody Press, 1989), 64-74.
[15]Lesslie Newbigin, quoted in Ed Stetzer, *Planting New Churches in a Postmodern Age* (Nashville, TN: Broadman and Holman Publishers, 2003), 128-29.

How does a church plant leader, like Paul, "become all things to all people" without slipping into cultural accommodation and distorting the message? Or, in the midst of the costs and the pressures, keep from falling into grave personal sin?

Additionally, contextualization inevitably leads to thorny questions of what faithfulness looks like in light of local conditions. How does one sort out these questions and practice pastoral theology that is wise, contextually sensitive, and faithful to the Bible's teachings?

I find it amazing that Paul was so attuned to the Spirit that he could look at Peter's backsliding into eating only with Jews and declare definitively, "No, this behavior is incompatible with the gospel!" (see Gal 2:14-16). Yet, no doubt to the great surprise of many of his hearers, Paul permits believers to eat food sacrificed to idols (idols!) under certain conditions (1 Cor 8–10). Similarly, Paul asks women to conform to some cultural norms yet not others. On the one hand, women can pray and preach in public worship, a cause of offense to many. Yet the women must not (as an expression of their freedom in Christ) do so with uncovered heads (1 Cor 11:5). This, Paul says, would be too much—the equivalent in our culture might be "if someone looked into a church and found the women all wearing bikinis."[16] How does one have the wisdom to know which adaptations are imperative even if they cause offense, which may be more optional, and which adaptations simply go too far?

I believe Paul directs us toward the answer in this passage, as he moves seamlessly from a discussion of contextualization (1 Cor 9:19-23) into a discussion of his own life in Christ (1 Cor 9:24-27). Paul "runs in such a way as to get the prize" and "beats his body and makes it his slave." Like an athlete striving for the top prize, Paul trains himself spiritually.

I would argue (and have done so extensively in chapter four) that intentional investment in one's own spiritual growth is the number one task of the church planter. Only as we pursue a life of abiding in Jesus will we find the power, peace, and wisdom to serve those we would seek to reach with the gospel. We must, as Paul says elsewhere, train ourselves to be godly (1 Tim 4:8).

What does such leadership look like in practice? In the remainder of this chapter, three church planters in three different places will tell their stories and discuss how they have learned to adapt their leadership styles in their unique contexts.

STORY 1: DAVID SWANSON, NEW COMMUNITY COVENANT CHURCH

I never expected to be the only white pastor in a black neighborhood. I was an associate pastor at a multiethnic church that had begun planning a church plant on

---

[16]N. T. Wright, "Women's Service in the Church: The Biblical Basis," paper delivered at St. John's College, Durham, England, September 4, 2004.

the South Side of Chicago. This area of the city is predominately African American, and Bronzeville, the specific neighborhood our leaders felt called to, is a historic black neighborhood where migrants from the Jim Crow South came looking for safety and work. It did not take an expert in contextual ministry to understand that this church plant required an African American pastor. As we moved into the planting process—praying, gathering, planning, and more—we earnestly searched for this pastor, only to meet one closed door after another. Finally, just weeks away from our first service, our leaders called me as the pastor.

Though I had been working with the planting team in a support capacity, it took some time for the significance of this crosscultural call to sink in. I wrestled with God in prayer. I poured out my anxieties and fears to my spiritual director. How could I—a white man—be the right person to lead a multiethnic church in this black neighborhood? Wouldn't my very presence be a hindrance to genuine gospel reconciliation across ethnic and racial lines of segregation? Slowly, in large part through the presence of African American friends and mentors, the Lord opened my heart to his call. I came to see the beauty of Paul's gospel-saturated words: "But God chose the foolish things of the world to shame the wise; God chose the weak things of the world to shame the strong" (1 Cor 1:27). As a white man I was used to leading from a place of wisdom and strength, but this context has forced me to acknowledge that God's power is best demonstrated through my foolishness and weakness.

This deep, internal shift in how I see myself in relation to God's mission is the most important thing I've learned through this ministry call. I remember sharing my deep anxieties about my place in our neighborhood with my spiritual director, an African American woman who grew up in Bronzeville. She listened to me talk about my discomfort in my own skin, about wondering whether I would ever be truly accepted, and about feeling like I had to fight the pervasive negative stereotypes of white male ministry leaders. She smiled and replied, "That's good, David. Now you have a small idea of what I've felt like most every day of my life." Her words created a paradigm-shifting moment as I realized that God was emptying me of my perceived strengths so that I could more authentically come alongside my new neighbors and the diverse members of our church.

There have been other important lessons along the way. Early on we decided not to launch any of our own outreach ministries. Though we were convinced that God had called us to be a racially diverse church in our segregated city, we were under no illusions that we were bringing the gospel to our neighborhood. For generations, faithful congregations have expressed God's grace and justice through faithful and innovative ministry. So rather than begin our own ministries we made friends with pastors and congregations and asked how we could assist their efforts. Not everyone was interested, but some were. Over the years those friendships have led to significant partnerships to reduce violence and trauma in our neighborhood, monthly prayer walks around our public schools, and many combined worship services. One of my mentors defines credibility as what others say about your faithfulness. Thanks to these friendships—nurtured by our decision to partner rather than do our own thing—our church has far more credibility in our community than I ever dared to expect.

As the years have passed, it has been essential to continue moving beyond my white bubble. I will always be a white man who carries specific cultural and racial memories within myself. Rather than denying this or pretending to be someone I'm not, I've learned to lean into friends and mentors who have deeply formed how I see our neighborhood, our ministry, and even myself. The authors I read and the preachers whose podcasts I listen to are a reflection of the experiences and concerns of our neighbors. It is a joyful realization to see the way my life has become intertwined with the diversity of the kingdom of God. The challenges and delights of multiethnic, crosscultural ministry are no longer theoretical; they have become my personal experiences. I get to show up to a street protest about neighborhood violence or to a meeting about an exciting community initiative because my life is now woven into the larger fabric of God's people and mission in our neighborhood. I wouldn't trade it for anything in the world.

STORY 2: JARED BOYD, FRANKLINTON ABBEY

While geography has impacted the way I've adapted my leadership, I find that over the past few years, my leadership has mostly been shaped by the women around me. I'm married, I have four daughters, and surprisingly (to me), the majority of the people who continue to emerge as leaders in our church plant—a contemplative faith community on the west side of Columbus, Ohio—are women.

And it's wonderful.

My natural leaning in leadership has historically been fairly top-down. I'm part of a church planting ethos that has effectively followed the CEO business model of the 1980s. As a church planting movement, the Vineyard in the USA has always been strong at releasing church planters as entrepreneurs who carry strong vision and a strong hustle to see that vision through. This entrepreneur-based church planting context is what has always been modeled for me and it's what I've mostly heard taught over the past twenty-five years of being a part of the Vineyard tribe (I showed up when I was sixteen): "The leader is the one with the vision, and everyone follows the leader."

Most of my leadership has also been shaped by men. While the Vineyard has been firmly in the egalitarian camp for most of the last twenty years, it's just in the past five or six years that I've been exposed to women in high levels of leadership. More particularly, it's just been recently that I've seen women displaying tremendous leadership that has pushed back against some of the more hierarchical models in favor of a more collaborative approach to leadership. At some point along the way, I decided that I wanted to develop more women leaders. Given that leadership is picked up through proximity, what I also noticed is that if this was going to be a part of my work, I was going to need to spend more time with women—one-on-one in mentoring and spiritual formation. This is how you grow leaders.

This conscious choice to invest time into nurturing women leaders has turned into a tremendous strength, given the location of our church plant. We are about two years into leading a handful of families into the poorest neighborhood of our city—one that is the epicenter of both Ohio's opioid crisis and a hub for human trafficking. Planting a church in a poor neighborhood (without any financial backing) is also forcing us to think through the economics of church planting in some new ways. My commitment to long-term bivocationalism has led to a leadership structure that is a bit flatter and a lot more collaborative. Here are a few things I'm learning.

First, collaboration dies when power is wielded. What I'm finding is that the women in our community are drawn to this collaborative leadership because we've begun with the assumption that there is no pyramid to climb. There is no power at the top because there is no power (or very little) at work in the system. We've chosen to operate according to our gifts, and what I keep hearing the women around me say is something like this: "I feel released in my gifting and supported to work it out within this community."

We haven't created leaders who happen to be women. *We've made a lot room for women wanting to serve and lead, and we've created no barriers to this happening.* My commitment to relinquishing power and empowering women, paired with my context for planting a church (the economics of our parish), has shaped our structure of leadership which has produced an environment where women can thrive. And this has further circled back and formed me as a leader in ways I was not expecting to be formed. I've become a better leader because of it.

Second, process is more important than outcome—it creates a future you never could have imagined. I lead with vision toward a specific (and often overly idealized) version of the world I want to live in. It's also the world I'm trying to create. What happens along the way and how things unfold contribute to the outcome far more than the original intentions I may set forth. I've become more flexible about what ends up happening in the end and have been taught (mostly by the women around me) to value the process over the outcome. And the truth is that the outcome ends up being a better version than I was thinking of to begin with.

Third, people are more important than the mission—because they are the mission. Emphasis on relationships makes things move much slower. And that's totally okay. There are things that I thought would be easily grasped and supported by everyone on my team that took far longer than I ever anticipated. This is not to say that I think the women (and men) were slow to get it. I think everyone was slow to catch some of the vision simply because I wasn't attending to it in the right way. There are assumptions I made about people's buy-in—and so many times it was the women who brought me back into conversations that I thought were finished. It was the vulnerability of those around me and their willingness to speak up and say, "Wait a minute. I don't think I fully understand what you've been saying," or, "I'm afraid to actually take this part of the vision on as a value of my own," that helped me see I needed to slow down even more and consider some new approaches to articulating what I felt I was leading us into. My experience has been that the women around me who are also developing as leaders have been more vulnerable with me about how they are experiencing the moving pieces of planting a faith community than the men have been.

Finally, discernment with other people is more important than articulating directives. When you know you're in it together, you'll get where you need to go. We've leaned hard into group discernment. We don't look for consensus, but we take time to discern what others within the community are sensing and seeing. Some of the leaders in our community have helped me see that I have a tendency to chew on things internally. Our practice (and commitment) to group discernment has helped me externalize my own process as a leader, get feedback, and bring extra sets of eyes and ears to chart a way forward. We listen together to discern God's will.

STORY 3: ADAM EDGERLY, NEW SONG LA COVENANT CHURCH

Newsong LA Covenant Church began as an effort to expand the ministry of Newsong Church in Irvine, California. When we planted in the Crenshaw district of Los Angeles, our congregation was mainly composed of second-generation Asian Americans who had been commuting from Los Angeles to Newsong Church in Irvine. There were members from about fourteen different Asian communities that made up over eighty percent of the congregation. The second largest group was Caucasian, followed by African Americans, Latinos, and others. Our challenge was to grow this congregation in a community that was predominantly African American with a rapidly growing Latino population. The challenge of contextualization has been a central theme of our ministry from day one. Today our congregation is broadly multicultural with no ethnic majority. There have been many lessons and adjustments along the way, but they all come back to leadership.

The first decision was to choose a team that would connect with a broad range of people. Our initial launch team included an African American creative director who also was a former rap artist, small group leaders who were all Asian American, a Caucasian children's pastor who had served in an African American megachurch, a young African American gospel music artist who became our worship leader, and an all Asian band (mostly second-generation Korean American). We chose our team based on who we believed we were called to reach. As an African American with an intercultural background, I was chosen to lead the team. Contextualization involves intentional leadership choices.

The next challenge was music style. There were members of our band who felt strongly that we should play the popular Hillsong-style songs that they liked and were accustomed to playing. Our worship leader, who had grown up with traditional black gospel music, wanted to play that. Our decision was to design our worship music based on the popular radio stations in the Crenshaw community. We challenged our worship team and band to cover popular R&B songs until they found their voice. So we worshiped to songs by Michael Jackson, Stevie Wonder, and Justin Timberlake, all with Christian lyrics written by our team. It was amazing! Today, we use a wide variety of styles of music, but our motivation remains the same—to give the outsider a feeling of familiarity and welcome.

Over the years the challenges have become much deeper. Perhaps the biggest challenge has been managing conflict. On one occasion, we had a significant disagreement involving two people from very different cultural backgrounds. We found that they also had different styles of engagement regarding conflict. One person was very emotionally reserved and indirect in her communication. She even sought the help of a mediator to communicate some bad news to the other person. This was entirely appropriate and respectful within her culture. However, the other person was very direct and emotionally expressive in her style of communication. She resented the fact that a mediator had come to her on behalf of someone she considered a close friend. So she went to her friend directly and asked her with a loud voice and tears in her eyes, "Why didn't you care enough about me to tell me yourself?"

The two different approaches to conflict caused both parties to be highly offended. Pretty soon, other church members got involved, and the accusations began to fly. One group was accused of being conniving and sneaky. The other group was called rude and emotionally immature. In order to resolve conflicts between different cultural groups I have had to learn to use different styles as I communicate with different parties.

I have also found it necessary to teach our congregation members how to understand and adapt to one another. For example, we have trained our leaders in cultural adaptability utilizing the Intercultural Development Inventory (IDI), the Intercultural Conflict Styles Inventory (ICS), and our own biblical model for cultural adaptability called the Third Culture Leadership Framework. This kind of training has been critical.

We have found that treating everyone with the same level of love and respect often requires us to treat people differently. We are attempting to live out the commitment of the apostle Paul with the same motivation he had, "I have become all things to all people so that by all possible means I might save some. I do all this for the sake of the gospel, that I may share in its blessings" (1 Cor 9:22-23).

DISCUSSION QUESTIONS

1. Contextualizing one's leadership requires giving attention to who you are. As you reflect on the story of Moses and on your own experiences as a leader, what are the foundational experiences that have shaped you? What are ways you can see God's hand was at work preparing you for your ministry?

2. Contextualizing one's leadership also requires giving attention to the place and people God has called you to serve. In your ministry context, what are the ways that who you are is a fit with those you are called to serve? In what ways does it feel like a mismatch? What in your leadership might need to change to better serve those to whom you are called?

3. This chapter includes three real-life stories of contextualized leadership in three very different contexts. What in these stories resonates with you most deeply? Do you feel compelled to take any particular actions in response?

4. What shifts may be taking place in your community—politically, socioeconomically, racially, or otherwise—and how would you say your leadership and your church plant are responding to those shifts?

9

HOW IS THE CHURCH GOOD NEWS FOR OUR WORLD?

LIVING AND SPEAKING THE GOSPEL NEAR AND FAR

CARRIE BOREN HEADINGTON

I SAT DOWN FOR COFFEE with the smiling, warm, church planting couple. "So how is it going?" I asked.

The husband and wife church planters began to systematically walk me through where they were in the planting process. They had moved into the neighborhood where they were planting and had been praying for their community, meeting their neighbors, having people over for meals, being present at community events, starting seeker Bible studies in local hangouts, feeding the homeless and cleaning up local parks, discipling a launch team, all the while rearing their son and seeking to hold fast to one day of sabbath rest.

They had been laboring for many months. They were joyful all the while battling discouragement and evident fatigue! Things were taking much longer than expected, they had not reached their personal goals of bringing in thirty new people, and their sponsoring denomination wanted to know the numbers. By this time they had hoped to have a more cohesive launch team. Some of the original members had already returned to their previous church, saying they "weren't called to plant after all," and the planter couple was having a hard time recruiting more leaders. Their community outreach days had been hit and miss—people who said they would be there were not showing up. Their seeker Bible study in the local hangout was significant for those attending, but the numbers were few. And to top it all off, their worship leader had been

Jesus went into Galilee, proclaiming the good news of God. "The time has come," he said. "The kingdom of God has come near. Repent and believe the good news!"

MARK 1:14-15

How beautiful are the feet of those who bring good news!

ROMANS 10:15

sick for the past few weeks. Lots of good was happening, but they were tired and needed some encouragement.

With an expectant, piercing gaze, the planters asked, "So what do you suggest?"

I took a breath, prayed for God's help, and our conversation began.

I am an evangelist who comes alongside church planters, as well as pastors of established churches, to explore how God is calling their community of believers to share the good news of Jesus with specific people in particular places.

Over the past fifteen years, my approach to evangelism has changed drastically. In chapter one, Charlie Cotherman highlighted how much our theology matters in church planting and how "bad theology kills." As I began my work as an evangelist coming alongside church planters and pastors, I had a solid theology of mission and a missional hermeneutic rooted in the *missio Dei*. I understood God as the great missionary and evangelist, reconciling all creation to himself. I grasped the sending nature of the triune God who sent his Son and his Spirit, and then sent his church to draw all people to himself. The good news emanates from a sending God who calls on us, his church, to be his hands, feet, and mouthpiece in the world. I had the right thinking, but I lacked the right practice. In practice, I was more shaped by being American than by belonging to the kingdom of God and participating in the *missio Dei*.

If you asked me a decade ago how to spread the gospel through your church plant, I would have touted the best new evangelistic training tools and seeker programs, the most innovative websites, the hippest local third space to meet people, and the slickest advertising campaigns and church slogans. My evangelistic impulse to communicate the good news of Jesus in a winsome, attractive, and relevant way was not wrong. As we discussed in chapter eight, we must be "all things to all people" in order to save some (1 Cor 9:22). However, I was not entering into the depth of God's missional nature and call. I had an anemic missional pneumatology (experiencing and listening to the Holy Spirit) and an underdeveloped missional hermeneutic (grounding in the Word). In reality, I (along with *our* missional teams) was asking God to bless *our* newest ideas on how to carry his good news in *our* strength into the context where *we* chose to plant.

As I have journeyed with God and his church planters over the years, I have come to a more humble and holistic practice of mission. The evangelistic endeavor is holy work which ventures to the very heart of God. It requires silence before God, deep listening to the Lord and his word, and a Holy Spirit–infused boldness to carry out God's mission in God's world through our small part of God's church. Our work is to draw as close as we can to the Lord, so that our hearts begin to beat with God's love for the specific mission field where he sends us.

Jesus said,

> I am the true vine, and my Father is the gardener. . . . Remain in me, as I also remain in you. No branch can bear fruit by itself; it must remain in the vine. Neither can you bear fruit unless you remain in me. I am the vine; you are the branches. If you remain in me and I in you, you will bear much fruit; apart from me you can do nothing. . . . You did not choose me, but I chose you and appointed you so that you might go and bear fruit. (Jn 15:1-5, 16)

Our work is to remain in the vine so that our church planting is a direct extension of it, infused with the vine dresser's DNA. There is nothing more thrilling than planting gospel seeds in a new community and watching a fresh branch on the vine begin to grow. As this book highlights, church plants need a healthy threefold root system of formation, theology, and mission to carry out the task of planting churches that are good news to the world.

The planting of these gospel seeds is the work of evangelism. God is the great evangelist. Only God can change hearts and draw people to himself (Jn 14:6; 1 Cor 12:3; Eph 3:5). Yet he invites the church to participate in this work through lavishly planting gospel seeds. The way the church is good news for our world is through speaking and living the good news wherever God plants us. This chapter will address how church planters cultivate an evangelistic church that brings, speaks, lives, and spreads good news.

EVANGELISM: BRINGING GOOD NEWS TO OUR WORLD

One of the primary motivations of church planters is the desire to share the good news of Jesus Christ with a broken and hurting world. Leading people to saving faith is one of the greatest joys and privileges that God allows us to experience, because the gospel is literally good news. The word *evangelism* comes from the Greek *euangelion*, meaning "good news." Evangelism is the sharing of the life-giving gospel of Jesus Christ in word (proclamation) and deed (actions) and inviting people to follow him. The same Jesus who said he came to preach the good news and "to seek and save the lost" (Mk 1:38; Lk 19:10) said that he came as the fulfillment of Isaiah's prophecy:

> The Spirit of the Lord is on me,
>> because he has anointed me
>> to proclaim *good news to the poor*.
> He has sent me to proclaim freedom for the prisoners
>> and recovery of sight for the blind,
> to set the *oppressed free*,
>> to proclaim *the year of the Lord's favor*. (Lk 4:18-19)

Verbal proclamation, social justice, and the works of mercy and charity are intertwined in and through our incarnate Savior. "For God was pleased to have all his fullness dwell in him" (Col 1:19) and in him we see the *euangelion* embodied in human flesh. The messenger Jesus Christ is also the message. Jesus heralds the good news, teaches the good news, shows us how to share the good news through his example, and invites us to receive the good news. Upon his ascension into heaven, Jesus commissions the church to continue his mission of spreading the good news in the same manner he did. The church is good news for a broken, hurting world as it lives out this call to speak, embody, and live the way of Jesus.

Jesus' example shows us the three dimensions of evangelism: proclamation, action, and invitation.

Proclamation. A key element of bringing good news to a community is to be a church plant that proclaims the good news of Jesus. Jesus began his ministry with the words, "Repent for the kingdom of heaven has come near" (Mt 3:2). Jesus said he came for the purpose to preach good news to the people (Mk 1:38; Lk 3:18; 4:43). It is evident that speaking the good news was central to the ministry of Jesus. Before he ascended into heaven, Jesus commissioned his followers to "Go into all the world and preach the gospel to all creation" (Mk 16:15).

As Paul emphasized, "How can they believe in the one of whom they have not heard? And how can they hear without someone preaching to them? And how can anyone preach unless they are sent? As it is written: 'How beautiful are the feet of those who bring good news!'" (Rom 10:14-15). Missiologist Christopher Wright notes, "The work of the 'gospel' (Phil 2:22), then seems to refer primarily to the task of making the good news known by all means of communication possible and at whatever cost. There is an intrinsically verbal dimension to the gospel. It is a story that needs to be told in order that its truth and significance may be understood."[17]

In our postmodern context, the church and even church planters tend to shy away from *speaking* the truth of the gospel, knowing that people are jaded and suspicious of any claims of absolute truth. As a result, the church often focuses more on social action. We all too easily give a drink of water without speaking of the Living Water himself. Without proclamation—verbally sharing the hope of Jesus—the church becomes merely a social agency, doing good works in the community. In our contentious and confused climate, where Christianity gets a bad rap, good works do not initially signal that we are followers of Jesus.

---

[17]Christopher J. H. Wright, *The Mission of God's People: A Biblical Theology of the Church's Mission* (Grand Rapids: Zondervan, 2010), 192-93.

A planter must discern the best way to embody good news in their context. For some it might begin with proclamation, letting the community hear the good news through events for seekers (such as seeker Bible studies, the Alpha course, Explore God, or talks on questions of faith) at local third spaces (like coffee shops, pubs, or restaurants) or by inviting people to worship services to hear the gospel message. For others, and what is most likely with many church planters, it might begin with serving and living in the way of Jesus to gain trust to be heard in gospel proclamation. When a group of us started a Bible study in a Los Angeles neighborhood densely populated with Guatemalan immigrants, no one came for weeks. It wasn't until we started serving them meals and caring for their needs that they then naturally wanted to explore Jesus with us. Evangelism includes *showing* and *telling* about the kingdom of God. The church is good news for the world as it shares the abundant life found in Jesus Christ. Often showing comes first, but the telling must soon follow. People need to know in whose name we serve and the good news that is for all.

THE STORY OF NEW LIFE COMMUNITY CHURCH

JOHN LO

The church I lead, Epicentre Church, helped plant New Life Community Church in the Lincoln Heights neighborhood of Los Angeles. Chris, the church planter, quickly realized that proclaiming good news needed to include addressing the practical issues of poverty and chaos in that context. So New Life formed In the City, a nonprofit aimed at meeting the needs of the community. Their first step was meeting and listening to members of the community to ask what was needed there. After much discussion, the feedback was to focus on providing holistic help to teenage boys. So New Life launched a ministry called Mission 3.0 to strengthen the character, relationships, and grades of teenage boys so they could maintain the GPA necessary to stay in athletics. Mission 3.0 was soon featured in the local news. After tragic acts of violence, they've organized peace and prayer marches, and then pulled together a coalition of faith leaders, government officials, and police officers committed to seeing shalom in the city. They have worked with organizations like LA Voice to organize meetings and votes to pass an affordable housing bill. They're now working with property owners and developers to see affordable housing built in the city.

Action. Jesus announced the good news of the arrival of the kingdom of God and he showed it through his actions. Jesus not only spoke about the good news, he embodied the good news as he healed the paralytic, gave sight to the blind, cast out demons, calmed the raging sea, gave life to the dead, treated women with dignity, ate with sinners, fed thousands, washed his disciples' feet, and forgave his persecutors as they nailed him to the cross. Jesus is the only person in human history who perfectly walked his talk. In Jesus, the good news breaks into the world not only in word but in deed:

> Jesus went through all the towns and villages, teaching in their synagogues, pro-claiming the good news of the kingdom and healing every disease and sickness. When he saw the crowds, he had compassion on them, because they were harassed and helpless, like sheep without a shepherd. Then he said to his disciples, "The harvest is plentiful but the workers are few. Ask the Lord of the harvest, therefore, to send out workers into his harvest field." (Mt 9:35-38)

This is a call to action from Jesus. He is asking his followers to be his co-laborers in our world. Christians should be on the frontlines of addressing the suffering of humanity. We must be on the forefront of reconciliation in the way of Jesus: feeding the hungry, clothing the naked, sheltering the homeless, welcoming the stranger, preventing violence, and breaking systems of injustice, prejudice, and systemic poverty. Social justice advocate Ron Sider, states that "Evangelism is the an-nouncement of good news in word and actions and an invitation to be part of the reconciling community as Christ followers."[18]

Our message has no power or authenticity if we do not live it out—caring, loving, and advocating for the least of these. People will not care about what we know until they know we care. They will know we are Christians by our love (Jn 13:35). The church is good news to the world as it embodies the justice and healing of God in places of personal and societal pain.

Invitation. Jesus announced the good news, showed good news in action, and invited people to repent, believe, and follow him. "Jesus went into Galilee, pro-claiming the good news of God. 'The time has come,' he said. 'The kingdom of God has come near. Repent and believe the good news!'" (Mk 1:14-15). Jesus was always inviting people into relationship with him and he asks us, his followers, to do the same. Jesus said to his disciples, "Follow me and I will make you fishers of men" (Mt 4:19). The word *repent* (Greek *metanoia*) means to "turn around." The word Jesus used for "belief" (Greek *pisteuō*) means "to trust, to commit to, to put your weight down on." Walter Brueggemann says evangelism is an invitation to turn toward Jesus and away from society's false gods of the day. He notes,

> Evangelism is an invitation and summons to reinstate our talk and walk according to the reality of God, a reality not easily self-evident in our society. The call of the gospel

---

[18]Ron Sider, "Evangelism, Salvation, and Social Justice: Definitions and Interrelationships," in *The Study of Evan-gelism: Exploring a Missional Practice of the Church,* ed. Paul W. Chilcote and Laceye C. Warner (Grand Rapids: Eerdmans, 2008), 200.

THE ART OF SHOWING THE GOOD NEWS

NICK WARNES

When we were starting Northland Village Church in northeast Los Angeles, we quickly learned that God was on the move within the lives of innumerable artists that we had met. This led us to create the Atwater Art Walk. We partnered with leaders in the neighborhood to create an event that would showcase the work of local artists. We did this for two reasons. First, we wanted to give space for the artists to share their story. Thus, for the Atwater Art Walk, with each piece of art that was submitted, the artist had to write about how this piece of art told a portion of their story. Second, we wanted to focus on racial reconciliation. Gentrification had been taking hold in the neighborhood, and divisions around race and economics were growing. We discerned that a way we could cooperate with God to bridge this gap was through creating this art walk for diverse peoples to be immersed in one another's stories. Northland Village Church hosted the Atwater Art Walk for five years and then passed the event on to a local business to keep the event moving forward. In the end, we learned that with each piece of art that was shared, the good news of the gospel was taking hold and the shalom of the city was enhanced.

includes the negative assertion that the technological-therapeutic-militaristic consumer world is false, not to be trusted or obeyed, and the positive claim that an alternative way in the world is legitimated by and appropriate to the new governance of God who is back in town.[19]

Essentially Jesus was inviting all to turn from their worldly crafted ways and to fully follow Jesus in his way. Evangelism involves an invitation to follow Jesus, to make him Lord, and to enter into the fellowship and call of the church.

Missiologists have affirmed the invitational aspect of evangelism. David Bosch defines evangelism as "that dimension of activity of the church's mission which seeks to offer every person, everywhere, a valid opportunity to be directly challenged by the gospel of explicit faith in Jesus Christ, with a view to embracing him as Savior, becoming a living member of his community, and being enlisted in his service of reconciliation, peace and justice on the earth."[20] Scott Sunquist also highlights the invitational aspect: "Evangelism is, at heart, introducing Jesus Christ to others and inviting them to become partakers in his Kingdom."[21]

---

[19]Walter Brueggemann, "Evangelism and Discipleship: The God Who Calls and the God Who Sends," in Chilcote and Warner, *Study of Evangelism,* 233.

[20]David Bosch, "Evangelism: Theological Currents and Cross-Currents Today," in Chilcote and Warner, *Study of Evangelism*, 17.

[21]Scott W. Sunquist, *Understanding Christian Mission: Participating in Suffering and Glory* (Grand Rapids: Baker Academic, 2013), 312.

Church planters and church planting teams need to be equipped to invite people to follow Jesus and to become a part of the body of Christ. I will share some equipping models later in this chapter. Evangelism is more than an announcement, a dialogue, and social action. Evangelism is more than being a friend, walking alongside someone in their spiritual journey, and caring for the poor. There is a point where an invitation to follow Jesus is made, and we need to equip our people for how to lead someone through this process of invitation. This a joyous endeavor of inviting people to follow Jesus Christ. It is offering the choice of abundant life over death. The church is good news to the world as it invites people to follow Jesus and join the community of faith.

In all this work we must remember that God is the great evangelist and we are his servants that speak, act, and invite on his behalf. J. I. Packer emphasizes that the essence of evangelism is not producing converts; rather, it is the communication of the gospel. "Evangelism is man's work but the giving of faith is God's."[22] God is the great evangelist and only the Holy Spirit can convict of sins and draw human beings to God. Jesus said, "I am the way and the truth and the life. No one comes to the Father except through me" (Jn 14:6). Only God can move a heart toward him, and yet he allows us to be "Christ's ambassadors, as though God were making his appeal through us" (2 Cor 5:20). What a privilege to be called to communicate in word and action this message of good news. The church has the high calling and honor to share the best news of salvation for all through Jesus Christ. As we engage in this work, we are good news for the world.

The gift of a church plant, in contrast to the perspective of many established churches, is that the plant must reach beyond itself to survive and reproduce. Evangelism is central to the life of any church plant that desires to grow. The church and our specific church planting communities are good news for the world as we hold together proclamation, social action, and invitation in the way of Jesus. Let us, like the early followers of Jesus, share in order to "make our joy complete" (1 Jn 1:4).[23]

WHAT IS THE GOOD NEWS?

Since the church is God's primary vessel to share good news with the world, we must ask: What is the good news that we as church planters are to share? How we shape the gospel message has direct ramifications on the life and ministry of the church plant.

---

[22]J. I. Packer, *Evangelism and the Sovereignty of God* (Downers Grove, IL: InterVarsity Press, 1991), 40.

[23]The content on the definition of evangelism was originally published by Carrie Boren Headington in the blog "What Is Evangelism" for the Covenant Blog of The Living Church, https://livingchurch.org/covenant/2016 /02/02/the-episcopal-churchs-e-word-what-is-evangelism.

The gospel is the message that in and through the life, death, and resurrection of Jesus Christ, salvation is made available to the world. It is the announcement that God has come to earth and revealed himself to us in human flesh in the person of Jesus. The long-awaited Messiah has come. In Jesus "God was pleased to have all his fullness dwell" (Col 1:19). God walked among us, taught us how to live, and showed us how to love. Jesus died for us on the cross, suffering the most brutal death, taking on all our sins on the cross, and he rose again, defeating death so that we could be fully reconciled to God forever. Christ has died. Christ is risen. Christ will come again.

This good news burst onto the scene of early Palestine and spread to much of the known world within thirty years.[24] Church plants sprang up all over the known world as new communities following Jesus emerged. The work you are doing as a church planter is a continuation of these first church planters.

Oxford scholar Michael Green notes:

> Christians did not go about proclaiming a new religion, new duties, a new ideology. They proclaimed good news. Not about what man is called to do but about what God has done. The first Christians believed, rightly or wrongly, that the life and death and raising to life again of their friend Jesus were the most important things that ever happened, and they wanted to tell everybody about them. That accounts for the astonishing burst of missionary activity that marked the infant church.[25]

George Hunsberger notes that

> the job of telling "gospel"—the good news of God—is always a fresh challenge that requires the teller to have ears to hear and eyes to see. Many of the older ways the story has been told are ready at hand, ways shaped by other times and places that demanded certain tones and accents if the story was to be heard in a way that was true to its first telling. But as the Christian story gets told over and over in a given place, it can as easily as not be overpowered by the other claims and visions that absorb it into their own agendas.[26]

The context of your church plant will determine how the gospel is expressed. The challenge is to not dilute the gospel in order to appease your hearers and capitulate to the reigning worldview. As the longtime chaplain to the U.S. Senate, Lloyd Ogilvie said, "We must be flexible in the non-essentials and graciously firm in the essentials."[27] The question is, what are the essentials of the gospel message with which church planters should equip their church to share the good news?

---

[24]For more on the spread of the gospel in the early church, see Michael Green, *30 Years That Changed the World* (Leicester, UK: Inter-Varsity Press, 2002) and *Evangelism in the Early Church* (Grand Rapids: Eerdmans, 1995).

[25]Michael Green, *Who Is This Jesus?* (Nashville: Thomas Nelson, 1992), 123.

[26]George R. Hunsberger, *The Story That Chooses Us: A Tapestry of Missional Vision* (Grand Rapids: Eerdmans, 2015), 2.

[27]Lloyd Ogilvie, First Presbyterian Church Bible Study, 2002.

The great missionary and missiologist Lesslie Newbigin said that the great challenge to Christians in the pluralistic West is to not dilute the gospel, domesticate it, privatize it, and make it one of the many options to know God.[28] I would add to this list of dangers the prosperity gospel which removes the cost of discipleship and makes God into a cosmic Santa Claus. In order to be seen as tolerant and loving, we can all too easily make Jesus into one great religious leader among many, the Christian faith into one of the many paths to God which can fill our personal "god-shaped hole," and our Lord into a kind deity who wants all people to be happy and calls all people to be nice so they can go to heaven.[29] Newbigin affirms that the best way to express the gospel is to stay rooted in the biblical story of God creating the world, revealing himself to the world, and redeeming the world in and through his Son Jesus Christ. Newbigin notes that "what is unique about the Bible is the story it tells, with its climax in the story of the incarnation, ministry, death and resurrection of the Son of God."[30] The story, rooted in human history, reveals a truth about the whole human story. "It is the beginning of a new creation. . . . Accepted in faith it becomes the starting point for a wholly new way of understanding human experience."[31] As church planters, we are storytellers and story inviters. We are inviting people into a whole new way of understanding human experience and God, a whole new way of life rooted in the life, death, and resurrection of Jesus.[32]

There are many ways to share the gospel and convey the Christian narrative. First and foremost, church planters must encounter the gospel afresh themselves as part of their own formation. We must experience what we preach and teach. All too easily the pressures of church planting can drive out the joy of the gospel in our lives. The gospel has been described as a multifaceted diamond since there are so many ways to experience its brilliance and beauty. Where you begin, how you tell it, all depends on context, but it is vital to note that the gospel is *the* good news, a truth and story to be shared publicly and universally.

The first followers of Jesus were announcing the gospel as news! In order for something to be news, N. T. Wright notes that there has to be "(1) an announcement of an event that has happened; (2) a larger context, a back story, within which this makes sense; (3) a sudden unveiling of the new future that lies ahead; and (4) a transformation of the present moment, sitting between the event that *has* happened

---

[28]Lesslie Newbigin, *The Gospel in a Pluralistic Society* (Grand Rapids: Eerdmans, 1989).

[29]"Moralistic Therapeutic Deism" was a term coined in Christian Smith and Melinda Lundquist Denton, *Soul Searching: The Religious and Spiritual Lives of American Teenagers* (New York: Oxford University Press, 2005).

[30]Newbigin, *Gospel in a Pluralistic Society*, 97.

[31]Newbigin, *Gospel in a Pluralistic Society*, 12.

[32]For more on the overarching narrative of the gospel story, see N. T. Wright, *Surprised by Hope: Rethinking Heaven, the Resurrection, and the Mission of the Church* (New York: HarperCollins, 2008).

and the future event that *will* happen."[33] With this framework in mind, we place the announcement of the good news of Jesus against the backdrop of a larger story, which, as Wright notes, is the same structure used by the first apostles (see 1 Cor 15:3-6). Being a theater major, I like to think of the parts of the gospel story like acts of a play. Again, it is vital that church planters and teams grasp the metanarrative (the bigger story) of why the news of Jesus Christ is *news* and why it is *good*. It is God's plan of salvation to redeem a wrecked and ruined world. There are many ways into the story and understanding the overarching story is helpful.

JR Woodward provides a helpful metanarrative of the six acts of God's story (see table 1).[34] As church planters, you are the chief storytellers who equip your congregation to tell the story. The stories we tell today shape our future tomorrow.

Table 1. The six acts of God's story

Acts	Summary
Creation	God creates the heavens and the earth and charges people made in his image to tend to creation and create culture.
Fall	People turn against God and the rebellion rips through all creation, personally, socially, and cosmically, creating a world of brokenness, sickness, decay, and death.
Israel	In a surprising response to the rebellion, God chooses to redeem the world by forming a nation to be a sign pointing to shalom, a foretaste embodying his presence, and an instrument bringing his justice and peace, seeking to bless all nations.
Jesus	Amid the rise and fall of Israel, God becomes flesh as Jesus of Nazareth, the ultimate sign, foretaste, and instrument of God's kingdom, displayed through his life, death, and resurrection.
Church	After Jesus' ascension into heaven, his followers are commissioned to carry on his work of being a sign, foretaste, and instrument through the indwelling of his Spirit as they continue to look ahead to his glorious return.
New Creation	At his appointed time, God makes his permanent home on earth, and Jesus' reign is consummated. The long-awaited renewal of creation takes place, bringing total justice, peace, and life.

WHERE TO TAKE THE GOOD NEWS

The whole church is called to take "the whole gospel to the whole world," as the Lausanne movement puts it. Jesus said, "Go into all the world and preach the gospel to all creation" (Mk 16:15). Newbigin uses a helpful image in thinking about the local church. The church universal is God's appointed and anointed kingdom embassy

---

[33]N. T. Wright, *Simply Good News: Why the Gospel Is News and What Makes It Good* (New York: HarperOne, 2015), 23.

[34]JR Woodward, *The Church as Movement: Starting and Sustaining Missional Incarnational Communities* (Downers Grove, IL: InterVarsity Press, 2016), 135.

on the earth. The church universal embodies the good news to the world. The local church is the local kingdom outpost in a specific locale with a specific kingdom call to share the good news contextually. The members of the local church are the local kingdom ambassadors. Church planters have a unique call to break new ground and plant where there is a need for a new kingdom outpost. Determining your mission field requires much prayer and communal discernment, as chapter seven shows. When Jesus discussed the spreading of the good news, he used images like salt (Mt 5:13), light (Mt 5:14-16), seed sowing (Mk 4:1-8), fishing (Mt 4:18), and shepherding lost sheep (Lk 15:1-7).

The whole church is called to the whole world, but how do we know where we should go? Here are some questions to help you discern:

- Where is there little or no sign of gospel flavor in our community? Who needs gospel flavor?
- Where is there no light of Christ? What people are in darkness and struggling?
- Where is there no kingdom outpost? Where is there no public gospel witness?
- Where is God at work and inviting you to join in the work?
- Who is hurting? Who is lost?
- Where would Jesus go?
- Where is there currently no presence of Jesus' followers?

Followers of Jesus need to be the first ones rushing to places where there is suffering. The people suffering most egregiously are those who do not know the good news of Jesus. As you examine the landscape, what moves your heart? How has God gifted and wired you to be good news where good news is needed? How has God gifted others on your church planting team to be good news? Where is God calling you and your team?

A call often comes when your passions and your team's passions meet the needs that God places in front of you. Perhaps these questions seem obvious to church planters, yet all too often we select locations based on where our specific kind of church plant style will mesh with affinity groups. Especially in mainline denominations, the church planter is asked to plant where people groups of that kind of denominational style and affinity will be attracted. This can become about propping up an institution rather than expanding the kingdom of God. It is not wrong to consider affinities, yet it certainly cannot be the only criterion. Searching where there is no sign of good news and witness should be paramount. This takes time, deep prayer, fasting, and confirmation from the wider body of Christ.

WHO TO REACH AND WHERE TO GO

NICK WARNES

After discerning that the mission of Northland Village Church would be reconciliation, we focused on creating a church that would reach people who had been de-churched. Early on we hoped that our meager efforts would be helpful for some to eventually reconcile with both God and the church. So we knew *who* we wanted to reach, but the next question was *where*. Our parent church, Glendale Presbyterian, was our starting place, but where would we go from there? The answer became clear in early meetings with the launch team. God guided us to two options for where we might focus our ministry. We could either move away from the city toward the suburbs north of Glendale or move toward the city. Through neighborhood exegesis, existing relationships, and lots of prayer, it became clear that God was calling us toward the city to reach de-churched people groups in northeast Los Angeles.

Once your church planting mission field is determined, Jesus provides a strategy of how the church is to bring good news to our context. Jesus' final words to his disciples before he ascended into heaven were "You will receive power when the Holy Spirit comes on you; and you will be my witnesses in Jerusalem, and in all Judea and Samaria, and to the ends of the earth" (Acts 1:8). Before we look into how we live and speak good news to our world, we must listen to God, our planting context, and ourselves. It is helpful to approach this noticing and listening on two levels—as individual members of the church plant and as the collective church plant body.

Jesus says we should begin in our *Jerusalem*. To the first followers of Jesus, Jerusalem was their immediate social network. Who are your and your church plant's closest neighbors, family, and friends? Who has God placed around you and your church? Who is in your immediate landscape and sphere of influence? This includes family, friends, acquaintances, work or school colleagues, volunteer groups, social groups, civic affiliations, and hobbies or special interests. Pray for these people and ask God how to best love, serve, and share the gospel with them.

Then Jesus says to go to our *Judea*. To the first followers, Judea was the surrounding region. Who is in your neighborhood and the community around your church? Where and among what people has God placed you? What is God doing in the neighborhood and in your town or city?

It is helpful to gather demographic data to know who is around you. It is also helpful to engage in neighborhood prayer walks, as discussed in chapter seven. When you walk the neighborhood and region surrounding your church plant, pray that God will open the eyes of your heart. Ask God to show you things about your region. What are people's needs, hurts, hopes, dreams, language, and ways of being? Ask God to show you ways to love, serve, and communicate in your Judea.

Then Jesus told his disciples to go to *Samaria*. For Jesus' disciples, Samaritans were the untouchables, the outcasts, the poor, and those with whom they should not associate. Jesus told his disciples to go to them and bear witness to the good news. Who is on the margins of your community? What groups, cultures, and generations do you *not* have a relationship with? Who are the forgotten, the outcasts, the alienated, the suffering in your midst? Who is the other through whom God might long to speak to you? Who is forgotten, broken-hearted, neglected, or suffering in your region?[35]

Then Jesus says to go to *the ends of the earth*. The spread of the good news through church plants has had a long history tied to human migration. Missionaries and church planters from one country would go to another country to share the good news and vice versa. In this book's preface, Scott Sunquist notes that in many ways America was founded as a church planting movement. Now, as missiologists and church planters note, the ends of the earth are coming to our shores. According to the United Nations, there are 258 million people living in a country other than their country of birth, an increase of 49 percent since 2000. Between 2000 and 2015, this influx of immigrants accounts for 42 percent of the population growth in North America.[36] God is moving people groups from countries around the world to key places in the West. Church planting and evangelism has frequently occurred as new immigrants come to meet followers of Jesus in their new land. As church planting leader Tim Keller suggests,

> All current signs lead us to believe that the world order of the twenty-first century will be global, multicultural and urban. . . . There are five million new people moving into the cities of the developing world every month—roughly the size of Philadelphia and San Francisco. . . . The people of the world are now moving into the great cities of the world many times faster than the church is.[37]

New churches are being planted by immigrants from the Global South in urban western/northern cities that have become secularized. "Most of the largest, well attended churches in London and Paris are led by Africans and in New York City we have seen hundreds of new churches started by Christians from Asia, Latin America,

---

[35]Stephanie Spellers and Carrie Boren Headington, "Cultivating an Evangelistic Church," www.kccathedral.org/wp-content/uploads/Cultivating-Evangelistic-Church_Booklet.pdf.

[36]United Nations Department of Economic and Social Affairs, accessed April 4, 2018, www.un.org/development/desa/publications/international-migration-report-2017.html.

[37]Timothy Keller, *Center Church: Doing Balanced Gospel-Centered Ministry in Your City* (Grand Rapids: Zondervan, 2012), 158-59.

the Caribbean and Africa."[38] In Dallas some of my denomination's most flourishing churches are Latino, Sudanese, Bhutanese, and Nigerian congregations.

The *ends of the earth* are coming to North America to study, work, and live. Church planters today need to have a global mindset and training. We need to know how to reach out to the diverse people groups coming to our towns and cities. Jim Ramsay of the Mission Society points out that 75 percent of international students who study in America never enter an American home.[39] Many of these international students return to be leaders in their home countries. My husband and I open our home every other Friday night to international students, and we have seen many young people come to Christ, including a woman from Saudi Arabia and a young man from China, who were recently baptized. This came from a gospel presentation at Christmas and Easter, bi-weekly meals in our home where we pray before the meals, and conversations driven by their curiosity about what we believed. Opening our home has started friendships which led to conversations and sharing life, which led to sharing Jesus. According to the US Census, there are over 66 million immigrants in the United States today from 180 countries, speaking 320 languages. Most will never enter the home of an American. Statistics show that an immigrant is invited into an American home once every fifteen years.

I recently met with an American church planter who said their plant didn't work because they planted too close to a Hindu Temple and a large South Asian community. I asked him how he engaged the Hindu community and he said they didn't even really try. His basic perspective was that they had their religion and didn't need evangelizing. My heart sank. I recalled being in a South Asian grocery store in the same area recently and had a small New Testament in my back pocket. I prayed as I walked the aisles and a man came up to me and said, "Excuse me, is that a Bible?" I said "Yes." He said, "I am Muslim and have never read the Bible. Can you tell me about it?" This led to a great discussion where he shared how his son was having such a hard time in his new American school. He said he wanted to know more so I connected him to a minister at a local church. This family has not become Christian, but they are making new Christian friends and in turn people at the church are meeting many new Pakistani families and sharing the love of Jesus. This was all from one encounter in a grocery store! Imagine if the entire church plant had been praying about how to bless and be blessed by their Hindu neighbors. New immigrants and refugees are often the most open to meeting new people and learning about Jesus.

---

[38]Keller, *Center Church*, 159.

[39]Jim M. Ramsay, "Welcoming the Foreigner," *The Good News Magazine*, March 5, 2013, www.goodnewsmag.org /2013/03/welcoming-the-foreigner/.

"Ends of the earth" also refers to planting churches in countries beyond our own. This kind of crosscultural planting is a vital part of gospel expansion. Often when our church plants in North America engage in mission abroad, we expand our experience of God and return with a fresh boldness and vision.

Now that we have addressed the question of where to plant and to take the good news of Jesus Christ, we will explore how best to form your church plant for living and speaking good news.

LIVING THE GOOD NEWS

The church becomes good news as it embodies the way of Jesus in the world. Since the church is called to "go and make disciples of all nations" teaching them to follow the commands of Jesus and baptizing them in the name of the Father, the Son, and the Holy Spirit (Mt 28:18-20), the church plant must be filled with students of the kingdom of God, being formed in the likeness of Christ. The apostle Paul said Jesus' followers should be the "fragrance of Christ" in the world (2 Cor 2:12-16). In the stench of a confused, broken, lost world of gross consumerism, poverty, injustice, violence, abuse, prejudice, war, and family breakdown, the church is intended to emanate the aroma of Jesus. We can transmit love, joy, peace, patience, kindness, goodness, faithfulness, gentleness, and self-control (Gal 5:22-23). Mahatma Gandhi once said to church planters in India, "Don't talk about it. The rose doesn't have to propagate its perfume. It just gives it forth, and people are drawn to it. Live it and people will come to see the source of your power."[40] How do we form a community that emanates the fragrance of Jesus? As this book has discussed, church plants must be rooted in the spiritual disciplines of prayer, Scripture reading and formation, worship, and action. From the first church plants in Acts to today, people have been drawn to follow Jesus not only by words but by people who are in a dynamic relationship with the living Jesus and who live according to his way.

In his book *The First Urban Christians*, Dr. Wayne Meeks discusses how the good news spreads through proclamation and through the embodied visible witness of the community.[41] The early church was markedly different from the world. They cared for the prisoners that society left to die; they loved the untouchables; they shared their resources with the poor; they cared for orphans and widows; they treated all people with dignity. In a highly stratified society, men and women from all social classes and races ate and worshipped together. They turned the other cheek, prayed for healings in the power of the Holy Spirit, and worshiped a living God who transforms all of life.

---

[40]Mahatma Gandhi, "Harijan, December 12, 1936," *Gandhi on Christianity* (Maryknoll, NY: Orbis, 1991).

[41]Wayne A. Meeks, *The First Urban Christians: The Social World of the Apostle Paul* (New Haven, CT: Yale University Press, 2003).

Church planting communities should radiate a radically different way of life. As Jesus said, "As I have loved you, so you must love one another. By this everyone will know that you are my disciples, if you love one another" (Jn 13:34-35). Newbigin noted that the best hermeneutic for the gospel is the church as it lives out the life, death, and resurrection of Jesus. The church "is the visible foretaste of what is to come."[42] There are five ways all church plants need to live out the good news—through motivating, praying, equipping, being, and speaking.

Motivating to share the good news. The first followers of Jesus and the church planters of the New Testament did not need to take an evangelism class to be able to share the good news. They had an encounter with the risen Lord and could not "help speaking about" what they had "seen and heard" (Acts 4:20). At every turn they gossiped the gospel, and the good news spread by one person telling another. Michael Green defines evangelism as "overflow."[43] Evangelism happens when believers are so filled with the good news of Jesus that it spills out of them. Just like someone newly in love, the lover cannot be silenced.

What church plants need more than methods is *motivation*. It is important to take the spiritual pulse of your congregation. There are a number of diagnostic surveys to assist with this.[44] In addition to spiritual disciplines and vibrant weekly corporate worship, it can also be helpful to have a form of spiritual renewal from time to time, such as congregational revivals, testimony sharing, spiritual retreats, weekends of faith sharing, devoted time to read Scripture together, praise and worship nights, corporate teaching and prayer, and healing services. We cannot give what we do not have. Evangelism often begins within the congregation as we "renew our minds" (Rom 12:2) and "encourage one another" (1 Thess 5:11) in the good news. Each church plant must assess what is needed to draw your congregation closer to Jesus. This is not about information but the deepening of an intimate relationship with God: Father, Son, and Holy Spirit. How can your church plant foster spiritual health and Christian formation? Does your plant have ways to deepen and strengthen a closer walk with Jesus? In what ways does your plant need to grow in zeal? Are you igniting people's encounter with the Holy Spirit and engaging people's spiritual gifts?

Praying the good news. Prayer is vital to living and sharing the good news. All evangelism and mission begins with prayer. When Jesus walked the earth, he drew away to a quiet place to pray before engaging in any mission. Prayer gave him the Holy Spirit-infused fuel he needed to align his will with the Father's will to heal,

---

[42]Newbigin, *Gospel in a Pluralistic Society,* 229.

[43]Michael Green, *Evangelism Through the Local Church* (London: Hodder and Stoughton, 1993), 8.

[44]See, for instance, "Reveal for Church Spiritual Life Survey," Reveal, accessed June 6, 2018, www.revealforchurch .com.

teach, cast out demons, listen, love, transfigure, and lay down his life for the world. Jesus said, "The harvest is plentiful, but the laborers are few. Therefore, pray earnestly to the Lord of the harvest to send out laborers into his harvest" (Lk 10:2 ESV).

In a grant funded by the Lilly Endowment, Martha Grace Reese analyzed five hundred of the fastest growing churches in the United States. The key common denominator in all of them was prayer, which drew them closer to Jesus and cultivated a heart for the lost in their mission field.[45] If you peel back the story of the most vibrant church plants, you find that they are communities who pray for one another, pray together, encourage personal prayer, and pray for the surrounding community.

One of the churches in our denomination, St. James, was about to close. One man began to pray for it and the mission field. People began to join him. This church grew two hundred times the size. I asked them what accounted for the growth and many responded, "We asked for God's help and God's vision. It changed our hearts as we became more unified in mission and we saw our surrounding community with God's eyes. We had courage to reach beyond ourselves."

Does your church plant have people praying for your leadership, your church (the laborers of the harvest), and the harvest? Do you take time for concerted corporate prayer before you engage in sharing good news in your community? Do you do neighborhood prayer walks, seeking God's perspective on your community?

Equipping for a good-news lifestyle. Jesus' final act before ascending into heaven was commissioning his believers to be his hands, feet, and mouthpiece in the world. The challenge to church planters is engaging the entire congregation in this missional call and equipping them for it. Evangelism is all too often professionalized in the church, relegating witness to outgoing personalities who have the gift to evangelize. As Paul highlights in Ephesians 4, some have indeed been given the spiritual gift of evangelism, and these evangelists are called, first and foremost, to build up the wider body of Christ to engage in witness. This means the evangelists should help teach your church plant team and budding congregation that all are called to witness, provide teaching to equip the congregation to evangelize and then model how to do this (Eph 4:11-14). Many called to plant a church have a natural evangelistic gift. If this is not the case (and that is okay), it will be important to know and understand this and to have an evangelist as part of your core launch team and to encourage the evangelist's leadership. Spiritual gift inventories are helpful in discerning gifts. No one has all the spiritual gifts, hence the need for shared leadership.

Here are some key areas that need to be included in equipping your congregation for evangelism: (1) Teach on the Great Commission through sermons, Bible studies,

---

[45]Unbinding the Gospel Project, accessed June 6, 2018, www.gracenet.info.

and book studies. All should grasp that they are called to be "Christ's ambassadors" (2 Cor 5:20). The emphasis is that all are called, and the biblical model shows there are many ways to evangelize depending on the believer and the people the Lord places in front of them. From the woman at the well saying "come, see a man who told me everything I ever did" (Jn 4:29), to Andrew simply saying "we have found the Messiah" (Jn 1:41), to the early church caring for those in need, to healings, to the proclamation of Peter and Paul, to apologetics in the Areopagus (Acts 17), to people inviting friends to agape meals in their homes—all are called to evangelize in their own way in the power of the Holy Spirit. Help your people find their style and particular call.[46]

(2) Have the church plant assess who is in their Jerusalem, Judea, Samaria, and the ends of the earth and then commit to pray for these people seeking God in how to care for them and share Jesus with them. This includes both the corporate church plant and individual members in their daily lives.

(3) Equip your church plant for how to tell the gospel story. This can be done in a variety of ways using verbal and visual techniques. I usually have people think of specific people or people groups with whom they are called to share and what aspects of the gospel message will connect with them. We then practice with one another with particular people in mind.

(4) Have people explore their own faith story and practice sharing this with others in the church plant body. This process can be faith building for the entire congregation as they hear the stories of God acting in the lives of their congregation. This should be done simply so all people feel they can do this. I sometimes simply have people complete the sentence Andrew used: "I have found _____."

(5) Equip people in basic conversation skills which include listening and meeting people where they are. Rebecca Manley Pippert, author of *Out of the Saltshaker and Into the World,* developed a conversational-skills model to guide people from points of interest to spiritual questions to God questions. Practicing these skills is helpful in our world that is losing its conversational abilities. This is not about manipulation but forming authentic relationships.[47]

(6) Pray for the harvest both corporately and individually, asking God to open the eyes of the hearts of those in your harvest field, to provide opportunities to naturally share the good news of Jesus, to open your eyes to the needs of the people

---

[46]Some helpful resources include "Spiritual Gifts Discovery" by Group; *Everybody Has a Part* by Ministry Tool Resource Center; www.spiritualgiftstest.com; "Gifted2Serve" by BuildingChurch.net; SHAPE Spiritual Gifts Assessment, www.sbpcshape.org; Spiritual Gifts Quiz on beliefnet, www.beliefnet.com/faiths/christianity/quiz /spiritual-gifts-quiz.aspx; Spiritual Gifts Survey by Lifeway Christian Resources, https://blog.lifeway.com /explorethebible/downloads/spiritual-gifts-inventory.

[47]Rebecca Manley Pippert, *Out of the Salt Shaker and Into the World: Evangelism as a Way of Life* (Downers Grove, IL: InterVarsity Press, 1999), chap. 17.

around you so you can care for them, and to give wisdom about the words you need to share with them.

(7) Have the evangelists within the plant model living and speaking the good news. Jesus did not immediately send out the seventy-two. He first had his disciples watch him do the work, then he verbally taught them, and then he had them participate in some way. For example, during the feeding of the five thousand he had them break people into small groups and hand them the food, then he sent them out to proclaim the gospel, cast out demons, and heal. Evangelism is better caught than taught. The best way to get people involved in this work is to have them apprentice by watching the evangelists share the gospel in various settings (small groups, personal conversation, workplace, home, etc.).

Being good news. Emulating the way of Jesus, every church plant should be good news in both word (proclamation) and deed (action). The church planting community should prayerfully assess how they can be a presence and blessing to those around them. There are three aspects to note here.

Being a presence. Have your church plant observe what is most important to the community around them and then participate as a presence. What do people in your surrounding community celebrate? What do they mourn? What do they protest? Be at these events and serve. Some examples include local festivals, parades, community marathons, rallies, cancer awareness events, anti-violence protests, school athletic events, arts events, and music concerts. The church is called to celebrate with those who celebrate and to weep with those who weep. One of our church plants handed out water at the local marathon, gave away hand fans at the local rodeo, walked in the annual MLK parade, and marched with the victims of gun violence in our city. Their service and quiet presence speaks volumes.

We also need to encourage individuals that one of the best ways to begin sharing good news in our personal daily lives is to be good news by simply being a presence and listening ear in our busy and hurried world.

Being a balm. Intricately tied to the Great Commission of Matthew 28 is the commandment of Matthew 25 to care for and love the sick, the poor, the neglected, and the outcasts. Jesus said, "Truly I tell you, whatever you did for one of the least of these brothers and sisters of mine, you did for me" (Mt 25:40). The church should be on the forefront of caring for those suffering in our midst. Serving the suffering in your community is also an opportunity to invite those who do not know Jesus to join you in the work. Sometimes people will be more likely to join you in service than in attending worship. Church plants should never miss an opportunity to have their members invite their non-Christians friends to join in outreach to the community.

Being a blessing. God said to Abraham regarding the call of Israel to evangelize the world, "I will bless you . . . so that you will be a blessing" (Gen 12:2). How can your church plant be a blessing to your community? It is important that your church plant find ways to connect and bless your community. These are opportunities for people to get to know you and your church planting family. The possibilities are endless. One church plant in an impoverished area discerned that the best way to bless the community was a great meal and piano concert. Another church plant surrounded by an aging community held a health fair where people could learn about healthy lifestyles to ameliorate the aging process. Another plant surrounded by single-parent households offered home repair, car repair, and Saturday childcare so that moms could run errands and have help with home needs. Another church plant in a hip millennial-filled area allowed local bands to use their space on Saturday nights. Another church filled with young families sponsored a pumpkin patch in the fall and offered parenting classes. The point of blessing is to show the love of Jesus in a tangible way to your community.

Speaking the good news. A key aspect to living the good news is speaking the good news. Jesus began his ministry with an announcement, "The kingdom of God has come near. Repent and believe the gospel" (Mk 1:15). Using words has always been central to the spread of the good news and the conversion of souls. The good news spread to much of the known world by people sharing their faith corporately and in personal daily life. Before radio, television, and internet the good news of Jesus spread like wildfire through word of mouth. As discussed earlier in this chapter, using words in evangelism can be a challenge in today's pluralistic culture. Yet it is crucial. How are they to believe unless someone tells them (Rom 10:14)?

All members of the church plant should have the good news on their lips in daily life. This primarily comes through engaging in spiritual conversations with others, asking questions, sharing our own faith stories and aspects of the gospel story, and verbally inviting people to more. As the apostle Peter wrote, "Always be prepared to give an answer to everyone who asks you to give the reason for the hope that you have. But do this with gentleness and respect" (1 Pet 3:15). One of the reasons believers do not want to engage in evangelism is because it has been done so disrespectfully in the past. Believers are also reluctant to engage in conversation because they want to avoid past mistakes. We must remember that only God draws people to himself; our work is to share. As human beings we share imperfectly, as Paul said we are broken "jars of clay" (2 Cor 4:7). Yet "when I am weak, then I am strong" (2 Cor 12:10). We must remember that God's word never returns void (Is 55:11). How people respond is not our work. Jesus tells the story of the master who prepared a banquet and sent his servant out to invite others to the feast. The master never admonished the servant when people declined the invitation, he simply said "Go back out and invite more" (Lk 14:12-24).

All verbal proclamation should be approached with humility and boldness, listening especially to how the Holy Spirit would have you engage each person and their needs. In his study over a ten-year period, Dr. Gary McIntosh interviewed over 1,100 Christians and found that roughly 60 percent of people became followers of Jesus through an interaction with family and friends; 17 percent through an interaction with a church staff member; and 11 percent through someone other than family, friends, or church staff. This means that roughly 88 percent come to faith through an interaction with a follower of Jesus.[48] The studies also found that conversion happened almost always through organic conversations about spiritual matters and not a method like the Romans Road, the Four Spiritual Laws, or Evangelism Explosion. The most effective way to share the good news is for your entire church planting congregation to know their personal call to go and make disciples and to be equipped and emboldened to share the good news naturally in their daily lives.

The church planting body also has a call to proclaim collectively. This can be done in a variety of ways including but certainly not limited to the following.

(1) Proclaim the gospel in the context of weekly worship, so the message can then be shared on social media and podcasts. Encourage your members to share relevant messages with friends. Hold special worship services where your congregation invites friends to worship and a meal afterward, where the message is focused on reaching seekers, agnostics, those of other faith traditions, and atheists.

(2) Go to places which people frequent (third spaces such as pubs, coffee shops, and local hang outs) and offer opportunities for seekers to engage the Christian faith through a seeker Bible study, public sharing of testimonies, or public presentations on a topic of faith. The key is for your church plant to have avenues where people can explore the faith, ask questions, and hear the gospel. Some effective tools are the Alpha Course, Christianity Explored, Explore God, Q Place, and Salt Shaker Seeker Bible Studies.

(3) At your blessing events (i.e., events that serve and celebrate the wider community and are not a church service), have members of your congregation briefly share their faith story.

(4) Foster a culture of personal invitation. Encourage all members to invite friends to church events, seeker series, opportunities to care for the poor and those

---

[48]Gary L. McIntosh, *Growing God's Church: How People Are Actually Coming to Faith Today* (Grand Rapids: Baker, 2016).

in need, and worship. One of our church plants tried multiple ways to reach out. They did a mass mailing, advertised in local newspapers, invested in great signage and a website to no avail. It was when they engaged in the TAKE 5 campaign, asking members of the congregation to invite five people weekly to worship and other church activities that the congregation doubled in size and many came to follow Jesus. Many of our church plants have nourishing events and ways to engage in the faith, but the church plant misses the opportunity to invite friends. LifeWay Research conducted a survey of fifteen thousand adults for the North American Mission Board. Of the thirteen evangelistic approaches listed, over 60 percent said they would best respond to a personal invitation to a church by a friend, neighbor, or family member. In a world where 80 percent of people say their primary source of pain is loneliness, this is an opportunity to invite people into our communities of faith. Church planters need to be passionate inviters.[49]

The key elements of speaking good news are igniting and equipping congregations to share their faith and empowering church plants to go into the community and provide multiple ways for people to hear and engage the gospel. Furthermore, we must be inviters, as God is always inviting. The Bible shows God inviting us to come to him, return to him, and follow him over six hundred times. Our church plants must have both a missional presence in the community and a boldness to invite people to church. How people respond is not our business, but it is our work to invite.

CONCLUSION

So how is the church to be good news for our world? By being a people who intentionally live and speak the good news of Jesus Christ. Every church plant I know begins with a missional impulse. Yet unless an intentional evangelism plan is marinated in prayer and developed, the evangelistic vision can get lost. All too easily a budding church plant turns inward and cares primarily for its close community of faith. This is understandable in an increasingly secular society sometimes hostile to matters of faith. Even I as an evangelist am tempted to remain coddled in my safe faith community at times. Yet this is not what we as the church have been called to do. Jesus said, "Whoever wants to be my disciple must deny themselves and take up their cross and follow me" (Mk 8:34). For church planters in places where Christians are persecuted, sharing the good news can mean actual death. For those of us in the West, it requires a different kind of death, but death nonetheless. Death to self is the

---

[49]"Americans Open to Outreach from Churches," LifeWay Research, March 23, 2009, www.lifewayresearch.com /2009/03/23/americans-open-to-outreach-from-churches/.

only route to abundant life in Christ. As the apostle Paul said, "For if we have been united with him in a death like his, we shall certainly be united in a resurrection like his" (Rom 6:5). As we die to self through sharing the good news and risking rejection and loss, we gain "an eternal glory that far outweighs them all" (2 Cor 4:17), and we find joy (1 Jn 1:4).

This world needs courageous Christian leaders who will boldly, humbly, and faithfully live and speak good news. Church planters must keep front and center the mission of the church to reconcile all people to God through Christ. Yes, we will certainly face persecution as Jesus predicted (Mt 5:10-12; Jn 15:20), but in the midst of this, we will receive the kingdom of heaven.

We hold the only true life-transforming news for which this world was made. As Saint Augustine said, "Thou hast made us for Thyself, O God, and our hearts are restless until we find rest in Thee."[50] What a privilege and high calling to share the only hope for the world. The church holds the news that God is real, God is alive, God is good, and God has revealed himself in and through Jesus Christ. Unconditional love, total forgiveness, Holy Spirit strength, and reunion with God for an eternity are available to all through the life, death, and resurrection of Jesus Christ. This is the good news for the whole of creation! "How beautiful are the feet of those who bring good news!" (Rom 10:15).

DISCUSSION QUESTIONS

1. If Jesus walked into the community where you are planting, what needs would he address and how would he take action?

2. How would Jesus communicate the gospel in your church planting context? What emphases, metaphors, stories, or questions might he use?

3. The whole church is called to the whole world, but how do we discern where we should go?

4. Who are your church plant's closest neighbors, family, and friends? Who is in your immediate landscape and sphere of influence?

5. Who is on the margins (e.g., the forgotten, brokenhearted, neglected, or suffering) of your community? Who is the other through whom God might long to speak to you?

---

[50] Augustine, *Confessions* 1.1

PART 4

HOW DO WE DEVELOP FRUIT THAT LASTS?

FAITHFUL PLANTERS AND FRUITFUL CHURCHES

THE TAG LINE OF FULLER'S CHURCH PLANTING PROGRAM is "Healthy roots leading to lasting fruit," based largely on Jesus' words in John 15:5: "I am the vine; you are the branches. If you remain in me and I in you, you will bear much fruit; apart from me you can do nothing." When our roots are deep and healthy, the nutrients sourced in Jesus himself can flow upward to the trunk, through the branches, and into bearing fruit. Connected to the vine of Jesus Christ, we want to help students and planters weave together the three roots of formation, theology, and mission so as to cultivate the fruit of new disciples and reproducing churches.

In this final section of the book, we want to help you begin with the end in mind. In chapter ten we discuss starting well by developing a prayerful, fully orbed church planting plan that practically takes you from nothing to something by reviewing and applying your learnings from the first three sections of the book. And we want you to plant your current church with a view to planting the *next* church—to think and pray and act in terms of bearing fruit that lasts. A faithful planter is not one who plants a church that lasts forever but one who makes disciples who give themselves away as God has given himself away in Jesus Christ. All fruit has a short shelf life and then goes bad. But when that fruit continues to fall to the ground, die, and then grow into another tree, God's purposes continue on even after the initial tree no longer exists. Chapter eleven asks the question "What are we really planting?" because we want to reflect deeply on the nature of the church as a living organism that keeps bearing fruit.

WHERE DO WE START?

DEVELOPING A HOLISTIC PLANTING PLAN

NICK WARNES

My wife and I are currently experiencing a unique season of life. We are consistently dwelling at the intersection of excitement and anxiety as we move toward the birth of our first child. The excitement is building as we imagine what will be, what may be, what will not be, and the limits of our imagination in all three. Contrasting with this excitement is the experience of a steady dose of anxiety. As I speak with other parents, I have been learning that most encounter this anxiety. Many share about new responsibilities that are at the center of a growing family and about their deep desires for their kids to flourish. The anxiety comes as parents want to foster this flourishing and minimize any parenting that will deplete potential.

Starting a new church has remarkable similarities to this intersection found in soon-to-be parents, as those involved anticipate with both excitement and anxiety the soon-to-be church. Also similar to being a part of the birth of a child, there is nothing like being a part of the birth of a church. In my work as the director of two church-starting networks (Cyclical LA and Cyclical INC),[1] I am fortunate to work with many churches as they find their beginning. Many people claim that starting a church is the most exciting time in their faith, and they marvel at the works of God as the church blossoms. That said, the most common question I receive as churches are organizing is, How do we go from nothing to something? In other words, how do we go from no community to community? From no small groups to small groups? From no organized

There is a time for everything, and a season for every activity under the heavens.

ECCLESIASTES 3:1

A startup is the largest group of people you can convince . . . to build a different future.

PETER THIEL

---

[1]For more on these ministries, see www.cyclicalLA.com and www.cyclicalchurches.com.

work toward justice to justice? From no communal engagement with neighbors to engaging neighbors? From no worship gathering to a worship gathering?

These questions filled my head as I met with Tim Morey, also a contributor to this book, to discuss how his church went from nothing to something. He encouraged me to marvel at the various dynamics to consider as we started Northland Village Church. All the questions above were in play, but Tim reminded me that at the heart of this process was a God who was and is still on the move in bringing the new church to life. Similarly during this time I was fortunate to sit with Dr. Ryan Bolger from Fuller Seminary to discuss the nuances of going from nothing to something. Dr. Bolger was generous to listen to my multitude of excitements and anxieties. In the end, I'll never forget that, just like Tim, he looked at me and reminded me that God was already on the move. "In fact," he said, "you need to remember, Nick, that you already are a part of a community. It is now your community's job to frame out what God is doing amongst our community." This was the fuel I needed to move forward.

In Peter Thiel's book *Zero to One*, he writes, "A startup is the largest group of people you can convince . . . to build a different future."[2] When it comes to the startup of a new church, the different future will be rooted in the priorities of the kingdom of God. I do not believe that any more important work exists in the cosmos. Working to encourage people deeper into the way of grace, mercy, forgiveness, justice, love, and all the other practices of Jesus can make exponential differences in the lives of individuals and communities. This work can be exponential because, as will be discussed in chapter eleven, within any seed lies the potential growth of not just one plant, but a new plant that will produce more fruit, which holds more seeds. From one simple seed comes the potential for thousands of new plants in just a few generations. In short, it is the generative potential, due to an inherent and necessary DNA of multiplication, that sets apart the exponential potential of any new church as a unique ministry within the kingdom of God.

Just like the birth of a seed into a plant, there are various stages within the life of a church that bring the new church to life. It is my hope that this chapter will be helpful for those who are beginning to jump into such an adventure.

This chapter will prioritize questions that will guide readers through a path of four seasons. These questions are rooted in practical narratives and have arisen from various contexts through which I have been fortunate to partner with a diversity of people in starting new churches. The four seasons, then, are a holistic guide for churches that will map a process from the earliest moments of a church's preexistence

---

[2]Peter Thiel, *Zero to One: Notes on Startups, or How to Build the Future* (New York: Crown Business, 2014), 10.

to its first moments of reproduction. These four seasons will be peppered with questions that will bring to light practical nuances that every new church faces.

The four seasons, moving from the church's earliest moments to becoming a seed-producing church plant, are

1. Discernment: Is God calling a people to start a new church? Is God calling a planter or a group of planters to start a new church?

2. Initial organization: How do we begin to gather well? How will we engage the Holy Spirit? How will we join the mission of God? How will we move toward sustainability?

3. Initial public expression: What will be the initial rhythms of the worship gathering? How will we equip people for community? How will we join in the mission of God together?

4. Adaptation of initial public expression: How do we create a pneumatological (Holy-Spirit shaped) culture of change and adaptation? How do we implement change and adaptation?

SEASON OF DISCERNMENT

In chapter one, we explored what it means to discern God's activity in both Scripture and the community. These are certainly essential works for any season of discernment and need consistent and ongoing attention. For the purposes of this chapter, we will keep God's activity in Scripture and the community in mind but will focus more on lenses of discernment for the two different groups of people who will start a new church—the leader or leaders (planters) and the participants. The participants are those who want to be involved in the church but don't necessarily intend to move directly into an active decision-making role at the onset.

The season of discernment for planters is a holy and critical space. It is downright difficult to start a new church. Planting a church without a clearly discerned call to do so is impossible. Innumerable questions and nuances sit at the foundation of any discernment process, and these questions are uniquely heavy for the church planter as decisions will impact large numbers of people. Our focus here will be on questions within two essential spheres of the planter's life: social base and preparation.

Social base is the network of relationships that hold an individual together. The social base for a Christian, and therefore a church planter, begins with God. Is God calling the leader to start a new church? John Calvin describes this as an "internal" call: "By the internal illumination of the Spirit He causes the word preached to take deep root in their hearts."[3] Is God calling the leader, through the Spirit, to start a new church? This is a key question for any planter. But Calvin also discusses the "external" call—the affirmation of the body of Christ that one is called to this ministry. Both are necessary. Is God, as I listen, calling me to start a new church? And are people around me, those closest to me—family, friends, pastors, the body of Christ—affirming the call that I need to lead in starting a new church? If both these elements of a social base are not in place, then a potential church planter ought to wait in patience for them to align prior to moving forward.

Along with social base, the preparation of the church planter is another essential center for discernment prior to starting a new church. The best way to understand preparation is to reflect on past experiences and pay attention to the trajectory of those experiences. For the discerning church starter, has God been consistently putting together experiences that build toward starting a new church? For instance, if a discerning church starter has experience starting multiple businesses or nonprofits, the trajectory of the planter's life may now be moving toward starting a new church. If, on the other hand, the discerning church starter's experience is with traditional and Christendom-oriented graduate studies and pastoral ministry, focused on office hours in church buildings and spending thirty hours a week writing sermons, his or her trajectory might not be pointing toward starting a new church.

The most important center for discerning preparation is the planter's ability to pay attention to God's call in their life. Referencing Moses' encounter with God in Exodus 3, Ruth Haley Barton says, "If spiritual leadership is anything, it is the capacity to see the bush burning in our own life and having enough sense to turn aside, take off our shoes, and pay attention."[4] A history of awareness of "burning bushes" is essential to the discernment process of the potential church planter. Whether one has become aware of a burning bush through listening to God in individual prayer time or through conversations with the body of Christ, a planter must have a historical trajectory of identifying burning bushes and taking off their shoes at their embers.

The season of discernment for those who plan on participating in but not actively leading the new church (parishioners) is equally as important as it is for the planter. The effort required will be unmatched. Again there are many questions, but we will highlight four here to create a framework for a season of discernment.

The first question is the same as that of the planter: Am I called to start a new church? The discernment of both internal and external call applies here too. The

---

[3]John Calvin, *Institutes of the Christian Religion*, trans. Ford Lewis Battles, ed. John T. McNeill (Louisville, KY: Westminster John Knox Press, 2006), 3.24.8; 2:247.

[4]Ruth Haley Barton, *Strengthening the Soul of Your Leadership: Seeking God in the Crucible of Ministry* (Downers Grove, IL: InterVarsity Press, 2008), 64.

parishioner should take time to pray and to listen to the inner workings of the Spirit in their heart. Is God calling? If the answer is yes, then this process of discernment should continue to its external portion. If the parishioner has a family, do they agree with the call? Do friends, colleagues, mentors, and mentees affirm it?

Connected to this internal and external process of discernment is a close look at an energy inventory. A high amount of energy is expended in starting a new church. Thus the second question is this: Does the parishioner have the energy resources to start the church? All church participation requires time and energy, but the time and energy required to start a new church will be significantly more. For instance, on a practical level, is there enough space in their schedule to put time into starting this new church? If not, is the parishioner prepared to change their weekly schedule? If so, then a calling to be part of a new church may be present.

Emotional and social energy will also be required to start a new church. Does the parishioner have the social and emotional energy required to start a new church? Church planting is not something that one does alone. There will be consistent collaboration, prayer, and decisions that need to be made with other people in order to get the church off the ground. Conflicts will arise and disagreements will be around every corner. Does the parishioner have the emotional and social energy to sit with another over coffee when a disagreement is at hand? Does the parishioner have the maturity to handle dealing with the passions and opinions of others that will be different than their own? These conversations and collaborations take a deep focus and sense of the Holy Spirit's presence.

Finally, spiritual energy is needed when starting a church. Does the parishioner have the spiritual energy to start a new church? One point of warning here: if the parishioner is looking to escape or break off a group of people from a current church to find more spiritual energy in a new church, then the calling should be reconsidered. Protestants come from a tradition of "protesting" and many new churches and denominations have arisen out of protest.[5] To be specific, there are now over thirty-three thousand Protestant denominations, many of which arose not out of a biblical frame or apostolic call, but rather out of disagreements that led to division. The biblical call for unity and oneness are important in today's culture, and displeased religious consumers starting new churches to escape specific distastes has been too common. If displeased people, low on spiritual energy, are at the center of new churches, then those churches will produce and reproduce similar people. Instead, spiritual energy rooted in the presence of God and God's sending nature for

---

[5]See Mark Lau Branson and Nicholas Warnes, eds., *Starting Missional Churches: Life with God in the Neighborhood* (Downers Grove, IL: InterVarsity Press, 2014).

the purposes of reconciling all things should be central to the called parishioner. If it is not, then a call may not be present.

Obviously, the call of the planter and the call of the parishioner overlap with one another. Equally as obvious, no one human will be in perfect condition for starting a new church, just as parents will never fully be ready to bring new life into the world. Thus the grace of God should undergird the whole process of discernment toward starting a new church. Once a new church begins to form, people will disappoint one another and a life of following in the forgiving sacrifice of Jesus will need to be at the center. The Spirit of God will heal and guide all callings of both church planters and parishioners. It is in this ongoing awareness of God's redeeming work that the church must find its birth.

Discernment exercises. Work through the essential questions provided for each of these seasons both on your own and with trusted family, friends, and colleagues as you develop a holistic planting plan.

When we were starting Cyclical LA we began by gathering all of the church starters that had emerged out of Northland Village Church. We promised three things in these monthly gatherings: the best food, the best drink, and the best training. As you might imagine, many people began to gather—some of them were church starters, but some were discerning church starters (that is, those who were still discerning whether God was calling them to start a church). We wanted to welcome the discerning church starters into this unique opportunity for training, but we also quickly noted that the season of discernment needs special attention. Thus we created another monthly gathering specifically for discerning church starters. We have found this space to be important for doing the essential and nuanced work of discerning a call to church starting.

1. How would you describe your church planting discernment process?

2. How much time have you spent on this process and are you satisfied with that amount of time?

3. Who have you invited into the process with you and what has been their response to your discernment?

In chapter four's opening section, Tim Morey wrote, "What undermines church planters is, more often than not, not underdeveloped skills in preaching or vision casting. It isn't a lack of motivation or passion for the kingdom of God. No, it is a spiritual life that is not sufficiently robust to deal with the challenges that church planting brings." Without a regular connection with the head of the church, it will be impossible to guide the body of the church.

4. How would you describe your spiritual life?

5. How does it match what you would desire in the life of a church planter?

6. How does your spiritual life fall short of this desire?

Many regularly notice the appeal of starting a new church. The excitement of starting something new and fresh, the opportunity for mutual transformation of the new church and its neighbors, tapping into God's image as people who create—the potential is endless. However, there are also hurdles that stand in the way of starting a church. From doubts about social base to economics, the challenges can be wide and diverse. That said, the most foundational question in the discernment process is often lost in the weeds.

7. Is God calling you to participate in starting a new church? Why?

8. Is God calling you to be a leader of a new church? Why?

SEASON OF INITIAL ORGANIZATION

The process of discernment may lead to the discovery that being a part of a new church is not a good fit. This is a good result. Not everyone is called to start a new church, and some are simply not in the right season for it. From social base considerations to vocational transitions, there are many good reasons why the Spirit will point people away from starting a new church. But the process may also end in discerning that the time is right to join in starting a new church. This is also a good result. If discernment leads to moving forward with the plant, then the next season for the new church will be one of initial organization.

It has been said that a golfer cannot win a golf match in the first two holes, but he or she can lose a golf tournament in the first two holes. In case you're unfamiliar with golf, after two holes there is still a long way to go—sixteen holes, to be specific. Regardless, the first two holes are essential to a round of golf, and two triple bogeys in the first two holes will almost certainly take the golfer out of contention.

This is a fitting metaphor for the first two seasons of a new church. There is still a long way to go after the first two seasons of a new church, but if the first two seasons are not attended to well, then the results of the new church will most likely not be positive. More specifically, if a proper season of discernment—for both planters and parishioners—is not stewarded well in the life of a new church, then a lack of calling may quickly lead to a toxic atmosphere. Similarly, a good start is essential in the work of organizing the called people who will make up the new church.

A good start to initial organization begins with the called people of God. Without the people of God, there is no church, because there is no communal discernment

of the Holy Spirit. Mark Lau Branson has pointed out that the initial work of organization is too often accomplished by a single individual: "We have been shaped by
cultural forces that emphasize individualism and that delegate to leaders the work
of providing directions. Our cultural norms set us up to look for the visionary, the
CEO, the charismatic leader."[6] Because they are shaped by the cultural forces of
individualism and the CEO mindset, the others called to the new church often act
as if the planter is uniquely set apart in his or her ability to connect with God and
make decisions. But this, of course, reveals a reductionistic pneumatology. Acts 15
is an important biblical narrative that reminds us of the importance of God's people
working together to discern God's guidance. Those gathered at the Council of Jerusalem were faced with an early missiological and ecclesiological decision: Then
certain individuals came down from Judea and were teaching the brothers, "Unless
you are circumcised, according to the custom taught by Moses, you cannot be saved"
(Acts 15:1). The question at hand is, will new believers, especially Gentile believers,
need to be circumcised in order to be welcomed into the church? Working together,
the apostles and elders meet to decide (Acts 15:6).

After praying, sharing stories, and considering theology and history, the apostles
and elders wrote a letter that shared how they had discerned the Spirit of God.

> The brothers, both the apostles and the elders, to the believers of Gentile origin in
> Antioch and Syria and Cilicia, greetings. Since we have heard that certain persons who
> have gone out from us, though with no instructions from us, have said things to
> disturb you and have unsettled your minds, we have decided unanimously to choose
> representatives and send them to you, along with our beloved Barnabas and Paul, who
> have risked their lives for the sake of our Lord Jesus Christ. We have therefore sent
> Judas and Silas, who themselves will tell you the same things by word of mouth. For
> it has seemed good to the Holy Spirit and to us to impose on you no further burden
> than these essentials: that you abstain from what has been sacrificed to idols and from
> blood and from what is strangled and from fornication. If you keep yourselves from
> these, you will do well. Farewell. (Acts 15:23-29 NRSV)

No single human was set apart, but all worked together to discern the Holy Spirit
and move forward accordingly.

Setting apart the planter over and against the called parishioners also reveals a
reductionistic understanding of giftedness and how the various gifts work with one
another (see 1 Cor 12). Does the planter have unique gifts to contribute to the body
of Christ and its discernment toward its mission? Absolutely. But so do the parishioners. All the diversity of gifts should be adopted within the season of the initial

---

[6]Branson and Warnes, *Starting Missional Churches*, 41.

organization of the church. All who are called to begin the new church should join in the activity. Will the process sometimes be messy? Yes. The Council of Jerusalem certainly had its messy moments. Will the body of Christ and the kingdom of God more fully be embodied with such collaboration? Yes. The parishioners and planters make up the body of Christ, and they need one another and their different gifts to be a whole system. The Spirit of God is moving in powerful, mysterious, and different ways in different contexts. Therefore, there is no prescription or industrial equation for how to join God in different cities and neighborhoods around the world to start churches. The consistency, instead, is found in God's called people, working together to discern God's initiatives in order that the church might become a sign and foretaste of the kingdom in its place.

The next step for a good season of initial organization is to begin to build communal habits and practices. The best way to build habits and practices isn't intuitive. One might initially think that the church needs to begin with a new set of patterns, but often the best way to begin to embody the activity of the Holy Spirit is to bolster habits and practices that are already present within the called people of the new church.

Someone once asked Michelangelo how he created a sculpture of an angel out of a huge slab of marble. The task had to be extremely difficult. To Michelangelo, however, it was quite simple. He is often quoted as saying, "The angel was already in the marble, and all I had to do was carve until I set him free." Similarly, God is already active in the habits and practices of the called people of God. God is active in the food that is eaten, the partnerships in the neighborhood that are already present, the spiritual practices, the passions, and in the common gathering places. The work in this second season becomes about chiseling out those practices that are already there, not necessarily creating completely new habits and practices.

From here, the work of connecting already existing habits and practices to what God is already doing is important.[7] JR Woodward writes, "God initiates mission. God is missionary in God's very nature. Because our triune God is actively on mission in our world today, our work shifts from initiating mission plans to discerning the work and whisper of God."[8] The initial organizing efforts of the new church are not about initiating mission but instead about cooperating with God's mission that is already active in context. Building the connection between the people's habits and practices and God's initiatives early in the plant will be sure to secure a healthy DNA for the new church.

---

[7]Branson and Warnes, *Starting Missional Churches*, 37.

[8]Dan White Jr. and JR Woodward, *The Church as Movement: Starting and Sustaining Missional-Incarnational Communities* (Downers Grove, IL: InterVarsity Press, 2016), 124.

One final imperative in this season is to create a framework for fiscal sustainability. Sustainability inevitably boils down to two things: joining in God's movement and God's resources. The financial life of the new church does not fit industrial models guided by equations across multiple contexts. Different expressions of church will require different financial frameworks. Prayerfully addressing the appropriate economic model to point the new church in the direction of sustainability is essential in the season of initial organization.

There are three fiscal considerations that need to be addressed and agreed on among the called people of the new church. The first is the compensation of the planter or planters, who will be central to the everyday work of the church. How much money do they require? Do they desire to be full-time vocational, bivocational, multivocational, or unpaid vocational?

The second consideration is the administrative and legal costs of the new church. Will the new church need to pay a lawyer to form a 501(c)3 nonprofit? How much will insurance cost? How about workers' compensation? Or denominational annual fees? These are just a few of the administrative questions that will need to be answered to determine the local budget of the new church.

The final fiscal consideration is the faith expression of the church. How much does the church plant want to spend on engaging with neighbors, the worship service, other staff, or generosity? Overall, it is imperative to remember that the entire budget is *the mission budget* and thoughtfully making early decisions on generosity (both inside and outside the new church) will set the DNA that will shape the life of the church for seasons to come.

Initial organization exercises. When Northland Village Church was initially gathering, we quickly concluded that we needed a common vocabulary around strengths. We considered using Myers-Briggs, Enneagram, the Spiritual Gifts Inventory, and APEST ideals from Ephesians 4. All were good frameworks, but in the end we found that StrengthsFinder would be the best fit for our community. Everyone took the test and the results were placed on a public document for all to see. Here we noted not only our individual gifts, but also who we were as a gifted community. We quickly saw overlaps in many of our themes and leaned in to these overlaps as we moved toward the next season in the life of the church.

1. How will your new group find a common language for giftedness?

2. What will be the framework for your common understanding of one another's giftedness?

In chapter two, beginning with the title, JR Woodward urged readers to ask the potent question, "What would the reign of God look like in my neighborhood?"

This question gets beyond lesser ecclesial ideals, typically centered around church growth and attractional programs. After the discernment process, gathering a group is essential, and the DNA that is set in the season of initial organization is critical. Keeping the focus on the reign of God in the context of the community will set a foundation that will carry the church to the next season.

3. What might the reign of God look like in your neighborhood?

4. Who is already joining that activity?

5. How might you, as a gifted person and community, join in that activity?

6. Does something need to be created to join the reign of God in your neighborhood?

With this season will come a network of generosity. This is one of the most exciting assets of any new church. There will be generosity in finances, time, resources, energy, and more. Stewarding this generosity then becomes an important task of the initial community as it looks to the sustainability of the new church.

7. How will a culture of generosity be cultivated?

8. What generosity will be prioritized in the budget of the church?

9. How will the pastor(s) be generously supported financially and in other ways?

10. How will moments of sustainability be accomplished?

SEASON OF INITIAL PUBLIC EXPRESSION

The church does not only exist for itself but also for those who don't identify as a part of the church. Therefore, the season of initial organization will need to transition to the season of initial public expression. The historical conversation about what makes the church *the church*, is an ongoing academic and practical one for all who identify as Christians. For the purposes of our discussion here, we will look to JR Woodward, who shares a helpful arrangement for what he calls "ecclesial architecture."[9] He connects three essential rhythms for a new church: (1) communion: a rhythm that guides us to abide in the love of God; (2) community: a rhythm that encourages people to share life together in the midst of a fiercely individualistic world; and (3) co-mission: a rhythm that guides our energies, bodies, and resources toward being a missional presence with the message of Jesus in a specific place. All three rhythms will need dynamic expression for the new church to unfold into its public expression.

---

[9]White and Woodward, *Church as Movement*, 147-49.

The rhythm of *communion* reminds us that God desires to be with us and invites humanity to abide in God's present love. Every year during the celebration of Christ's birth the universal church remembers that Emmanuel came to be with us in the flesh. Like the wise men who knelt before Jesus in worship, we are now invited to do the same. While no two expressions of communal worship will look identical, deciding how the church would like to regularly gather together to express its worship is important.

Whether the new church is a house church, a low church, a high church, or a church that is deemphasizing the communal worship gathering, when those gathered are initially putting together their expression of faith in public worship, they should be mindful of preconceived notions about how liturgy is "supposed" to unfold. Many new churches gather together diverse groups of people who have different ideas, typically based on past experiences, of what a typical worship gathering should be. For instance, some who come from a lower church background will assume that liturgy is meant to produce an existential experience. They may expect lots of music, probably led by a band, with hands raising and a passionate sermon. Another might come from a higher church background and anticipate a certain pattern and rhythm, a homily, and an entire liturgy pointing toward the sacrament of the Eucharist. This type of diversity can produce hurdles when a new church is working to find its rhythm in worship.

In order to navigate these hurdles, the new church should be clear about who sets the initial framework for how the church will worship and then decide who will plan worship weekly. Again, the assumption may be that the church planter or a staff person such as a worship director will do this regular work. But all should be careful of such an assumption. At Northland Village Church, which was planted in Los Angeles in 2010, a larger team has always gathered to plan worship. The team was charged to be creative and test different liturgical tools to find appropriate expressions for the context of the new church. Meeting in local coffee shops to this day, they work together to shape local and contextual liturgy for their parishioners and neighbors. This practice has led to a diversity of voices that has helped navigate the hurdles around different preconceived notions of how worship should look.

The time, pace, and place of the communion of worship is also an essential element for new churches to decide. Where will the church gather for worship—in a home, a church building, a coffee shop? Regarding time and pace, how often will the church meet for worship—daily, weekly, monthly? And what day and time will they gather? The way these questions are answered will impact the future ministry and mission of the church.

In the early church's first expressions of communion, we see a distinct time, pace, and place of worship.

> Awe came upon everyone, because many wonders and signs were being done by the apostles. All who believed were together and had all things in common; they would sell their possessions and goods and distribute the proceeds to all, as any had need. Day by day, as they spent much time together in the temple, they broke bread at home and ate their food with glad and generous hearts, praising God and having the goodwill of all the people. And day by day the Lord added to their number those who were being saved. (Acts 2:43-47 NRSV)

The places of worship were in the temple and in homes. The times and pace were very different than the traditions of many churches today. In this first church in Jerusalem, people were together every day and for many hours a day. Does this mean that all new churches should do the same? No. The Holy Spirit led this church to find a pattern and rhythm in such a way, and the same Spirit guided different churches in different cities to worship differently. The essential habits here are following the Holy Spirit with faithfulness and not allowing the worship service to be the end of the local expression of the church. As we see in Acts 2, the moments of communion with God should inform both the community life of the new church and the co-mission of the new church.

Community is the rhythm that encourages people to share life together in the midst of a fiercely individualistic world. The community element of the ecclesial architecture also emerged in the early church: "All who believed were together and had all things in common; they would sell their possessions and goods and distribute the proceeds to all, as any had need" (Acts 2:44-45 NRSV). They were together, they shared, and they would sell possessions to give resources to any who had need. These are very distinct ways of functioning as a community together, which provide a helpful frame for new churches. Community meant sharing time, space, and goods with one another.

In our globalizing world, filled with new opportunities at every turn, time is an essential asset. To give and be given time by another is a great gift. The initial public expression of the church will require giving and being given the gift of time by others. JR Woodward highlights *availability* and *spontaneity* as essentials of time.[10] If people are not willing to make themselves available, or to be spontaneous with others, the community aspect of ecclesial architecture is sure to fall flat.

---

[10]White and Woodward, *Church as Movement*, 148.

Sherry, a new member of a new church in a local neighborhood on the East Coast, came across Tina at the grocery store. Tina was having a difficult time with her job and her marriage. Sherry knew this as she saw her from across the aisle of the grocery store. Tina approached Sherry to make small talk. Sherry quickly asked Tina about her job and she broke into tears. Sherry demonstrated spontaneity and availability for her sister in Christ by asking her if she would like to go to the local coffee shop for some tea.[11] Tina was encouraged by the invitation and they entered into a new level of friendship. Jesus gave time and availability and spontaneity over and over again throughout the Gospels. By joining the life of Jesus, Sherry did the same for Tina. A healthy community, especially in the midst of increasing demands on time in our current culture, will need such generosity.

Space is also an essential for community. In Acts 2, the church shared space with one another at the temple and in their homes. Being present with one another was important. Much has been written about social media and ministry in the past ten years. There are certainly assets in social media, but there are also shortfalls. Social media can assist in creating community, but it also needs to be a priority for people to be physically present with one another. The new church should work together to create this type of space with intentionality and also be open to spontaneity. Whether enjoying a meal or going to a baseball game together, space to be present is essential for community.

In Acts 2, the church also shared goods with one another. Culture too often teaches people to hoard goods for themselves to create safety nets and comfortability. This was not the case in the first church of Jerusalem and should also not be the case in the new church that is trying to foster healthy community. How can the church members share with one another? How can the church take care of those who have need in any given moment? There are various ways to answer these questions, and again these decisions should be made with Spirit-led intentionality.

Commission, or co-mission, is the rhythm that is the foundation of the church. As JR Woodward notes, commission guides our energies, bodies and resources toward being a missional presence with the message of Jesus in a specific place. Without the consistent outpouring of energies, bodies, and resources into mission, the church ceases to be the church. Thus new churches need to be continually asking themselves how they can be living into this primary call. As Carrie Boren Headington noted in chapter nine, the church's commission begins with the reality that Jesus has ushered in the kingdom of God and that this is the good news. This is the

---

[11]Proper boundaries are also a priority here. For a look at creating healthy boundaries, see Peter Scazzero, *The Emotionally Healthy Church: A Strategy for Discipleship That Actually Changes Lives* (Grand Rapids: Zondervan, 2003).

gospel, the news that every new church should found itself on as it moves deeper into mutual relationship with the neighborhood. Integral to this good news is that God is already present in any place that a new church is emerging. God has already been expressing this good news in innumerable ways prior to any particular new church arriving on the scene. The work for the new church in its primary vocation as co-missioner with God is to jump into God's gospel activity.

First impressions are important. One does not get a second chance at making a first impression. Within this season of initial public expression, the new church will also make many first impressions within its context. How does a church do this well?

It begins with remembering that God is already on the move and that God brings with God the good news of the gospel. If the new church would like to make a good first impression, and the church believes that the goods news really is good, then it will work to establish itself as a movement of people connected with this goodness. Oak Life Church, a new church in Oakland, California, quickly realized that to many in their context, the good news of the gospel was not good news at all. Unfortunately, many had experienced or had been taught a lesser gospel. The result then was that many had unsubscribed to this reductionist form of the good news. Oak Life wanted to reverse people's preconceived notions of this lesser gospel and join with God once again in what God was doing in the context of Oakland. So the people of Oak Life showed up with their neighbors to clean up the park. Is God about beauty? Absolutely, and Oak Life Church was there to join in the gospel activity. Oakland is also a city with a long history of effective protest. When protests arise around actions that are opposed to God's gospel activity, guess who was there? Every time, Oak Life had representation. This work made a very positive first impression on many in Oakland, from neighbors to community leaders, and has given Oak Life an increasing opportunity for shaping shalom in their context.

New churches only get one shot at a first impression with its neighbors. Many new churches have fallen short in their first impressions and have jeopardized the life of the church due to poor decisions. For example, the church mentioned in chapter seven thought that going to clean up the beach with their neighbors was a reasonable way to build healthy relationships. Unfortunately, they also decided that it would be a good idea to bring plastic water bottles with their church's logo printed on the labels. Yes, they brought plastic water bottles, to a beach cleanup, where they were picking up thousands of empty plastic water bottles. The good news wasn't good to neighbors that day and no one was better for it.

The initial public expression is a key step in the life of the church. People called to join in creating the church will have to make important decisions regarding the church's worship (communion), fellowship (community), and witness (co-mission). The most important thing to remember in the midst of this season is that the initial expression is not final. The church is alive, and that which is alive is dynamic. The next season needs to reflect the dynamic nature of the life of the new church.

Initial public expression exercises. JR Woodward noted the importance of joining God in God's commission, or co-mission. God is on the move. Developing a deep sense of companionship with God in order that we might better join in God's mission is primary for every new church.

1. What regular practices are you developing as a new church to grow in companionship with God?

2. How does that companionship help you partner with God in God's mission in your context?

The Artist's Outlet (TAO) is a new church focused on Moorpark, California. At the end of 2017 the giant Thomas Fire sparked in TAO's backyard. Thousands of people were affected as the fire burned almost three hundred thousand acres in Southern California. The leadership of TAO had already been tuned in to God's care for those who were pushed to the edges of their community, and all those who were now displaced by the fire certainly fit into that category. Over the course of a month, TAO, leading other community stakeholders, put together an art auction to raise money for those who had lost so much. The event brought the community together: thousands of dollars were raised and new relationships were ignited.

3. What reality in your context breaks your heart?

4. With what aspects of God's character do you most identify?

5. How might your heartbreak and your identification with God's character lead toward joining God in your context?

Most churches in our Western culture have preconceived notions of both life and faith rooted in individualism. Individualism is very complex but is founded on self-reliance. Someone who has individualistic priorities might commonly say or think, "If you want the job done right, then do it yourself." Preservation of the self—looking out for one's own interests—is also central to the ideology of individualism. While this philosophy and way of life can be a hurdle for new faith communities, there is also an opportunity to demonstrate that nothing could be further from the life that God invites God's people to live.

6. How have you subscribed to our fiercely individualistic culture?

7. How have your previous faith experiences submitted to the crown of individualism?

8. How has your faith pushed against the sinful side of individualism?

9. How might your new church speak truth to the power of individualism?

SEASON OF ADAPTATION OF INITIAL PUBLIC EXPRESSION

Peter Thiel writes of all startups, "No one can predict the future exactly, but we know two things: it's going to be different, and it must be rooted in today's world."[12] While Thiel is generally speaking of for-profit organizations, his book translates well into the work of starting a new church. When it is assumed that we cannot know the future, but that we can know both that the future is going to be different *and* that our expression of the church needs to fit in today's world, we begin to understand that our expressions of faith need to be constantly adapting. In existing churches, we can better predict the future. While not perfectly, we can predict attendance in worship services, challenges to certain commission-oriented events, and annual financial giving. In a new church, these patterns have not yet developed, thus requiring adaptive leadership.

In *Leadership on the Line: Staying Alive Through the Dangers of Leading*, Ronald A. Heifetz and Marty Linsky famously note the difference between adaptive and technical leadership. Technical leadership happens when, "people have problems for which they do, in fact, have the necessary know-how and procedures."[13] On the flip side, and on the side of leadership that most new churches encounter, there is adaptive leadership. This happens when "there is a whole host of problems that are not amenable to authoritative expertise or standard operating procedures."[14] Again, in an existing church, this type of leadership is less necessary as time often provides opportunity to create authoritative expertise or standard operating procedures. The time necessary to develop such authoritative expertise or standard operating procedures has not yet existed for the new church. Thus a higher ratio of adaptive leadership will be necessary. Of course, this is not to say that technical leadership is not important or needed in a church, new or old. (Who doesn't want the good technical leadership of someone with an accounting background on their planting team?!) What a new church needs to be careful of, however, is the type of technical leadership that answers every "Why are we doing it this way?" question with "Because we have done it this way before and we know that it works!" This classic technical leadership response can stifle or even kill a church if adaptation doesn't happen. One of the luxuries of a church plant is that technical leadership can be

---

[12]Thiel, *Zero to One*, 6.

[13]Ronald A. Heifetz and Marty Linsky, *Leadership on the Line: Staying Alive Through the Dangers of Leading*, rev. ed. (Boston: Harvard Business Review Press, 2017), 13.

[14]Heifetz and Linsky, *Leadership on the Line*, 13.

used where needed (finances, building practicalities, etc.) without as great of a temptation that it will become the *only* leadership framework for the community. In church planting, adaptive leadership and experimentation comes with the territory!

In *The Lean Startup* Eric Ries discusses adaptive leadership and the importance of experiments. Any new venture should continuously experiment, measure the experiment, and then either pivot (change the practice) or persevere (continue the practice) based on the results of the experiment. This, for Ries, will produce *resiliency*.

> A pivot is not just an exhortation to change. Remember, it is a special kind of structured change designed to test a new fundamental hypothesis about the product, business model and engine of growth. It is the heart of the Lean Startup method. It is what makes the companies that follow Lean Startup resilient in the face of mistakes: if we take a wrong turn, we have the tools we need to realize it and the agility to find another path.[15]

In any new church, resiliency will be key and Ries's model for adaptive leadership, while a bit reductionistic, is important in the face of inevitable change.

Alan Roxburgh gives theological legs to the conversation on adapting the initial public expression of faith. He spends over half his book *Joining God, Remaking Church, Changing the World* building a similar but more robust adaptive leadership process than Ries. He begins his process with listening. He observes that generally "listening is directed either toward the front (the altar or pulpit), where we've ritualized our relationships to the Holy; or to the head of the table (as in committee meetings), where we've formalized relationships around agendas and tasks. We've lost the practice of listening to one another outside of these structured interactions."[16] A great first step in adapting the initial expression of the church is placing a higher priority on listening to neighbors, others in the church, and God.

Roxburgh's second step is discerning. Listening is not an end in itself. The move to discernment is the shift from understanding what the neighborhood, the people, and God are saying to what the Spirit of God is inviting the church to join or create. Should we join in a local initiative that is already happening? Should we create a new initiative? The Holy Spirit will guide us. Discerning the Spirit is an essential aspect of adaptive leadership.

Interestingly, the third, fourth, and fifth steps in Roxburgh's framework connect with Ries's steps. The third is to experiment, the fourth is to reflect, and the fifth is to decide. The most important thing to note here is the movement toward creating

---

[15]Eric Ries, *The Lean Startup: How Today's Entrepreneurs Use Continuous Innovation to Create Radically Successful Businesses* (New York: Crown Business, 2011), 173.

[16]Alan J. Roxburgh, *Joining God, Remaking the Church, and Changing the World: The New Shape of the Church in Our Time* (New York: Morehouse, 2015), 58.

habits of working through this cycle in the church. As soon as this cycle ceases, the church will soon see the end of its lifecycle.

Agility in this season is also essential: listen, discern, experiment, evaluate, and pivot or persevere. And then, repeat.[17] The church is ultimately trying find its way toward moments of sustainability (homeostasis) because in moments of sustainability, reproduction is possible. Like a new baby becoming a toddler, the process is messy and filled with many accidents. However, if the toddler can one day become a child and then an adult who experiences moments of homeostasis, then reproduction is possible. While no single, particular church has ever been fully sustainable, particular churches regularly achieve moments of homeostasis, and the question then becomes what the church does with those moments. One of the most important questions a church can ask in its adulthood is, How do we expend our energy in these moments of homeostasis? Work to grow larger through building programs? Hire more staff? Build a building? Build a bigger building? Start a new youth group?

We can learn a lot from biology here. For instance, plants in homeostasis produce flowers, which then become fruit, which then allows the plant to reproduce its DNA through the seeds in the fruit. Plants understand that their time is limited and often prioritize reproduction over and against other options, such as more growth. There are many options that a church needs to discern at this sacred moment in its lifecycle. As we discuss in chapters three and eleven, starting new churches out of existing churches experiencing homeostasis ought to become a more regular practice.

Unfortunately, most churches in today's Western world don't prioritize reproduction on a regular basis and instead choose to work on various levels at growing their congregation. This then threatens homeostasis and lessens the possibility of reproducing. An ecclesial shortsightedness keeps too many churches from taking note of the larger ecosystem of both historical and geographical churches in their contexts. Churches end up only thinking about themselves, not the next generation of churches. There is a scarcity mindset in many ecclesial settings, which unfortunately keeps the church from starting the number of churches necessary to keep up with global population growth.[18] Until this changes, fewer and fewer people will connect with churches in North America.

The reality is that every church that has ever existed started, grew, shrank, and then eventually dissolved. Thus, sustainability for the church ultimately happens not by fully sustaining every church. This simply isn't possible. It instead happens

---

[17]For another change cycle, see Branson and Warnes, *Starting Missional Churches*, 182.

[18]For more on this, see Dave Olsen, *An American Church in Crisis: Groundbreaking Research Based on a National Database of Over 200,000 Churches* (Grand Rapids: Zondervan, 2008).

through developing more leaders who are called and willing to take on the historical work of starting the next generation of churches.

Adaptation exercises. In chapter nine's first section, Carrie Boren Headington writes about her adapted understanding of the work of evangelism, "The evangelistic endeavor is holy work which ventures to the very heart of God. It requires silence before God, deep listening to the Lord and his Word, and a Holy Spirit–infused boldness to carry out God's mission in God's world through our small part of God's church. Our work is to draw as close as we can to the Lord, so that our hearts begin to beat with God's love for the specific mission field where he sends us." Church planting requires consistent and pneumatological adaptations. Some of the adaptations are large and some are small. Regardless of the size, the essential element in all adapting is a deep and intimate relationship with God.

1. How is your church opening itself to God's dynamic guidance?

2. What may need to adapt in the near future?

3. What may need to adapt in the not-so-near future?

Cyclical LA has partnered to start dozens of new churches around Southern California and all of them need help through their first season of adaptation. The reality is that many more seasons of adaptation are on the horizon, but the first time through this season can be difficult due to a diversity of ideas from a diversity of people who have different thoughts on what needs to change and what needs to stay the same in the original planting plan.

4. How are you giving voice to all committed participants in the church regarding what needs to be adapted?

5. How are final decisions made regarding what needs to change and what needs to stay the same?

6. What needs to be adapted in your new church right now?

There is no such thing as sustainability for any particular church. There are certainly moments of sustainability, but true sustainability is reserved for the universal church. That said, different churches will prioritize different elements to achieve moments of sustainability for their context. Some will work toward sustainability through generativity, or economics, or global outreach. All of these efforts require adaptation to work toward the goals of having moments of homeostatic sustainability.

7. How would you describe sustainability for your church?

8. Are you satisfied with the efforts that are being made to achieve moments of sustainability?

9. How does your church plan to reproduce in moments of homeostasis?

FOUR SEASONS, ONE NARRATIVE: OIL CITY VINEYARD CHURCH

Oil City Vineyard, a local church in Oil City, Pennsylvania, has recently gone through the first four seasons of a new church. The pastor of Oil City Vineyard is Charlie Cotherman, who is also a contributor to this book. He was interviewed in November 2017 to get his perspective on the nuances within each of the four seasons.

Discernment. The season of discernment began with Charlie and his wife, Aimee, in 2014. The first step of their discernment process was a desire to find an ecclesial family in which they could do the hard work of discernment. Based on their research of ecclesiology and theology, the Vineyard Church, specifically Multiply Vineyard's Small Town USA initiative, quickly emerged as a good fit. Within this partnership, two main questions emerged in Aimee and Charlie's discernment process. First, would God confirm this call in their lives? This was indeed confirmed through prayer, conversations with friends, and especially through various corporate worship settings. Second, was there desire in the community for a new church? Charlie and Aimee began meeting with people with whom they had grown up. An extensive and long-standing network of people were also compelled by the Spirit in these meetings. Within months, about twenty people, most of whom were not connected with local churches or were effectively de-churched, had moved from discerning a call to start a new church to discerning how to start a new church with one another.

Initial organization. Since Charlie was finishing his PhD in Charlottesville, Virginia, an immediate empowering of leadership naturally emerged. With Aimee and Charlie hundreds of miles away, the group began meeting twice a month for a meal, Bible study, and prayer. A Facebook group was created for people to communicate with one another, and the larger Vineyard Church was given frequent space to orient the new group of people to the larger tradition. Through this process, the group naturally began to talk very openly about sustainability. It was decided that, since there was not an abundance of money coming from an outside source, Charlie would be a bivocational pastor, and those who had discerned a call to start the church would begin tithing their resources into a pool until the official public launch of the church. They also wanted to keep things simple. No fancy lights or smoke machines. No large-scale fundraising campaigns or publicity stunts. Just people, relationships, and food. Some preconceived notions had to be shed in this process as people had encountered other ways that churches had started. As these notions, largely around industrial models, waned, following the Holy Spirit became a priority and the group continued to grow.

With regard to simplicity, in the season of initial organization the church gathered a group of people who wanted to leverage food as a central unifier of people. Every time they met, the people who would soon be known as Oil City Vineyard Church met around shared food—sometimes meals, sometimes snacks, sometimes communion. This was quite prophetic in the local context because usually only biological family and close friends shared food like this. (Even in the local church culture most small group ministries take place through Sunday school programs in the church building. Home Bible studies and home groups are relatively uncommon.) People found energy, encouragement, and a natural cooperation with the mission of God by extending the imagination of family into the ecclesial sphere. Week in and week out, the group would bond over a meal. This also extended beyond the organized gatherings of the budding local church. People were encouraged to spend time with each other one-on-one outside of the Sunday gatherings over coffee and meals. This activity would thicken the network of relationships and build trust as the church moved toward the public expression of their faith.

Initial public expression. Season three is framed by JR Woodward's trifold ecclesiological frame of communion, community, and commission. It took Oil City about two years to move from the initial discernment of the first leaders to the public launch of the expression of faith with all three of these elements of ecclesiology in place. The church began its public ministry in October 2016 with sixteen people present at a public worship service.

This worship service was not publicized in any way except through word of mouth, an announcement on the church's Facebook group page, and through a princess party at a local coffee shop a few weeks after the initial launch. The original parishioners invited neighbors to attend this princess party, and many people connected to the church through this effort. Charlie, working with others in the church, created a low-church liturgy around weekly communion. Charlie organizes the liturgy every week. After one year of ministry, approximately a hundred people gather for worship on a weekly basis and the budget has grown to $100,000 annually.

The communal aspects of the church continued with a call to food and celebration. During the first year, food was connected to every worship service to build community within the church. A woman in the church with a heart for hospitality organized a brunch spread each week and several others volunteered to brew coffee. The church also hosted community meals after worship on a regular basis. Each of these meals had a highly celebratory atmosphere and provided adequate space for others to get to know one another. As mentioned earlier, this was a prophetically essential space because people in this context do not typically invite one another into their homes for meals. This local hesitancy to see the church as extending into one's home has hindered attempts at building community in more traditional small group settings. Overall, homes are for biological family, not ecclesial family. Charlie notes that over time this reality is beginning to change as more families open up their homes for small groups, but there is still plenty of room for growth in this area. The leadership of Oil City Vineyard sees opportunity for increased small group involvement in years to come, but in the meantime has found traction is simply creating communal spaces over food before and after worship services.

An overlapping place of community, communion, and commission has been worshiping in an art gallery and building art into the liturgy. Local artists are invited into the liturgy to share their performance, visual, and culinary art within the worship service. These semi-regular spaces created by the church have been a powerful way to reach out to neighbors and invite them into what God is doing with the church. The church has also done well in its commission through partnership with a local school. Activities as simple as providing Kleenex to classrooms and basketball nets for the school's playground after the budget was cut have been meaningful steps into the school. An annual Easter morning donut giveaway has also provided the church with a public means of blessing the community and teaming up with other nearby churches. Overall, Charlie is clear that relationships in the neighborhood are just beginning to flourish and the church is focused on working on these as it continues to grow.

Adaptation of initial public expression. With Oil City Vineyard being only one year old at the time of the writing of this book, Charlie was quick to note that the church is just jumping into this season. As he and the leaders of the church look out to the horizon of adaptations, there are three elements that stand out. The first, as previously noted, is around small groups. The church sees a real prophetic opportunity to encourage hospitality in the lives of the people of Oil City through small groups. With a couple of small groups already up and running, and a couple of small groups currently failing, they understand that they will have to do some hard work to appropriately frame how these small groups will actually work. They look forward to the challenge. The church is also looking to adjust as they move spaces. Due to growth, the church is moving to a weekly worship gathering in a gym. In doing so they are leaving the hip space in town, and many in the church are aware of the challenges and opportunities that this will bring. Finally, due to its quick growth, the church will need to regularly adapt the budget. Charlie notes that movement on their budget will need to happen nimbly as the early stages of a new church require quick decision making. All three of these ecclesiological essentials are closely tied together. The healthiest communities will have substantial overlap in each of the three and they feed into one another. Oil City Vineyard is a good example of all three working with one another to further the witness of the church (see oilcity vineyard.org for further information).

11

WHAT AM I REALLY PLANTING?

FROM TREE TO ORCHARD

**JOHN LO, NICK WARNES,
AND CHARLES E. COTHERMAN**

For over 2,000 years, the lifespan of greater than 99.9 percent of all local churches is less than 100 years (most are less than 50 years). . . . The legacy of all 300,000-plus churches in the United States will ultimately be measured not by what they accumulated during their 100-year (or less) lifespan, but rather by what they released and sent.

TODD WILSON

THE PREVIOUS CHAPTER SOUGHT TO ANSWER the intensely practical church planting question, Where do we start? In this final chapter, we (Charlie, Nick, and John) conclude with the highly teleological question, What am I really planting? We want to step back, begin with the end in mind, and consider how the *missio Dei* might shape and inform that end. What is our goal? How do we actually flourish over the long haul as church planters and local communities? What does success look like?

In contemporary life I (Charlie) find few words more slippery than *success*. In part, this is because success is so easy to compartmentalize. We all can think of "successful" celebrities whose athletic, cinematic, or political careers have been marked with one achievement after another, even as their relational, physical, or mental health deteriorate. But it's not just the folks whose airbrushed faces beam at us from magazine racks in the checkout aisle who struggle with success. We live in what French philosopher Jacques Ellul famously described a half century ago as a "technological society" where efficiency and specialization are esteemed over more holistic methods of assessing value.[1] In this technological world the compartmentalization of success impacts all of us. Like the celebrities we simultaneously admire and shake our heads at, we are often tempted to focus on success in isolated areas (jobs, parenting, fitness, academics) and forget that in the kingdom of God, true success

---

[1]Jacques Ellul, *The Technological Society*, trans. John Wilkinson (New York: Vintage Books, 1964), 5, 21.

is putting on Christ and being formed holistically by his Spirit in such a way that our lives overflow in tangible ways with the Spirit's fruit—love, joy, peace, patience, kindness, goodness, faithfulness, gentleness, and self-control (Gal 5:22). While we still might want our surgeons to be specialists, in the area of success we should all be generalists. Our whole lives matter.

Of course, pastors and church planters are not immune to the cultural forces that shape life in a compartmentalized, twenty-first-century world. Misguided and idolatrous narratives of so-called success beckon us in a myriad of ways. Fortunately, we are not without time-tested tools to fight these cultural half-truths. As earlier chapters in this book have highlighted, the church has always emphasized the importance of deep spiritual formation through practices like prayer, reflection on Scripture, partaking in the sacraments, and regular involvement in Christian community. Furthermore, as demonstrated in the preface and chapter one, a historical consciousness can also be a helpful tool for confronting the predominant lies of any given age, including lies about the nature of success. As C. S. Lewis noted in his introduction to Athanasius' *On the Incarnation* (c. 318 CE), the only way to avoid "the characteristic blindness" of our age is "to keep the clean sea breeze of the centuries blowing through our minds."[2]

Prayer, scriptural reflection, Christian community, historical consciousness—these are all great tools for maintaining equilibrium in any age. In a fallen world, however, even these tools are not failproof. As leaders in the church, making sure that we gauge our understanding of success and set our future hopes well takes continual vigilance.

Confronting my hidden assumptions is something I found to be especially true in my experience as a church planter. At the end of chapter ten, Nick gave the basic outline of our community's journey to plant Oil City Vineyard Church. He laid out the hopes and practices that shaped our community in its formative years. Hidden from his account, however, are the ways our planting team struggled to (a) define success and then (b) hold our definition of success against the multiple counter-definitions that others subtly imposed on our community.

My wife and I had come into our church plant with hearts attuned to the necessity of deep spiritual formation. Well before we planted we had established patterns of prayer and scriptural reflection. Individually, I also had a coach, a spiritual director,

---

[2]C. S. Lewis, "Preface," in Athanasius, *On the Incarnation*, translated by John Behr (Yonkers, NY: St. Vladimir's Seminary Press, 2011), 11. Lewis suggested that this knowledge of history could only be garnered "by reading old books." For Lewis, it was "not that the past has any magic about it," but rather that the person "who has lived in many places is not likely to be deceived by the local errors of his native village." See also C. S. Lewis, "On Learning in War Time," in *The Weight of Glory* (San Francisco: HarperSanFrancisco, 2000), 58-59.

and people praying with and for me throughout most of the early phases of our plant. My own experience within American evangelicalism as well as my training as a historian of religion had given me plenty of time to reflect on the misguided frameworks of success that all too often accompanied efforts to build ministries. I knew all of this, and yet as Oil City Vineyard grew in its first year, I found it easy to adopt the ideal of success that others in my town, the larger church culture, and sometimes my own heart wanted to use as measuring rods. Were people coming to a worship gathering? How many were coming? Were they giving? What was the budget? These questions constantly pushed for priority of place in my mind. While these questions were perfectly fine as part of the quantifiable features of church life, they were incapable of defining the success or holistic health of a church.

I tried (hard) to be intentional about keeping equilibrium. When people asked about the church I told them that the quantifiable things (numbers, giving, etc.) were good, but I also stressed that the qualitative measures seemed to be good too. I told stories about how people felt loved in our community. I shared about how two women who had held a grudge against each other for a decade had found themselves at Oil City Vineyard together one Sunday and had gone out to lunch the next week and forgiven each other. I talked about a former drug dealer who had been six months clean, about a new Narcotics Anonymous group, and about a baptism service that rippled with power through the lives of many in our congregation. In all of this I was determined to do all I could to keep a holistic, kingdom-centered framework for success. What I did not realize at the time, however, was that even with all my intentionality I had still allowed some alternate narratives of success to color my thinking.

A little over a year after our public launch I found myself describing the journey of Oil City Vineyard to another pastor who had years of experience as a church planter with a focus on church multiplication. It felt good to recount the story of God's provision throughout Oil City Vineyard's first year, a time filled with some disappointments but far more moments of joy. As I narrated what had been one of the more exciting stages of the journey—our move from our initial public space to a larger space, necessitated by higher attendance in worship—my friend asked me a question no one (and I mean, *no one*) had asked: "Is that a good thing?"

Was growing and moving to a new space a good thing? I had never thought about the possibility that it might not be. Suddenly, I realized that all along I had made a subtle assumption about the relationship of congregational growth and success. While the two are not necessarily opposed, neither are they intrinsically linked. I had simply worked along the assumption that growing out of our old space was good. People were coming. People were giving. People were getting baptized. At least a few lives seemed to be changed. It took a seasoned church planter with a heart for multiplication to help me see that in some areas my sense of success had been adopted unexamined from larger cultural norms.

TOWARD A BIBLICAL MODEL OF SUCCESS

My friend's question made me wrestle with my own unexamined assumptions about success in new ways. A little over a year into church planting a large part of me was simply happy that the church was growing, that people seemed to be positively impacted by the church's presence in the community, that the church budget had expanded to the point that the church could pay me a partial salary to help me support my family. In short, I think I was primarily excited that on some level the experiment of church planting seemed to work. Simply being part of following the Spirit's lead and helping to create a community that had not existed previously seemed a big enough accomplishment.

But my friend's question prompted me to consider that mere existence and even growth, as good as both had been, were not the end of the story. Like any living thing, life and growth were stages to be celebrated, but they were not the only telos (end goal) of anything planted—be it an apple tree or a church. In nature, growth is naturally followed by reproduction, the passing on of DNA to the next generation. Perhaps Oil City Vineyard was not called to grow large but to reproduce? Perhaps we did not need a new space but needed to help launch a new community? Because I was, for all practical purposes, functioning under norms of success that saw the continuing survival, growth, and maintenance of the original church plant as the primary markers of community health, I had missed the call to pass on God's blessing through multiplication.

After my conversation with my friend I began to see more clearly than ever that my role in helping to plant and nurture the growth of our community was not a one-time or one-location endeavor. In the Bible God regularly urges God's people to rejoice over God's provision in major events, like the call of Abram (Gen 12:1-3), the crossing of the Jordan (Joshua 3–4), or the dedication of the temple (2 Chron 6:32-33), but these events, as significant as they are, are never meant to be ends in themselves. They are always meant to spread—to expand out in place and time. Abram's blessing is not only for his family but for "all the nations." So too, Solomon's temple is intended to be a place of worship for Israelites as well as God-fearing foreigners, or as Isaiah would later describe it, "a house of prayer for all nations" (Is 56:6-7). When Israel crosses the Jordan and enters into the Promised Land on dry ground, Joshua instructs them to multiply the story of God's goodness by regularly repeating the story of their miraculous deliverance to their children, who will then do the same for their own children. In each of these instances there might be a temptation to personally revel in God's goodness in the moment with little thought toward spreading the blessing beyond one's immediate family, one's immediate time and place, or even one's own nation, but time and time again God reminds his people that his blessings require action; they required spreading God's goodness and glory beyond one's own family and friends—even beyond one's own lifetime. God's blessings are for the world. They are meant to multiply.

The clearest example of this imperative is also the most natural. In Mark 4 Jesus tells the story of a sower who did something humans have done for millennia: he planted seeds. His seeds fell in four different kinds of soil. Of the four types of soil, only the fourth soil was conducive to sustained growth and multiplication. As John Lo noted in chapter three, the call of the church is to be "fourth-soil" plants that not only thrive and "grow up" but also reproduce thirtyfold, sixtyfold, and a hundredfold (Mk 4:8). Just as Jesus explicitly ties spiritual health to reproduction and multiplication, we argue that this type of spiritual multiplication is *the normal expectation* and *a significant indicator of true health and success* not only in our individual lives but also in the larger life of our churches.

What would it look like if the church in North America and around the world discovered anew the significance of reproduction and multiplication as the norm of church life essential to any evaluation of overall church health or success? That is the question that frames the rest of this chapter. Our entry point will be the stories of two church planters (and co-authors) who have experience in creating cultures of multiplication that reach across North America and around the world. Together Nick's and John's stories show the importance of helping planters and local communities develop a larger ecclesiological vision that renormalizes church planting and provides a framework for raising up leaders whose lives are defined by character, grit, and sensitivity to the Holy Spirit's leading. As their lives and stories demonstrate, with prayer and intentionality, multiplication can move from a vague hope to a vibrant reality and a key component for evaluating the holistic health of our worshiping communities and our efforts as church planters.

RENORMALIZING CHURCH STARTING

As someone who started a church-planting church and now leads a church planting network, I (Nick) have observed that there are two types of churches in North America: churches that understand and practice the importance of starting new churches, and churches that do not. For churches that do not understand the importance of starting new churches, there is one perversely false mode of thought that undergirds this disjointed view of historical ecclesiology: There are already enough churches. Why would we need to plant anymore? This church-building-centered, Christendom-oriented, ecclesial competition-based mode of thought is underdeveloped on multiple levels, the most glaring of which is that it does not take into account that the church is alive.

There are three common seasons within the life of anything that has ever lived: birth, opportunity to reproduce (homeostasis), and death. From minute bacteria to enormous elephants, every living organism shares these three seasons. Because the church is also alive, every particular church also experiences these three seasons. Unfortunately, it has become all too common for local churches to enjoy the second season of homeostasis for its own purposes, rather than spending any energy to reproduce. This is ultimately to the detriment of the universal church, since every particular church will one day cease to exist. This is why the notion that "there are already enough churches" isn't congruent with a desire for the church to continue beyond the current generation of ecclesial life. What would happen if we didn't start more churches? The slow and inevitable end of the church in the United States would begin. For instance, this year in the United States approximately 3,700 churches will close.[3] There are approximately 400,000 churches in America. One might argue that without starting new churches, the end of the church in America could come within a hundred years or so. While it's difficult to be precise about the math, the spirit of the reality is clear.

The good news is that approximately 4,000 churches per year are started in America. To the churches and the individuals in these churches who do the hard work of starting them, we commend you! To the churches and the individuals in these churches who are ready to begin this work, we are with you! To the churches and the individuals in these churches who have planted a church but are ready for the exponential, mustard-seed-like transition from a single plant to a forest, please read on.

BECOMING A CHURCH-PLANTING CHURCH

When I (John) turned thirty-nine, I remember thinking, *I love being an assistant pastor. Why would anyone want the stress of being a senior pastor?* I also remember thinking, *I don't think I'm going to have a mid-life crisis.* I had been on staff for eleven years at the ethnic Chinese church that I had grown up in, and in that time I had

---

[3]Ed Stetzer and Daniel Im, "Multiplication Today, Movements Tomorrow" (Nashville: Lifeway Christian Resources, 2016), 4.

pioneered new ministries to reach out to youth, college students, and young adults. Then early in 2001, my senior pastor asked me to consider taking on the church as its next senior pastor, saying "I'll take the next five years to get you ready." The honor (and shock) of his request threw me right into the crisis I didn't think I was going to have!

Through a process of prayer, what God impressed on my heart was "I didn't create you to reform existing churches but start new ones." This was a mission statement I didn't know I had! Once I accepted these words from God, however, a number of new convictions began to fill my heart. One was that the Great Commission would never be accomplished simply by starting one church, but by churches that started other churches. Becoming a church-planting church—one that would start a movement—became the goal of the church we planted, Epicentre Church. We wanted to start our church with this priority because *movements* are what I read about in the Gospels and Acts. Launching *movements* is not only what Jesus came to do and what was eventually passed on to the apostle Paul, but what I believe is the baton handed to today's church as well. Planting a church is a means to a harvest that will eventually result in Revelation 7:9, and this requires fourth-soil plants that reproduce other fourth-soil trees, which lead to orchards, which virally spring up from person to person, town to town, and people group to people group.

I wanted to be part of this great gospel movement, but I knew that inspiring this type of movement took intentionality. Churches seldom fell into multiplication. In my planning process, I read the statistic that "if a church does not plant another church in their first three years they likely never will."[4] Churches that multiplied seemed to start with that emphasis as part of their DNA from the beginning. With this in mind, even as we began to plan on how to plant Epicentre, I also asked God how we were to plant our first church.

Because my sending church had a history of church planting, they were glad to send part of the young adult congregation I had started as a new church to focus on reaching second-generation Asian Americans. "But what do we do about planting our own church?" I wondered. In prayer, I began to think immediately about people, which led me to think about Chris Rattay, a church member who had married one of the young leaders in our church. He was serving as staff for a local InterVarsity chapter, where he'd not only helped them become more multiethnic but had also launched a new African American chapter. So Chris and I began to pray and dream about planting a church-planting church.

---

[4]Ed Stetzer, "7 Top Issues Church Planters Face: Issue #1: Leadership Development and Reproducing Culture," *The Exchange* (blog), January 12, 2011, www.christianitytoday.com/edstetzer/2011/january/7-top-issues-church-planters-face-issue-1-leadership.html.

Epicentre was planted in September 2003, and we brought on Chris as our first assistant pastor in 2004. I found his vision compelling: "the justice of God requires that we plant a church in the poorest area of Los Angeles that doesn't have strong evangelical churches." Our research indicated the spot: Lincoln Heights, a gang-infested neighborhood located a few miles northwest of downtown LA. That was a vision our young church could get behind.

Aside from helping our young church stabilize and grow, I realized that with the church-planting church goal in mind, a key component of my own calling was training Chris to become the church planter he was called to be. So I poured my life into him, helping him to grow in his formation, skills, and character, and helping him identify and train his church planting team from among our young church.

We were blessed to send them into Lincoln Heights in January 2007. While we technically missed the three-year window by three months, our church responded to our call, to what was written in our DNA: to be a church-planting church.

RAISING UP LEADERS

As our story shows, a key aspect of participating in a multiplying church movement is identifying, equipping, and sending leaders that God has already brought to our communities. But even though church planters know that raising up leaders is an essential part of church planting, moving from this knowledge to consistently developing leadership is seldom as natural and intuitive as we expect. It starts with a philosophy of how we expect leaders to actually lead (top-down or bottom-up?) and moves into a range of practical considerations and skills. From start to finish the whole process requires intentionality and sensitivity to the Spirit's leading.

Top-down or bottom-up? Being a church-planting church can sometimes be complicated when it comes to raising leaders. Young leaders can be wary of a church that feels too top-down and vision driven. They don't want to feel used or be treated as a cog in an organizational machine. Instead, they (rightly) want to know that the church is there to equip and resource them for God's call on their lives. How do we resolve this conflict?

In my mind, if it's clear that (a) the church that I'm planting is called to be a church- planting church, and (b) we trust that God will bring future church planters into the church, then (c) my joyful discipling, equipping, and resourcing of those whom God brings into our fellowship will result, in the big picture, with equipped church planters who can plant churches that plant more churches.

Starting with the right people. As noted in chapter three, starting with the right people is key. Jesus' discipleship of fourth-soil people of influence is key to seeing his missional movement move toward the fulfillment of Matthew 24:14 and Revelation 7:9. He teaches the disciples to do the same, and we see this same focus in the apostle Paul. As Neil Cole writes wryly,

> When he tells the disciples to pray for workers, where do you think they were expecting these leaders to come from? Seminary or Bible colleges? Of course not. Other churches? None existed. The passage is about farming leaders, not robbing other ministries of them. No, there is no other solution than that the leaders for the harvest must come from the harvest itself. We must farm our leaders, not recruit them. The new disciples are the new workers, and the seed of the next generation is found in the fruit of the current one.[5]

For me, keeping in mind the end vision of being a church-planting church means that one of my primary roles is focusing on identifying and equipping future church planters. This is why I focused on Chris two years before he came on our church staff and five years before they planted.

Farm system. Helpfully, there's already one part of our world where this sort of preplanning is happening: professional baseball. The farm system was developed by sports executive Branch Rickey as a way to find and develop young talent through a system of minor league teams, ranked from rookie ball to AAA, just a short step from the major leagues. In this developmental system, potential future major leaguers have coaches and competitions to test and train them at each level so that those who really have the talent are given the best possible opportunity to make it to the major leagues. All of this depends on coaches whose job it is to find and develop raw young talent. Indeed, the early success of the St. Louis Cardinals, New York Yankees, and Brooklyn Dodgers was directly tied to successful farm systems. In God's church the local congregation is the farm system of the church planters of tomorrow.

One of my mentors, Carol Davis, said to me, "Don't make training a program in your church. Train people by the way you do church." So that's what we did. We figured that the best way to find future church planters was to develop a structure which would give potential planters an opportunity to do what church planters do: pray, lead people to Christ, disciple, build a team, and multiply. We decided on a cell church structure to accomplish this. We wanted to build a farm system–style developmental process into our church structure.

Chris led small groups, and he was able to grow in some basic church planter skills. When we sent Chris and his team to Lincoln Heights, we were a church of 150 people.

---

[5]Neil Cole, *Organic Leadership: Leading Naturally Right Where You Are* (Grand Rapids: Baker, 2010), 136.

A CHURCH-PLANTING FARM SYSTEM

A. A process to identify future planters

1. As a local church, identify fourth-soil disciples. Epicentre Church focuses specifically on high schoolers, college students, graduate students, and young adults with an eye to reach nonbelievers and new believers. This means targeting ministries at specific high schools, colleges, and seminaries where we believe we can find undeveloped, future church planters. (Note: we sometimes send out church planters who are older—we recently commissioned two women in their 50s and 60s.)

2. Because church planting is our DNA, finding future church planters is an explicit part of our church's ministry plan.

B. A process to develop a scout's eye for the characteristics we're looking for

1. As a local church, we train our staff and leaders to look for men and women who respond readily to God and who have circles of relationships with nonbelievers and are hungry to reach them.

2. We have also found that sometimes future church planters have an edge to them: they want to change the world and often come across as disgruntled. Underneath, however, is a passionate, idealistic world changer. We have to know what to look for.

C. A process and system to disciple and raise up future planters

1. When we identify individuals as potential planters, we personally disciple them in areas of their character and in the competencies of prayer, evangelism, and discipleship.

2. We also help train them in the basics of starting and nurturing small groups.

D. A process and system to plant them locally and globally

1. While each church, denomination, or movement must develop its own process to plant or send church planters, it is important that a young church planter has clarity, knowing that (a) there is a clear path and (b) we, as a church family, are behind you.

2. Develop a network of relationships with other church planting networks and seminaries to help place planters in the contexts they are well suited for.

A REPRODUCING CULTURE

As discussed previously, growth and reproduction need to be normal parts of congregational life. Every living organism on the planet reproduces, whether it's bacteria and viruses, mushrooms, plants or animals, so it is right for us to begin with the expectation that true life in Christ should reproduce—unless something is amiss!

When we are not reproducing, we must look to see either where we've added DNA that is causing us to be sterile and infertile, or where there are factors in the soil of our people and culture, such as fear, a poor understanding of the gospel and submission to the Word of God, or an inadequate understanding of the goodness of God as our heavenly Father. In such cases, we must focus on recapturing a vibrant, reproducing Christianity and spirituality so that it becomes normal for Christians to reproduce Christians, small groups to reproduce small groups, leaders to reproduce leaders, and churches to reproduce churches.

As noted above, part of restoring a sense of normalcy to church multiplication is tied to our *expectation*. We need to expect God to increase the harvest. But expectation is not the only factor that influences our ability to multiply. Our ability to be communities that multiply also stems in large part from our *habits*. We have to ask ourselves if we and the leaders in our congregations instinctively and effectively pull others into what we are doing, equip them to do the work of ministry, and teach them to do the same thing with others. This is the means to unleashing the viral nature of the gospel that we read about in the Gospels and Acts. When the gospel is unleashed, the reproduction can be amazing—even in places one might not expect.

When Jim first arrived in the Middle East, he knew God was calling him to reach Palestinians in refugee camps. But how was a young, white American going to do that? Through coaching by some of the older church planters in the region, he met Samuel, a young Palestinian man who had recently come to follow Isa Al-Masih ("Jesus" in Arabic) as Lord and Savior.

Jim began to disciple Sam in how to do a Discovery Bible Study (DBS), a simple, reproducible inductive study of the Scriptures aimed at establishing the truths of the Scriptures as seekers obey what they learn and see that this is indeed the way of truth. Sam began a DBS with his friends, and after nine months, they decided that what they were reading must be true and they must give their lives to it. Sam came to Jim one day and said, "We want to get baptized." With great joy, Jim helped them to learn how to baptize each other. They then decided that they must start new groups to tell their friends. So they did and began the process again. Because some of Sam's friends were imams in their mosques, new studies of the Injil (Arabic New Testament) were started in these mosques. Over time, many in these groups got baptized. Today more than thirty groups in this area are meeting. And Jim never set foot in those refugee camps. His role was to unleash the viral nature of the gospel through those he discipled.

HOW DO PLANTERS FOLLOW THE HOLY SPIRIT?

About now you might be feeling overwhelmed with the enormity of starting a multiplying church planting movement. While starting with the right leaders developed in our ecclesial contexts is essential, how do we operate in the Spirit's power and not our own? What defines a Spirit-led, church-multiplying movement? We think it starts with leaders who have cultivated hearts that are sensitive to the Spirit of God. In our experience, this cultivation often shapes leaders with similar traits.

If we understand that one of the main goals of the Holy Spirit's work in the Gospels and Acts is starting new churches, then a key trait for church planters must be discerning and joining in what the Holy Spirit is doing in future church planting activity. As a matter of fact, it must be more than a trait—it must become a habit, part of the church planter's modus operandi. And as noted in chapter three, the key is looking for ripe fields: places where the Holy Spirit is already moving. This is not a brute-force, crunch-the-numbers process, but one that hinges on the ability of a church planter to see with whom God is working and how God is working as she steps into her context.

A willingness to take Spirit-led risks. Taking risks and jumping into what someone else might consider a leap of faith is a necessary trait in a church planter because we do not simply plant churches through strategy. If the assumption is that the Lord of the harvest is present in an area, then a planter's most important trait is their ability to see what the Holy Spirit is doing and follow wholeheartedly. While this might look silly or scary to someone else, to the church planter who sees God moving, it is natural because she has made following God her habit.

At Epicentre Church we have had a chance to watch firsthand as church planters have taken steps of faith to follow the Holy Spirit. Based on individual and community discernment of what the Spirit was doing in our city, Chris and Maggie Rattay took a step of faith by moving with their two young children from a nice suburb of Los Angeles to a gang-infested apartment complex littered with graffiti and used drug needles. Maggie's mother, an upper-middle-class Chinese woman, nearly disowned the family for taking her two young grandchildren to Lincoln Heights. This is not what she had in mind for her suburban-raised daughter. But Chris had the conviction that if Jesus was calling him here, Jesus would be with him.

It was this same sort of conviction that inspired two couples from our church to move to northern Iraq in early 2015. It was my privilege to accompany them to a city nearby the refugee camps where the Yazidis had fled after ISIS invaded Mosul. For these couples, they sensed the Holy Spirit was calling them and their combined six children under the age of five to Iraq. They were faithful to what they discerned to be the leading of the Spirit, and God has been faithful to them. They've seen many house churches started there among Yazidi and Syrian refugees.

Spirit-inspired grit, passion, and perseverance. When Chris first began his work in Lincoln Heights, he found the ground very difficult. At first his neighbors thought he worked for the police—why else would a white person move into *this* neighborhood? Over time, Chris led many people to Christ but found it difficult to find true persons of influence who, in the fractured brokenness of gang culture, could function in a healthy way to lead others to faith. Sadly, the first ten people who were led to Christ each experienced dramatic relapses into their prior lifestyles of sin and suffering. Some ended up getting thrown in jail for past offenses; others relapsed into their addictions; still others moved out of the area because of issues with immigration or the lack of affordable housing. The chaos of the inner city seemed to reign.

I (John) had many tearful conversations with Chris in those days and assured him that if Jesus had sent him there, there was a harvest field that was ripe. Though he moved into the neighborhood in 2007, by early 2010 he had still just gathered a few people. Church planting is not easy work. It requires grit, passion, and perseverance. This is because the battle we are fighting is not just natural but spiritual. This means that there are real spiritual forces keeping people bound in darkness. As I often tell those whom we're sending into dark places: Don't forget—there's a reason why it's dark there!

Throughout those early years Chris and his family experienced the darkness firsthand, but through it all they demonstrated immense levels of Spirit-aided grit and perseverance. But as strong as the Rattays were, we knew that we, their sending church, had a duty to aid them in their efforts to stand faithfully against the darkness. We did all we could to encourage them. We also prayed—a lot. Throughout those years we sent multiple waves of prayer teams to prayer walk the streets of Lincoln Heights, asking that God's kingdom come on earth as it is in heaven.

One day, after years of perseverance and prayer, Chris stumbled on the Holy Spirit's platform for church planting—football. Chris had grown up with football. His older brother Tim played in the NFL, his dad was a coach, and Chris had played quarterback in college. To Chris all of this seemed like a part of his past until he volunteered to be a coach for the high school football team. In this new role as a coach, he quickly realized how much football was a focal point of East LA. It seemed like every local boy played football, and each high school team was deeply united, creating a sense of *us*. As a coach for the local varsity team, Chris was now part of that *us* too.

"The Hulk" gets saved. One of the first indications that the Holy Spirit was about to turn the tide in Lincoln Heights was the conversion of another assistant football coach named Chuck. Chuck was a broad-shouldered man whose muscular build, huge Hulk tattoo on his back, and propensity to get physical during his drunken rages had earned him the nickname "The Hulk." During Chris's early days in Lincoln Heights everyone had warned him to "stay away from that man." But led by the Spirit, and more than a little intrigued, Chris found himself drawn to Chuck and his wife, Isabel.

One day, Chuck and Isabel mentioned that in a short while they were going to turn forty.

"What are your plans?" Chris inquired.

"We're going to buy a whole bunch of 40-oz kegs of beer, have everyone who comes drink them, and then party!" they replied excitedly.

Little did they know that the Holy Spirit was about to change their plans. God was at work in their lives, and before they reached their birthday milestone, Chris had an opportunity to be part of the Spirit's drawing them to a new birth as members of God's family.

A few weeks later they came to Chris with a question. "Hey Chris, instead of our buying all that beer, what do you think about baptizing us on our fortieth birthdays and letting us tell our friends what Jesus has done for us?"

They did not have to ask twice. Chris jumped at the opportunity and helped them get everything in place for a birthday celebration like no one in Lincoln Heights had seen before.

What a glorious day it turned out to be! Chuck and Isabel shared their testimonies with their family and friends before getting baptized, starting a domino effect of one person after another finding truth and transformation in Jesus. Because Chuck was an assistant football coach, and Isabel one of the team moms, a Spirit-directed strategy on how to grow this church began to emerge.

Chuck began to befriend a few of the other assistant coaches, eventually helping to lead many of them to faith. Over time, he initiated a "character counts" camp to help football players with their character. He also started a character- and discipline-based tutoring program to help students stay on the team by keeping their grades up. As these players' and coaches' lives became salt and light, the good news spread to their families, and a church began to form.

Nearly ten years after Chris and his family moved to Lincoln Heights, Chuck is now one of the elders of the church, and his life and ministry have multiplied many times over. In 2016, in addition to his ministry as a football coach, he co-led a short-term mission team composed of young Latinos from Chris's church, some young people from Epicentre Church, and a group of Mandarin Chinese from our Chinese church to serve Syrian refugees in Germany, where many were healed and came to know Jesus as Lord and Savior. It was a foretaste of Revelation 7:9 made possible in large part by Chris's grit, perseverance, and sensitivity to the Spirit.

FROM A TREE TO AN ORCHARD—MATURE, HUB, AND EXTEND

As I (Nick) reflect stories like those of Chuck in Lincoln Heights and Jim in the Middle East, I find a powerful principle at work: the propensity of the gospel to multiply when church leaders take time to discern where the Spirit is calling us to join in the work of the kingdom. Leaders can then faithfully commit themselves to persevering in the joys and risks that following the Spirit entails. As we do this, multiplication is a natural—though not necessarily easy—result. Once again, we need look no further than the book of Acts to catch a glimpse of this immense potential.

As the story rolled out in the book of Acts, the original disciples, filled with the Holy Spirit, began the powerful work of being witnesses of the gospel of Christ and the movement of what soon became Christianity was on its way. There is great power in a seed. In fact, one seed can turn into a tree, which then produces dozens of fruits per year, which each contain seeds that can turn into reproducing trees. In short, not just one orchard, but innumerable orchards exist in the potential of any given seed.

Dan Steigerwald frames this potential in his book *Dynamic Adventure,* noting three phases that point a new church (or seed) toward an orchard: mature, hub, and extend. During the *maturing* phase the church moves toward sustainability. Steigerwald writes, "Maturing happens as a faith community intentionally develops into a more sustainable form, giving appropriate attention to systems and processes that support its growth and health." Within these systems comes growth and maturity in public witness, finances, governance, and discipleship. As these practices move toward sustainability, the church will experience moments of homeostasis. *Hubbing* is the next phase and is characterized by "creating or participating in environments locally that foster the multiplication of new missional initiatives and church plants." Steigerwald notes that hubbing can happen through developing partnerships for church planting across the city or internally as a local church focuses its energy on new pioneering initiatives. The final phase in moving from a seed to an orchard is *extending,* which involves "intentionally developing wider connections and networks that reach beyond a church's host city."[6] The extending phase is where the exponential growth of an orchard is most likely to occur.

---

[6]Dan Steigerwald, *Dynamic Adventure: A Guide to Starting and Shaping Missional Communities* (Centennial, CO: Communitas International, 2017), 5.

I have been fortunate to experience these three phases over the past eight years. The maturing phase happened with Northland Village Church as we transitioned from a church plant to an established church.[7] In line with Steigerwald's model, we matured as we figured out our best public witness, our internal economics, how we would govern ourselves, and how we would do discipleship. After three years and a number of hiccups, Northland Village Church began to start new churches. By year five, we had partnered with others to start ten new worshiping communities. The most successful partnership was with a denominational church planting ministry called 1001 New Worshiping Communities. Together we created a cohort for discerning church starters where we gathered ten people every summer to participate in a praxis-oriented discernment process. The ten potential planters gathered weekly for training and then were sent out into the community as church planters. They were asked to wear the primary lens of a church starter as they went about the pattern of their days. After the ten weeks, each member of the cohort was asked to reflect on their short-term experience as a church planter. Many discovered that the difficult work was not for them, but others learned that the vocation of church starting was a perfect match. This cohort program still gathers each summer and has resulted in over twenty new churches around North America.

After we had started ten new churches through Northland Village Church, I was invited by our denomination's regional governing body to work with them half-time to understand what God was doing with all these new churches. After lots of prayer with our elders and my wife, we decided that it was a good time to grow in this way. Nine months later we launched Cyclical LA (see cyclicalLA.com), a practical example of the hubbing phase. We created a local environment that fostered the multiplication of new churches. The mission statement for Cyclical LA is developing leadership toward sustainability in a church-starting ecosystem. Within Cyclical LA, we spend our time and resources on three aspects of a cycle that we have determined to be essential: discerning church starters, church starters, and churches. When we started Cyclical LA, we had a hunch that other governing bodies may be interested in our postindustrial frameworks. This Spirit-guided hunch came to fruition as new Cyclical networks began to emerge in San Diego, Orange County, Seattle, and in Spanish with the creation of Ciclica Southern California.

With all this activity we quickly created Cyclical INC (see cyclicalchurches.com). The trans-local work of Cyclical INC, a 501c3 nonprofit, embodies Steigerwald's

---

[7]For more about Northland Village Church, see www.northlandvillagechurch.com; and Nicholas Warnes, "Growing Roots in a Secularized Context: Northland Village Church," in *Starting Missional Churches: Life with God in the Neighborhood*, ed. Mark Lau Branson and Nicholas Warnes (Downers Grove, IL: InterVarsity Press, 2014), 120-39.

extending phase. We created a contextualized framework to develop wider networks in multiple cities. Ecosystems are now popping up across North America with the calling to start new churches. From San Diego to Winnipeg, Cyclical networks are now creating space to identify, equip, and empower leaders to do the essential work of opening opportunities for transformative impact in people's lives. The single seed of Northland Village Church has turned into a generative and decentralized orchard of thousands of people now connected to these new churches.

There are innumerable local churches and denominational governing bodies who will unintentionally or intentionally shy away from starting new churches for any number of reasons. For those who do prioritize a focus on starting new churches, it is too easy to think about starting just one or two new churches at a time. This will inevitably lead to a zero-sum game as new churches will replace closing churches. The key for the future of the church in America is for congregations, church planting networks, and denominations to not create one or two new churches at a time, but to create entire ecosystems of orchards for multiple churches to begin and reproduce. With this refocusing, the potential for exponential transformation in the lives of countless people may once again find deep roots in North America.

CONCLUSION

From images of deep roots to seeds, trees, and orchards, this chapter and indeed this whole book has used organic language to describe the Spirit-led process of joining God in God's cosmic mission of redemption as we plant churches defined by spiritual formation, missional theology, and an expectation of multiplication as a normal part of congregational life.

It makes perfect sense to use the nature-based imagery of a seed, tree, and orchard. Not only does this imagery spring readily from the pages of the New Testament where Jesus frequently uses familiar agricultural images to teach spiritual truths, but it also gets at the heart of church planting as we understand it. Just as making disciples is the natural outgrowth of healthy spiritual life for the individual, so church planting and multiplication are the natural outgrowth of life in a healthy church community. The gospel and the church are built for Spirit-led multiplication. Like Abraham, God's people are always blessed not only for our own growth and satisfaction but also to be a blessing for the world. Any understanding of success or flourishing, whether in church planting, ministry, or our personal lives, that does not account for this multiplying mandate is missing one of the Bible's primary themes. The Spirit of the sending God is with us and in front of us. Christ's church is still alive. Our prayer is that more and more will take the joy-filled risk of joining in on what our missional God is doing and, in the process, find out what it means to truly flourish.

DISCUSSION QUESTIONS

1. How would you and your church define a successful church plant? Would it be one large church or a church that plants many other churches?

2. How would thinking in terms of multiplication affect the way you approach each aspect of church planting—finances, leadership development, staffing, etc.?

3. As you consider developing a farm system, are there particular leaders you can invest in right now with the goal of sending them out?

4. Does your church, network, or denomination have a plan or structure to multiply?

5. Is God's Spirit calling you to take any risks or leaps of faith now?

CONTRIBUTORS

Charles E. Cotherman planted Oil City Vineyard in Oil City, Pennsylvania. Charles is married to Aimee and they have three children. Charles serves on the advisory board for Fuller's church planting program.

Carrie Headington is an evangelist with the Episcopal Diocese of Dallas and is the founder of the Good News Initiative, an evangelistic ministry. Carrie serves on the advisory board of Fuller's Church Planting Program. She is married to Greg.

John Lo planted Epicentre Church in Pasadena, California. He is married to Evelyn and they have one son. John serves on the advisory board of Fuller's Church Planting Program.

Tim Morey planted Life Covenant Church in Torrance, California. Tim is the author of *Embodying the Faith: Becoming a Living, Sharing, Practicing Church* and serves on the advisory board of Fuller's Church Planting Program. He is married to Samantha and they have two daughters.

Johnny Ramírez-Johnson is professor of anthropology at Fuller Theological Seminary and serves on the advisory board of Fuller's Church Planting Program. He is married to Clara and they have three grown children.

Scott Sunquist served as dean and professor of intercultural studies at Fuller Theological Seminary. He is the author of numerous books, including *Understanding Christian Mission: Participation in Suffering and Glory*. He is married to Nancy and they have four grown children and nine grandchildren.

Len Tang planted Cedar Creek Church in Sherwood, Oregon, and is currently planting Missio Community Church in Pasadena, California. He is the director of the Church Planting Program at Fuller Theological Seminary. Len is married to Amy and they have three teenage boys.

Nick Warnes planted Northland Village Church in Los Angeles and is the founding director of Cyclical LA and the executive director of Cyclical INC. Nick is on the advisory board of Fuller's Church Planting Program. He cowrote *Starting Missional Churches: Life with God in the Neighborhood*. Nick is married to Whitney and they have one son.

JR Woodward planted two churches and is the national director of the V3 Church Planting Movement. He cofounded Ecclesia Network and Missio Alliance and is the author of *The Church as Movement: Starting and Sustaining Missional-Incarnational Communities*.

NAME INDEX

SUBJECT INDEX

SCRIPTURE INDEX

ALSO AVAILABLE FROM IVP ACADEMIC AND THE FULLER CHURCH PLANTING PROGRAM

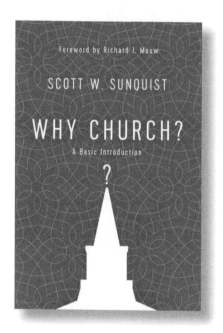

EQUIPPING YOU TO PLANT
MISSIONAL CHURCHES

Fuller Seminary's Church Planting Program prepares men and women to plant and multiply missional churches. Our renowned faculty and experienced practitioners provide you with the healthy root system you'll need to plant a flourishing church that makes disciples and helps transform communities. We believe the three roots needed are (1) a biblical theology of church planting, (2) the spiritual formation of the planter, and (3) the missional skills to reach a post-Christian culture.

Outside the classroom, our apprenticeships, church planter student group, luncheons, and conferences introduce you to a variety of church planters and church planting networks to give you on-the-ground training for planting in a diverse, post-Christendom world.

**LEARN MORE AT FULLER.EDU/CHURCHPLANTING
OR CHURCHPLANTING@FULLER.EDU.**

Finding the Textbook You Need

The IVP Academic Textbook Selector
is an online tool for instantly finding the IVP books
suitable for over 250 courses across 24 disciplines.

---

ivpacademic.com